The Seven Books of Augustine on Baptism, Against the Donatists

The Seven Books of Augustine on Baptism, Against the Donatists

St. Augustine

The Seven Books of Augustine on Baptism, Against the Donatists

© Lighthouse Publishing 2018

Written by: St. Augustine (Nov.13 354 – Aug.28 430)
Translated by: Rev. J.R. King M.A
Updated into Modern U.S English by A.M. Overett (b. 1960)

All rights reserved. Without limiting the rights under copyright reserved above, no part of this publication may be reproduced, stored in a retrieval system, or transmitted, in any form or by any means (electronic, mechanical, photocopying, recording or otherwise), without the prior written permission of the copyright owner of this book.

Published by
Lighthouse Christian Publishing
SAN 257-4330
5531 Dufferin Drive
Savage, Minnesota, 55378
United States of America

www.lighthousechristianpublishing.com

Preface

The schism of the Donatists, with which the treatises in the present volume are concerned, arose indirectly out of the persecution under Diocletian at the beginning of the fourth century. At that time Mensurius, bishop of Carthage, and his archdeacon Cæcilianus, had endeavored to check the fanatical spirit in which many of the Christians courted martyrdom; and consequently, on the death of Mensurius in 311, and the elevation of Cæcilianus to the see of Carthage in his place, the opposing party, alleging that Felix, bishop of Aptunga, by whom Cæcilianus had been consecrated, had been a traditor, and that therefore his consecration was invalid, set up against him Majorinus, who was succeeded in 315 by Donatus. The party had by this time gained strength, through the professions that they made of extreme purity in the discipline which they maintained, and had gone so far, under the advice of another Donatus, bishop of Casæ Nigræ in Numidia, as to accuse Cæcilianus before the Roman Emperor Constantine, —thus setting the first precedent for referring a spiritual cause to the decision of a civil magistrate. Constantine accepted the appeal, and in 313 the matter was laid for decision before Melchiades, bishop of Rome, and three bishops of the province of Gaul. They decided in favor of the validity of the consecration of Cæcilianus; and a similar verdict was given by a council held at Arles, by direction of the Emperor, in the following year. The party of Majorinus then appealed to the personal judgment of the Emperor, which was likewise given against them, not without strong expressions of his anger at their pertinacity. This was followed by severe laws directed against their schism; but so far from crushing them, the attack seemed only to increase their enthusiasm and develop their resources. And, under the leadership of Donatus, the successor of Majorinus, their influence spread widely throughout Africa, and continued to prevail, despite various efforts at their forcible suppression, during the whole of the fourth century. They especially brought on themselves the vengeance of the civil powers, by the turbulence of certain fanatical ascetics who embraced their cause, and who, under the name of Circumcelliones, spread terror through the country, seeking martyrdom for themselves, and offering violence to everyone who opposed them.

Towards the close of the century, this schism attracted the attention of Augustin, then a priest of Hippo Regius in Numidia. The controversy seems to have had for him a special attraction, not merely because of its intrinsic importance, but also because of the field which it presented for his unrivalled powers as a dialectician. These the Donatists had recently provoked, by inconsistently receiving back into their body a deacon of Carthage named Maximianus who had separated himself from them, and by recognizing as valid all baptism administered by his followers. Hence they naturally shrank from engaging in a contest with an antagonist who was sure to make the most of such a deviation from the very principles on which they based their schism; and, on the other hand, Augustin was so firmly convinced that his own position was impregnable, that he seems to have thought that if he could only secure a thorough and dispassionate discussion of the matter, the Donatists must necessarily be brought to acknowledge not only their theoretical errors, but also the practical sinfulness of their separation from the Church. Throughout the controversy, however, he appears to have put out of sight two considerations: first, the influence of party spirit and prejudice in blinding men to argument; and, secondly, the necessity of treating his opponents in a logical discussion as on an equal footing with himself. The first was in some degree an unavoidable element of disappointment; but Augustin made concession yet more difficult on the part of his opponents, by expecting them to acknowledge his superior position as a member of the Catholic Church, whose duty it was to expose the error of their views. He practically begs the very point at issue, by assuming that he, and not the Donatists, was in the Catholic communion; and though his argument is conducted independently of this premise, yet it naturally rendered them more unwilling to admit its force.

This dogmatism was of less consequence in the first pamphlet which Augustin published on the subject, —his Alphabetical Psalm, in which he set forth the history and errors of the Donatists in a popular form, —since it was not intended as a controversial treatise, but only as a means of enlightening the less educated as to the Catholic tenets on the question in dispute. His next work, written in answer to a letter of Donatus of Carthage, in which the latter tried to prove that the baptism of Christ existed only in his communion, is unfortunately lost; and we can only gather hints as to the further part which he took in the controversy during the next few years from certain of his letters, especially those to the Donatist Bishops Honoratus and Crispinus. From the former he claims the admission that the exclusiveness of the Donatists proves that they are not the Church of Christ; and his letter to the latter contains an invitation to discuss the leading points at issue, which Crispinus seems to have declined.

In the year 400 he wrote two books Against the Party of Donatus, which are also lost; and about the same time he published his refutation of the letter of Parmenianus in answer to Tichonius, in which he handles and solves the famous question, whether, while abiding in unity in the communion of the same sacraments, the wicked pollute the good by their society.

Then followed his seven books On Baptism, included in this volume, in which he shows the emptiness of the arguments of the Donatists for the repetition of baptism; and proves that so far was Cyprian from being on their side, that his letters and conduct are of the highest value as overthrowing their position, and utterly condemning their separation from the Church.

Not long after this, Petilianus, bishop of Cirta or Constantina, the most eminent theologian among the Donatist divines, wrote a letter to his clergy against the Catholics, of which Augustin managed to obtain a copy, though the Donatists used their utmost care to keep it from him; and he replied to it in two books, written at different times, —the first in the year 400, before he was in possession of the whole letter, the remainder in 402. To the first book Petilianus made an answer, of which we gather the main tenor from a third book written by Augustin in reply to it. It appears to have been full of vehement abuse, and to have assumed the question in dispute, that the existence of the true Church, and the catholicity of any branch of it, depended on the purity and orthodoxy of all its ministers; so that the guilt or heresy of any minister would invalidate the whole of his ministerial acts.

Hence, he argued that Cæcilianus being the spiritual father of the so-called Catholics, and having been a traditor, none of them could possibly have been lawfully baptized, much less rightfully ordained.

Augustin admits neither of his assumptions; but, leaving the guilt or innocence of Cæcilianus as a point which was irrelevant (though practically the case against him utterly broke down), he addresses himself to the other point, and argues most conclusively that all the functions of the clergy in celebrating the rites of the Church being purely ministerial, the efficacy of those rites could in no way depend upon the excellence of the individual minister, but was derived entirely from Christ. Hence there was a certainty of the grace bestowed through the several ordinances, which otherwise there could not possibly have been, had their virtue depended on the character of any man, in whom even an unblemished reputation might have been the fruit of a skilled hypocrisy.

The third treatise in this volume belongs to a later period, being a letter written to Bonifacius, the Roman Count of Africa under Valentinian the Third. He had written to Augustin to consult him as to the best means of dealing with the Donatists; and Augustin in his reply points out to him his mistake in supposing that the Donatists shared in the errors of the Arians, whilst he urges him to use moderation in his coercive measures; though both here and in his answer to Petilianus we find him countenancing the theory that the State has a right to interfere in constraining men to keep within the Church. Starting with a forced interpretation of the words, "Compelthem to come in," in Luke xiv. 23, he enunciates principles of coercion which, though in him they were subdued and rendered practically of little moment by the spirit of love which formed so large an element in his character, yet found their natural development in the despotic intolerance of the Papacy, and the horrors of the Inquisition. It is probable that he was himself in some degree misled by confounding the necessity of repressing the violence of the Circumcelliones, which was a real offense against the State, with the expediency of enforcing spiritual unity by temporal authority.

The Donatist treatises have met with little attention from individual editors. There is a dissertation, De Aur. Augustino adversario Donatistarum, by Adrien Roux, published at Louvain in 1838;1144but it is believed that no treatises of this series have ever before been translated into English, nor are they separately edited. They are in themselves a valuable authority for an important scene in the history of the Church, and afford a good example both of the strength and the weakness of Augustin's writing,—its strength, in the exhaustive way in which he tears to pieces his opponent's arguments, and the clearness with which he exposes the fallacies of their reasoning; its weakness, in the persistency with which he pursues a point long after its discussion might fairly have been closed, as though he hardly knew when he had gained the victory; and his tendency to claim, by right of his position, a vantage ground which did not in reality belong to him till the superiority of his cause was proved.

J. R. King
Oxford, March, 1870.

This treatise was written about 400 A.D. Concerning it Aug. in Retract. Book II. c. xviii., says: I have written seven books on Baptism against the Donatists, who strive to defend themselves by the authority of the most blessed bishop and martyr Cyprian; in which I show that nothing is so effectual for the refutation of the Donatists, and for shutting their mouths directly from upholding their schism against the Catholic Church, as the letters and act of Cyprian.

Book I.

He proves that baptism can be conferred outside the Catholic communion by heretics or schismatics, but that it ought not to be received from them; and that it is of no avail to any while in a state of heresy or schism.

Chapter 1. —1. In the treatise which we wrote against the published epistle of Parmenianus to Tichonius, we promised that at some future time we would treat the question of baptism more thoroughly; and indeed, even if we had not made this promise, we are not unmindful that this is a debt fairly due from us to the prayers of our brethren. Wherefore in this treatise we have undertaken, with the help of God, not only to refute the objections which the Donatists have been wont to urge against us in this matter, but also to advance what God may enable us to say in respect of the authority of the blessed martyr Cyprian, which they endeavor to use as a prop, to prevent their perversity from falling before the attacks of truth. And this we propose to do, in order that all whose judgment is not blinded by party spirit may understand that, so far from Cyprian's authority being in their favor, it tends directly to their refutation and discomfiture.

2. In the treatise above mentioned, it has already been said that the grace of baptism can be conferred outside the Catholic communion, just as it can be also there retained. But no one of the Donatists themselves denies that even apostates retain the grace of baptism; for when they return within the pale of the Church, and are converted through repentance, it is never given to them a second time, and so it is ruled that it never could have been lost. So those, too, who in the sacrilege of schism

depart from the communion of the Church, certainly retain the grace of baptism, which they received before their departure, seeing that, in case of their return, it is not again conferred on them whence it is proved, that what they had received while within the unity of the Church, they could not have lost in their separation. But if it can be retained outside, why may it not also be given there? If you say, "It is not rightly given without the pale;" we answer, "As it is not rightly retained, and yet is in some sense retained, so it is not indeed rightly given, but yet it is given." But as, by reconciliation to unity, that begins to be profitably possessed which was possessed to no profit in exclusion from unity, so, by the same reconciliation, that begins to be profitable which without it was given to no profit. Yet it cannot be allowed that it should be said that that was not given which was given, nor that anyone should reproach a man with not having given this, while confessing that he had given what he had himself received. For the sacrament of baptism is what the person possesses who is baptized; and the sacrament of confer ring baptism is what he possesses who is ordained. And as the baptized person, if he depart from the unity of the Church, does not thereby lose the sacrament of baptism, so also he who is ordained, if he depart from the unity of the Church, does not lose the sacrament of conferring baptism. For neither sacrament may be wronged. If a sacrament necessarily becomes void in the case of the wicked, both must become void; if it remain valid with the wicked, this must be so with both. If, therefore, the baptism be acknowledged which he could not lose who severed himself from the unity of the Church, that baptism must also be acknowledged which was administered by one who by his secession had not lost the sacrament of conferring baptism. For as those who return to the Church, if they had been baptized before their secession, are not rebaptized, so those who return, having been ordained before their secession, are certainly not ordained again; but either they again exercise their former ministry, if the interests of the Church require it, or if they do not exercise it, at any rate they retain the sacrament of their ordination; and hence it is, that when hands are laid on them, to mark their reconciliation, they are not ranked with the laity. For Felicianus, when he separated himself from them with Maximianus, was not held by the Donatists themselves to have lost either the sacrament of baptism or the sacrament of conferring baptism. For now he is a recognized member of their own body, in company with those very men whom he baptized while he was separated from them in the schism of Maximianus. And so others could receive from them, whilst they still had not joined our society, what they themselves had not lost by severance from our society. And hence it is clear that they are guilty of impiety who endeavor to rebaptize those who are in Catholic unity; and we act rightly who do not dare to repudiate God's sacraments, even when administered in schism. For in all points in which they think with us, they also are in communion with us, and only are severed from us in those points in which they dissent from us. For contact and disunion are not to be measured by different laws in the case of material or spiritual affinities. For as union of bodies arises from continuity of position, so in the agreement of wills there is a kind of contact between souls. If, therefore, a man who has severed himself from unity wishes to do anything different from that which had been impressed on him while in the state of unity, in this point he does sever himself, and is no longer a part of the united whole; but wherever he desires to conduct himself as is customary in the state of unity, in which he himself learned and received the lessons which he seeks to follow, in these points he remains a member, and is united to the corporate whole.

Chapter 2. —3. And so the Donatists in some matters are with us; in some matters have gone out from us. Accordingly, those things wherein they agree with us we do not forbid them to do; but in those things in which they differ from us, we earnestly encourage them to come and receive them from us, or return and recover them, as the case may be; and with whatever means we can, we lovingly busy ourselves, that they, freed from faults and corrected, may choose this course. We do not therefore say to them, "Abstain from giving baptism," but "Abstain from giving it in schism." Nor do we say to those whom we see them on the point of baptizing, "Do not receive the baptism," but "Do not receive it in schism." For if anyone were compelled by urgent necessity, being unable to find a Catholic from whom to receive baptism, and so, while preserving Catholic peace in his heart, should receive from one without the pale of Catholic unity the sacrament which he was intending to receive within its pale, this man, should he forthwith depart this life, we deem to be none other than a Catholic. But if he should be delivered from the death of the body, on his restoring himself in bodily presence to that Catholic congregation from which in heart he had never departed, so far from blaming his conduct, we should praise it with the greatest truth and confidence; because he trusted that God was present to his heart, while he was striving to preserve unity, and was unwilling to depart this life without the sacrament of holy baptism, which he knew to be of God, and not of men; wherever he might find it. But if anyone who has it in his power to receive baptism within the Catholic Church prefers, from some perversity of mind, to be baptized in schism, even if he afterwards bethinks himself to come to the Catholic Church, because he is assured that there that sacrament will profit him, which can indeed be received but cannot profit elsewhere, beyond all question he is perverse, and guilty of sin, and that the more flagrant in proportion as it was committed willfully. For that he entertains no doubt that the sacrament is rightly received in the Church, is proved by his conviction that it is there that he must look for profit even from what he has received elsewhere.

Chapter 3. —4. There are two propositions, moreover, which we affirm, —that baptism exists in the Catholic Church, and that in it alone can it be rightly received, —both of which the Donatists deny. Likewise, there are two other propositions which we affirm, —that baptism exists among the Donatists, but that with them it is not rightly received, of which two they strenuously confirm the former, that baptism exists with them; but they are unwilling to allow the latter, that in their Church it cannot be rightly received. Of these four propositions, three are peculiar to us; in one we both agree. For that baptism exists in the Catholic Church, that it is rightly received there, and that it is not rightly received among the Donatists, are assertions made only by ourselves; but that baptism exists also among the Donatists, is asserted by them and allowed by us. If anyone, therefore, is desirous of being baptized, and is already convinced that he ought to choose our Church as a medium for Christian salvation, and that the baptism of Christ is only profitable in it, even when it has been received elsewhere, but yet wishes to be baptized in the schism of Donatus, because not they only, nor we only, but both parties alike say that baptism exists with them, let him pause and look to the other three points. For if he has made up his mind to follow us in the points which they deny, though he prefers what both of us acknowledge, to what only we assert, it is enough for our purpose that he prefers what they do not affirm and we alone assert, to what they alone assert. That baptism exists in the Catholic Church, we assert and they deny. That it is rightly received in the Catholic Church, we assert and they deny. That it is not rightly received in the schism of Donatus, we assert and they deny. As, therefore, he is the more ready to believe what we alone assert should be believed, so let him be the more ready to do what we alone declare should be done. But let him believe more firmly, if he be so disposed, what both parties assert should be believed, than what we alone maintain. For he is inclined to believe more firmly that the baptism of Christ exists in the schism of Donatus, because that is acknowledged by both of us, than that it exists in the Catholic Church, an assertion made alone by the Catholics. But again, he is more ready to believe that the baptism of Christ exists also with us, as we alone assert, than that it does not exist with us, as they alone assert. For he has already determined and is fully convinced, that where we differ, our authority is to be preferred to theirs. So that he is more ready to believe what we alone assert, that baptism is rightly received with us, than that it is not rightly so received, since that rests only on their assertion. And, by the same rule, he is more ready to believe what we alone assert, that it is not rightly received with them, than as they alone assert, that it is rightly so received. He finds, therefore, that his confidence in being baptized among the Donatists is somewhat profitless, seeing that, though we both acknowledge that baptism exists with them, yet we do not both declare that it ought to be received from them. But he has made up his mind to cling rather to us in matters where we disagree. Let him therefore feel confidence in receiving baptism in our communion, where he is assured that it both exists and is rightly received; and let him not receive it in a communion, where those whose opinion he has determined to follow acknowledge indeed that it exists, but say that it cannot rightly be received. Nay, even if he should hold it to be a doubtful question, whether or not it is impossible for that to be rightly received among the Donatists which he is assured can rightly be received in the Catholic Church, he would commit a grievous sin, in matters concerning the salvation of his soul, in the mere fact of preferring uncertainty to certainty. At any rate, he must be quite sure that a man can be rightly baptized in the Catholic Church, from the mere fact that he has determined to come over to it, even if he be baptized elsewhere. But let him at least acknowledge it to be matter of uncertainty whether a man be not improperly baptized among the Donatists, when he finds this asserted by those whose opinion he is convinced should be preferred to theirs; and, preferring certainty to uncertainty, let him be baptized here, where he has good grounds for being assured that it is rightly done, in the fact that when he thought of doing it elsewhere, he had still determined that he ought afterwards to come over to this side.

Chapter 4. —5. Further, if any one fails to understand how it can be that we assert that the sacrament is not rightly conferred among the Donatists, while we confess that it exists among them, let him observe that we also deny that it exists rightly among them, just as they deny that it exists rightly among those who quit their communion. Let him also consider the analogy of the military mark, which, though it can both be retained, as by deserters, and, also be received by those who are not in the army, yet ought not to be either received or retained outside its ranks; and, at the same time, it is not changed or renewed when a man is enlisted or brought back to his service. However, we must distinguish between the case of those who unwittingly join the ranks of these heretics, under the impression that they are entering the true Church of Christ, and those who know that there is no other Catholic Church save that which, according to the promise, is spread abroad throughout the whole world, and extends even to the utmost limits of the earth; which, rising amid tares, and seeking rest in the future from the weariness of offenses, says in the Book of Psalms, "From the end of the earth I cried unto Thee, while my heart was in weariness: Thou didst exalt me on a rock." But the rock was Christ, in whom the apostle says that we are now raised up, and set together in heavenly places, though not yet actually, but only in hope. And so the psalm goes on to say, "Thou was my guide, because Thou art become my hope, a tower of strength from the face of the enemy." By means of His promises, which are like spears and javelins stored up in a strongly fortified place, the enemy is not only guarded against, but overthrown, as he clothes his wolves in sheep's clothing, that they may say, "Lo, here is Christ, or there;" and that they may separate many from the Catholic city which is built upon a hill, and bring them down to the isolation of their own snares, so as utterly to destroy them. And these men, knowing this, choose to receive the baptism of Christ without the limits of the communion of the unity of Christ's body, though they intend afterwards, with the sacrament which they have received elsewhere, to pass into that very communion. For they propose to receive Christ's baptism in antagonism to the Church of Christ, well knowing that it is so even on the very day on which they receive it. And if this is a sin, who is the man that will say, Grant that for a single day I may commit sin? For if he proposes to pass over to the Catholic Church, I would fain ask why. What other answer can he give, but that it is ill to belong to the party of Donatus, and not to the unity of the Catholic Church? Just so many days, then, as you commit this ill, of so many days' sin are you going to be guilty. And it may be said that there is greater sin in more days' commission of it, and less in fewer; but in no wise can it be said that no sin is committed at all. But what is the need of allowing this accursed wrong for a single day, or a single hour? For the man who wishes this license to be granted him, might as well ask of the Church, or of God Himself, that for a single day he should be permitted to apostatize. For there is no reason why he should fear to be an apostate for a day, if he does not shrink from being for that time a schismatic or a heretic.

Chapter 5. —6. I prefer, he says, to receive Christ's baptism where both parties agree that it exists. But those whom you intend to join say that it cannot be received there rightly; and those who say that it can be received there rightly are the party whom you mean to quit. What they say, therefore, whom you yourself consider of inferior authority, in opposition to what those say whom you yourself prefer, is, if not false, at any rate, to use a milder term, at least uncertain. I entreat you, therefore, to prefer what is true to what is false, or what is certain to what is uncertain. For it is not only those whom you are going to join, but you yourself who are going to join them, that confess that what you want can be rightly received in that body which you mean to join when you have received it elsewhere. For if you had any doubts whether it could be rightly received there, you would also have doubts whether you ought to make the change. If, therefore, it is doubtful whether it be not sin to receive baptism from the party of Donatus, who can doubt but that it is certain sin not to prefer receiving it where it is certain that it is not sin? And those who are baptized there through ignorance, thinking that it is the true Church of Christ, are guilty of less sin in comparison than these, though even they are wounded by the impiety of schism; nor do they escape a grievous hurt, because others suffer even more. For when it is said to certain men, "It shall be more tolerable for the land of Sodom in the day of judgment than for you," it is not meant that the men of Sodom shall escape torment, but only that the others shall be even more grievously tormented.

7. And yet this point had once, perhaps, been involved in obscurity and doubt. But that which is a source of health to those who give heed and receive correction, is but an aggravation of the sin of those who, when they are no longer suffered to be ignorant, persist in their madness to their own destruction. For the condemnation of the party of Maximianus, and their

restoration after they had been condemned, together with those whom they had sacrilegiously, to use the language of their own Council, baptized in schism, settles the whole question in dispute, and removes all controversy. There is no point at issue between ourselves and those Donatists who hold communion with Primianus, which could give rise to any doubt that the baptism of Christ may not only be retained, but even conferred by those who are severed from the Church. For as they themselves are obliged to confess that those whom Felicianus baptized in schism received true baptism, inasmuch as they now acknowledge them as members of their own body, with no other baptism than that which they received in schism; so we say that that is Christ's baptism, even without the pale of Catholic communion, which they confer who are cut off from that communion, inasmuch as they had not lost it when they were cut off. And what they themselves think that they conferred on those persons whom Felicianus baptized in schism, when they admitted them to reconciliation with themselves, viz., not that they should receive that which they did not as yet possess, but that what they had received to no advantage in schism, and were already in possession of, should be of profit to them, this God really confers and bestows through the Catholic communion on those who come from any heresy or schism in which they received the baptism of Christ; viz., not that they should begin to receive the sacrament of baptism as not possessing it before, but that what they already possessed should now begin to profit them.

Chapter 6. —8. Between us, then, and what we may call the genuine Donatists, whose bishop is Primianus at Carthage, there is now no controversy on this point. For God willed that it should be ended by means of the followers of Maximianus, that they should be compelled by the precedent of his case to acknowledge what they would not allow at the persuasion of Christian charity. But this brings us to consider next, whether those men do not seem to have something to say for themselves, who refuse communion with the party of Primianus, contending that in their body there remains greater sincerity of Donatism, just in proportion to the paucity of their numbers. And even if these were only the party of Maximianus, we should not be justified in despising their salvation. How much more, then, are we bound to consider it, when we find that this same party of Donatus is split up into many most minute fractions, all which small sections of the body blame the one much larger portion which has Primianus for its head, because they receive the baptism of the followers of Maximianus; while each endeavors to maintain that it is the sole receptacle of true baptism, which exists nowhere else, neither in the whole of the world where the Catholic Church extends itself, nor in that larger main body of the Donatists, nor even in the other minute sections, but only in itself. Whereas, if all these fragments would listen not to the voice of man, but to the most unmistakable manifestation of the truth, and would be willing to curb the fiery temper of their own perversity, they would return from their own barrenness, not indeed to the main body of Donatus, a mere fragment of which they are a smaller fragment, but to the never-failing fruitfulness of the root of the Catholic Church. For all of them who are not against us are for us; but when they gather not with us, they scatter abroad.

Chapter 7. —9. For, in the next place, that I may not seem to rest on mere human arguments,—since there is so much obscurity in this question, that in earlier ages of the Church, before the schism of Donatus, it has caused men of great weight, and even our fathers, the bishops, whose hearts were full of charity, so to dispute and doubt among themselves, saving always the peace of the Church, that the several statutes of their Councils in their different districts long varied from each other, till at length the most wholesome opinion was established, to the removal of all doubts, by a plenary Council of the whole world:—I therefore bring forward from the gospel clear proofs, by which I propose, with God's help, to prove how rightly and truly in the sight of God it has been determined, that in the case of every schismatic and heretic, the wound which caused his separation should be cured by the medicine of the Church; but that what remained sound in him should rather be recognized with approbation, than wounded by condemnation. It is indeed true that the Lord says in the gospel, "He that is not with me is against me; and he that gathered not with me scattered abroad." Yet when the disciples had brought word to Him that they had seen one casting out devils in His name, and had forbidden him, because he followed not them, He said, "Forbid him not: for he that is not against us is for us. For there is no man which shall do a miracle in my name, that can lightly speak evil of me." If, indeed, there were nothing in this man requiring correction, then anyone would be safe who, setting himself outside the communion of the Church, severing himself from all Christian brotherhood, should gather in Christ's name; and so there would be no truth in this, "He that is not with me is against me; and he that gathered not with me scattered abroad." But if he required correction in the point where the disciples in their ignorance were anxious to check him, why did our Lord, by saying, "Forbid him not," prevent this check from being given? And how can that be true which He then says, "He that is not against you is for you?" For in this point he was not against, but for them, when he was working miracles of healing in Christ's name. That both, therefore, should be true, as both are true,—both the declaration, that "he that is not with me is against me, and he that gathered not with me scattered abroad;" and also the injunction, "Forbid him not; for he that is not against you is for you,"—what must we understand, except that the man was to be confirmed in his veneration for that mighty Name, in respect of which he was not against the Church, but for it; and yet he was to be blamed for separating himself from the Church, whereby his gathering became a scattering; and if it should have so happened that he sought union with the Church, he should not have received what he already possessed, but be made to set right the points wherein he had gone astray?

Chapter 8. —10. Nor indeed were the prayers of the Gentile Cornelius unheard, nor did his alms lack acceptance; nay, he was found worthy that an angel should be sent to him, and that he should behold the messenger, through whom he might assuredly have learned everything that was necessary, without requiring that any man should come to him. But since all the good that he had in his prayers and alms could not benefit him unless he were incorporated in the Church by the bond of Christian brotherhood and peace, he was ordered to send to Peter, and through him learned Christ; and, being also baptized by his orders, he was joined by the tie of communion to the fellowship of Christians, to which before he was bound only by the likeness of good works. And indeed, it would have been most fatal to despise what he did not yet possess, vaunting himself in what he had. So too those who, by separating themselves from the society of their fellows, to the overthrow of charity, thus break the bond of unity, if they observe none of the things which they have received in that society, are separated in everything; and so any one whom they have joined to their society, if he afterwards wish to come over to the Church, ought to receive everything which he has not already received. But if they observe some of the same things, in respect of these they have not severed themselves; and so far they are still a part of the framework of the Church, while in all other respects they are cut off from it. Accordingly, any one whom they have associated with themselves is united to the Church in all those points in which they are not separated from it. And therefore, if he wishes to come over to the Church, he is made sound in those points in which he was unsound and went astray; but where he was sound in union with the Church, he is not cured, but recognized, —lest in desiring to cure what is sound we should rather inflict a wound. Therefore, those whom they baptize they heal from the wound of idolatry or unbelief; but they injure them more seriously with the wound of schism. For idolaters among the people of the Lord were smitten with the sword; but schismatics were swallowed up by the earth opening her mouth. And the apostle says, "Though I have all faith, so that I could remove mountains, and have not charity, I am nothing."

11. If anyone is brought to the surgeon, afflicted with a grievous wound in some vital part of the body, and the surgeon says that unless it is cured it must cause death, the friends who brought him do not, I presume, act so foolishly as to count over to the surgeon all his sound limbs, and, drawing his attention to them, make answer to him, "Can it be that all these sound limbs are of no avail to save his life, and that one wounded limb is enough to cause his death?" They certainly do not say this, but they entrust him to the surgeon to be cured. Nor, again, because they so entrust him, do they ask the surgeon to cure the limbs that are sound as well; but they desire him to apply drugs with all care to the one part from which death is threatening the other sound parts too, with the certainty that it must come, unless the wound be healed. What will it then profit a man that he has sound faith, or perhaps only soundness in the sacrament of faith, when the soundness of his charity is done away with by the fatal wound of schism, so that by the overthrow of it the other points, which were in themselves sound, are brought into the infection of death? To prevent which, the mercy of God, through the unity of His Holy Church, does not cease striving that they may come and be healed by the medicine of reconciliation, through the bond of peace. And let them not think that they are sound because we admit that they have something sound in them; nor let them think, on the other hand, that what is sound must needs be healed, because we show that in some parts there is a wound. So that in the soundness of the sacrament, because they are not against us, they are for us; but in the wound of schism, because they gather not with Christ,

they scatter abroad. Let them not be exalted by what they have. Why do they pass the eyes of pride over those parts only which are sound? Let them condescend also to look humbly on their wound, and give heed not only to what they have, but also to what is wanting in them.

Chapter 9. —12. Let them see how many things, and what important things, are of no avail, if a certain single thing be wanting, and let them see what that one thing is. And herein let them hear not my words, but those of the apostle: "Though I speak with the tongues of men and of angels, and have not charity, I am become as sounding brass, or a tinkling cymbal. And though I have the gift of prophecy, and understand all mysteries, and all knowledge; and though I have all faith, so that I could remove mountains, and have not charity, I am nothing." What does it profit them, therefore, if they have both the voice of angels in the sacred mysteries, and the gift of prophecy, as had Caiaphas and Saul, that so they may be found prophesying, of whom Holy Scripture testifies that they were worthy of condemnation? If they not only know, but even possess the sacraments, as Simon Magus did; if they have faith, as the devils confessed Christ (for we must not suppose that they did not believe when they said, "What have we to do with Thee, O Son of God? We know Thee who Thou art"; if they distribute of themselves their own substance to the poor, as many do, not only in the Catholic Church, but in the different heretical bodies; if, under the pressure of any persecution, they give their bodies with us to be burned for the faith which they like us confess: yet because they do all these things apart from the Church, not "forbearing one another in love," nor "endeavoring to keep the unity of the spirit in the bond of peace," insomuch as they have not charity, they cannot attain to eternal salvation, even with all those good things which profit them not.

Chapter 10. —13. But they think within themselves that they show very great subtlety in asking whether the baptism of Christ in the party of Donatus makes men sons or not; so that, if we allow that it does make them sons, they may assert that theirs is the Church, the mother which could give birth to sons in the baptism of Christ; and since the Church must be one, they may allege that ours is no Church. But if we say that it does not make them sons, "Why then," say they, "do you not cause those who pass from us to you to be born again in baptism, after they have been baptized with us, if they are not thereby born as yet?"

14. Just as though their party gained the power of generation in virtue of what constitutes its division, and not from what causes its union with the Church. For it is severed from the bond of peace and charity, but it is joined in one baptism. And so there is one Church which alone is called Catholic; and whenever it has anything of its own in these communions of different bodies which are separate from itself, it is most certainly in virtue of this which is its own in each of them that it, not they, has the power of generation. For neither is it their separation that generates, but what they have retained of the essence of the Church; and if they were to go on to abandon this, they would lose the power of generation. The generation, then, in each case proceeds from the Church, whose sacraments are retained, from which any such birth can alone in any case proceed, —although not all who receive its birth belong to its unity, which shall save those who

persevere even to the end. Nor is it those only that do not belong to it who are openly guilty of the manifest sacrilege of schism, but also those who, being outwardly joined to its unity, are yet separated by a life of sin. For the Church had herself given birth to Simon Magus through the sacrament of baptism; and yet it was declared to him that he had no part in the inheritance of Christ. Did he lack anything in respect of baptism, of the gospel, of the sacraments? But in that he wanted charity, he was born in vain; and perhaps it had been well for him that he had never been born at all. Was anything wanting to their birth to whom the apostle says, "I have fed you with milk, and not with meat, even as babes in Christ"? Yet he recalls them from the sacrilege of schism, into which they were rushing, because they were carnal: "I have fed you," he says, "with milk, and not with meat: for hitherto ye were not able to bear it, neither yet now are ye able. For ye are yet carnal: for whereas there is among you envying and strife, are ye not carnal, and walk as men? For while one saith, I am of Paul; and another, I am of Apollos; are ye not men?" For of these he says above: "Now I beseech you, brethren, by the name of our Lord Jesus Christ, that ye all speak the same thing, and that there be no divisions among you; but that ye be perfectly joined together in the same mind, and in the same judgment. For it hath been declared unto me of you, my brethren, by them which are of the house of Chlöe, that there are contentions among you. Now this I say, that every one of you saith, I am of Paul, and I of Apollos, and I of Cephas, and I of Christ. Is Christ divided? was Paul crucified for you? or were ye baptized in the name of Paul?" These, therefore, if they continued in the same perverse obstinacy, were doubtless indeed born, but yet would not belong by the bond of peace and unity to the very Church in respect of which they were born. Therefore, she herself bears them in her own womb and in the womb of her handmaids, by virtue of the same sacraments, as though by virtue of the seed of her husband. For it is not without meaning that the apostle says that all these things were done by way of figure.

But those who are too proud, and are not joined to their lawful mother, are like Ishmael, of whom it is said, "Cast out this bond-woman and her Son: for the son of the bond-woman shall not be heir with my son, even with Isaac." But those who peacefully love the lawful wife of their father, whose sons they are by lawful descent, are like the sons of Jacob, born indeed of handmaids, but yet receiving the same inheritance. But those who are born within the family, of the womb of the mother herself, and then neglect the grace they have received, are like Isaac's son Esau, who was rejected, God Himself bearing witness to it, and saying, "I loved Jacob, and I hated Esau;" and that though they were twin-brethren, the offspring of the same womb.

Chapter 11. —15. They ask also, "Whether sins are remitted in baptism in the party of Donatus:" so that, if we say that they are remitted, they may answer, then the Holy Spirit is there; for when by the breathing of our Lord the Holy Spirit was given to the disciples, He then went on to say, "Baptize all nations in the name of the Father, and of the Son, and of the Holy Ghost." Whose soever sins ye remit, they are remitted unto them; and whose soever sins ye retain, they are retained." And if it is so, they say, then our communion is the Church of Christ; for the Holy Spirit does not work the remission of sins except in the Church. And if our communion is the Church of Christ, then your communion is not the Church of Christ. For that is one, wherever it is, of which it is said, "My dove is but one; she is the only one of her mother;" nor can there be just so many churches as there are schisms. But if we should say that sins are not there remitted, then, say they, there is no true baptism there; and therefore ought you to baptize those whom you receive from us. And since you do not do this, you confess that you are not in the Church of Christ.

16. To these we reply, following the Scriptures, by asking them to answer themselves what they ask of us. For I beg them to tell us whether there is any remission of sins where there is not charity; for sins are the darkness of the soul. For we find St. John saying, "He that hated his brother is still in darkness." But none would create schisms, if they were not blinded by hatred of their brethren. If, therefore, we say that sins are not remitted there, how is he regenerate who is baptized among them? And what is regeneration in baptism, except the being renovated from the corruption of the old man? And how can he be so renovated whose past sins are not remitted? But if he be not regenerate, neither does he put on Christ; from which it seems to follow that he ought to be baptized again. For the apostle says, "For as many of you as have been baptized into Christ have put on Christ;" and if he has not so put on Christ, neither should he be considered to have been baptized in Christ. Further, since we say that he has been baptized in Christ, we confess that he has put on Christ; and if we confess this, we confess that he is regenerate. And if this be so, how does St. John say, "He that hated his brother remained still in darkness," if remission of his sins has already taken place? Can it be

that schism does not involve hatred of one's brethren? Who will maintain this, when both the origin of, and perseverance in schism consists in nothing else save hatred of the brethren?

17. They think that they solve this question when they say: "There is then no remission of sins in schism, and therefore no creation of the new man by regeneration, and accordingly neither is there the baptism of Christ." But since we confess that the baptism of Christ exists in schism, we propose this question to them for solution: Was Simon Magus endued with the true baptism of Christ? They will answer, Yes; being compelled to do so by the authority of holy Scripture. I ask them whether they confess that he received remission of his sins. They will certainly acknowledge it. So, I ask why Peter said to him that he had no part in the lot of the saints. Because, they say, he sinned afterwards, wishing to buy with money the gift of God, which he believed the apostles could sell.

Chapter 12. —18. What if he approached baptism itself in deceit? were his sins remitted, or were they not? Let them choose which they will. Whichever they choose will answer our purpose. If they say they were remitted, how then shall "the Holy Spirit of discipline flee deceit," if in him who was full of deceit He worked remission of sins? If they say they were not remitted, I ask whether, if he should afterwards confess his sin with contrition of heart and true sorrow, it would be judged that he ought to be baptized again. And if it is mere madness to assert this, then let them confess that a man can be baptized with the true baptism of Christ, and that yet his heart, persisting in malice or sacrilege, may not allow remission of sins to be given; and so let them understand that men may be baptized in communions severed from the Church, in which Christ's baptism is given and received in the said celebration of the sacrament, but that it will only then be of avail for the remission of sins, when the recipient, being reconciled to the unity of the Church, is purged from the sacrilege of deceit, by which his sins were retained, and their remission prevented. For, as in the case of him who had approached the sacrament in deceit there is no second baptism, but he is purged by faithful discipline and truthful confession, which he could not be without baptism, so that what was given before becomes then powerful to work his salvation, when the former deceit is done away by the truthful confession; so also in the case of the man who, while an enemy to the peace and love of Christ, received in any heresy or schism the baptism of Christ, which the schismatics in question had not lost from among them, though by his sacrilege his sins were not remitted, yet, when he corrects his error, and comes over to the communion and unity of the Church, he ought not to be again baptized: because by his very reconciliation to the peace of the Church he receives this benefit, that the sacrament now begins in unity to be of avail for the remission of his sins, which could not so avail him as received in schism.

19. But if they should say that in the man who has approached the sacrament in deceit, his sins are indeed removed by the holy power of so great a sacrament at the moment when he received it, but return immediately in consequence of his deceit: so that the Holy Spirit has both been present with him at his baptism for the removal of his sins, and has also fled before his perseverance in deceit so that they should return: so that both declarations

prove true,—both, "As many of you as have been baptized into Christ have put on Christ;" and also, "The holy spirit of discipline will flee deceit;"—that is to say, that both the holiness of baptism clothes him with Christ, and the sinfulness of deceit strips him of Christ; like the case of a man who passes from darkness through light into darkness again, his eyes being always directed towards darkness, though the light cannot but penetrate them as he passes;—if they should say this, let them understand that this is also the case with those who are baptized without the pale of the Church, but yet with the baptism of the Church, which is holy in itself, wherever it may be; and which therefore belongs not to those who separate themselves, but to the body from which they are separated; while yet it avails even among them so far, that they pass through its light back to their own darkness, their sins, which in that moment had been dispelled by the holiness of baptism, returning immediately upon them, as though it were the darkness returning which the light had dispelled while they were passing through it.

20. For that sins which have been remitted do return upon a man, where there is no brotherly love, is most clearly taught by our Lord, in the case of the servant whom He found owing Him ten thousand talents, and to whom He yet forgave all at his entreaty. But when he refused to have pity on his fellow-servant who owed him a hundred pence, the Lord commanded him to pay what He had forgiven him. The time, then, at which pardon is received through baptism is as it were the time for rendering accounts, so that all the debts which are found to be due may be remitted. Yet it was not afterwards that the servant lent his fellow-servant the money, which he had so pitilessly exacted when the other was unable to pay

it; but his fellow-servant already owed him the debt, when he himself, on rendering his accounts to his master, was excused a debt of so vast an amount. He had not first excused his fellow-servant, and so come to receive forgiveness from his Lord. This is proved by the words of the fellow-servant: "Have patience with me, and I will pay thee all." Otherwise he would have said, "You forgave me it before; why do you again demand it?" This is made clearer by the words of the Lord Himself. For He says, "But the same servant went out, and found one of his fellow-servants which was owing him a hundred pence." He does not say, "To whom he had already forgiven a debt of a hundred pence." Since then He says, "was owing him," it is clear that he had not forgiven him the debt. And indeed it would have been better, and more in accordance with the position of a man who was going to render an account of so great a debt, and expected forbearance from his lord, that he should first have forgiven his fellow-servant what was due to him, and so have come to render the account when there was such need for imploring the compassion of his lord. Yet the fact that he had not yet forgiven his fellow-servant, did not prevent his lord from forgiving him all his debts on the occasion of receiving his accounts. But what advantage was it to him, since they all immediately returned with redoubled force upon his head, in consequence of his persistent want of charity? So the grace of baptism is not prevented from giving remission of all sins, even if he to whom they are forgiven continues to cherish hatred towards his brother in his heart. For the guilt of yesterday is remitted, and all that was before it, nay, even the guilt of the very hour and moment previous to baptism, and during baptism itself. But then he immediately begins again to be responsible, not only for the days, hours, moments which ensue, but also for the past, —the guilt of all the sins which were remitted returning on him, as happens only too frequently in the Church.

Chapter 13. —21. For it often happens that a man has an enemy whom he hates most unjustly; although we are commanded to love even our unjust enemies, and to pray for them. But in some sudden danger of death he begins to be uneasy, and desires baptism, which he receives in such haste, that the emergency scarcely admits of the necessary formal examination of a few words, much less of a long conversation, so that this hatred should be driven from his heart, even supposing it to be known to the minister who baptizes him. Certainly, cases of this sort are still found to occur not only with us, but also with them. What shall we say then? Are this man's sins forgiven or not? Let them choose just which alternative they prefer. For if they are forgiven, they immediately return: this is the teaching of the gospel, the authoritative announcement of truth. Whether, therefore, they are forgiven or not, medicine is necessary afterwards; and yet if the man lives, and learns that his fault stands in need of correction, and corrects it, he is not baptized anew, either with them or with us. So, in the points in which schismatics and heretics neither entertain different opinions nor observe different practice from ourselves, we do not correct them when they join us, but rather commend what we find in them. For where they do not differ from us, they are not separated from us. But because these things do them no good so long as they are schismatics or heretics, on account of other points in which they differ from us, not to mention the most grievous sin that is involved in separation itself, therefore, whether their sins remain in them, or return again immediately after remission, in either case we exhort them to come to the soundness of peace and Christian charity, not only that they may obtain something which they had not before, but also that what they had may begin to be of use to them.

Chapter 14. —22. It is to no purpose, then, that they say to us, "If you acknowledge our baptism, what do we lack that should make you suppose that we ought to think seriously of joining your communion?" For we reply, We do not acknowledge any baptism of yours; for it is not the baptism of schismatics or heretics, but of God and of the Church, wheresoever it may be found, and whithersoever it may be transferred. But it is in no sense yours, except because you entertain false opinions, and do sacrilegious acts, and have impiously separated yourselves from the Church. For if everything else in your practice and opinions were true, and still you were to persist in this same separation, contrary to the bond of brotherly peace, contrary to the union of all the brethren, who have been manifest, according to the promise, in all the world; the particulars of whose history, and the secrets of whose hearts, you never could have known or considered in every case, so as to have a right to condemn them; who, moreover, cannot be liable to condemnation for submitting themselves to the judges of the Church rather than to one of the parties to the dispute,—in this one thing, at least, in such a case, you are deficient, in which he is deficient who lacks charity. Why should we go over our argument again? Look and see yourselves in the apostle, how much there is that you lack. For what does it matter to him who lacks charity, whether he be carried away outside the Church at once by some blast of temptation, or remain within the Lord's harvest, so as to be separated only at the final winnowing? And yet even such, if they have once been born in baptism, need not be born again.

Chapter 15. —23. For it is the Church that gives birth to all, either within her pale, of her own womb; or beyond it, of the seed of her bridegroom, — (either of herself, or of her handmaid.) But Esau, even though born of the lawful wife, was separated from the people of God because he quarreled with his brother. And Asher, born indeed by the authority of a wife, but yet of a handmaid, was admitted to the land of promise because his brotherly good-will. Whence also it was not the being born of a handmaid, but his quarrelling with his brother, that stood in the way of Ishmael, to cause his separation from the people of God; and he received no benefit from the power of the wife, whose son he rather was, inasmuch as it was in virtue of her conjugal rights that he was both conceived in and born of the womb of the handmaid. Just as with the Donatists it is by the right of the Church, which exists in baptism, that whosoever is born receives his birth; but if they agree with their brethren, through the unity of peace they come to the land of promise, not to be again cast out from the bosom of their true mother, but to be acknowledged in the seed of their father; but if they persevere in discord, they will belong to the line of Ishmael. For Ishmael was first, and then Isaac; and Esau was the elder, Jacob the younger. Not that heresy gives birth before the Church, or that the Church herself gives birth first to those who are carnal or animal, and afterwards to those who are spiritual; but because, in the actual lot of our mortality, in which we are born of the seed of Adam, "that was not first which is spiritual, but that which is natural, and afterward that which is spiritual." But from mere animal sensation, because "the natural man received not the things of the Spirit of God," arise all dissensions and schisms. And the apostle says that all who persevere in this animal sensation belong to the old covenant. that is, to the desire of earthly promises, which are indeed the type of the spiritual; but "the natural man received not the things of the Spirit of God."

24. At whatever time, therefore, men have begun to be of such a nature in this life, that, although they have partaken of such divine sacraments as were appointed for the dispensation under which they lived, they yet savor of carnal things, and hope for and desire carnal things from God, whether in this life or afterwards, they are yet carnal. But the Church, which is the people of God, is an ancient institution even in the pilgrimage of this life, having a carnal interest in some men, a spiritual interest in others. To the carnal belongs the old covenant, to the spiritual the new. But in the first days both were hidden, from Adam even to Moses. But by Moses the old covenant was made manifest, and in it was hidden the new covenant, because after a secret fashion it was typified. But so soon as the Lord came in the flesh, the new covenant was revealed; yet, though the sacraments of the old covenant passed away; the dispositions peculiar to it did not pass away. For they still exist in those whom the apostle declares to be already born indeed by the sacrament of the new covenant, but yet capable, as being natural, of receiving the things of the Spirit of God. For,

as in the sacraments of the old covenant some persons were already spiritual, belonging secretly to the new covenant, which was then concealed, so now also in the sacrament of the new covenant, which has been by this time revealed, many live who are natural. And if they will not advance to receive the things of the Spirit of God, to which the discourse of the apostle urges them, they will still belong to the old covenant. But if they advance, even before they receive them, yet by their very advance and approach they belong to the new covenant; and if, before becoming spiritual, they are snatched away from this life, yet through the protection of the holiness of the sacrament they are reckoned in the land of the living, where the Lord is our hope and our portion. Nor can I find any truer interpretation of the scripture, "Thine eyes did see my substance, yet being imperfect" considering what follows, "And in Thy book shall all be written."

Chapter 16. —25. But the same mother which brought forth Abel, and Enoch, and Noah, and Abraham, brought forth also Moses and the prophets who succeeded him till the coming of our Lord; and the mother which gave birth to them gave birth also to our apostles and martyrs, and all good Christians. For all these that have appeared have been born indeed at different times, but are included in the society of our people; and it is as citizens of the same state that they have experienced the labors of this pilgrimage, and some of them are experiencing them, and others will experience them even to the end. Again, the mother who brought forth Cain, and Ham, and Ishmael, and Esau, brought forth also Dathan and others like him in the same people; and she who gave birth to them gave birth also to Judas the false apostle, and Simon

Magus, and all the other false Christians who up to this time have persisted obstinately in their carnal affections, whether they have been mingled in the unity of the Church, or separated from it in open schism. But when men of this kind have the gospel preached to them, and receive the sacraments at the hand of those who are spiritual, it is as though Rebecca gave birth to them of her own womb, as she did to Esau; but when they are produced in the midst of the people of God through the instrumentality of those who preach the gospel not sincerely, Sarah is indeed the mother, but through Hagar. So, when good spiritual disciples are produced by the preaching or baptism of those who are carnal, Leah, indeed, or Rachel, gives birth to them in her right as wife, but from the womb of a handmaid. But when good and faithful disciples are born of those who are spiritual in the gospel, and either attain to the development of spiritual age, or do not cease to strive in that direction, or are only deterred from doing so by want of power, these are born like Isaac from the womb of Sarah, or Jacob from the womb of Rebecca, in the new life and the new covenant.

Chapter 17. —26. Therefore, whether they seem to abide within, or are openly outside, whatsoever is flesh is flesh, and what is chaff is chaff, whether they persevere in remaining in their barrenness on the threshing-floor, or, when temptation befalls them, are carried out as it were by the blast of some wind. And even that man is always severed from the unity of the Church which is without spot or wrinkle, who associates with the congregation of the saints in carnal obstinacy. Yet we ought to despair of no man, whether he be one who shows himself to be of this nature within the pale of the Church, or whether he more openly opposes it from without. But the spiritual, or those who are steadily advancing with pious exertion towards this end, do not stray without the pale; since even when, by some perversity or necessity among men, they seem to be driven forth, they are more approved than if they had remained within, since they are in no degree roused to contend against the Church, but remain rooted in the strongest foundation of Christian charity on the solid rock of unity. For hereunto belongs what is said in the sacrifice of Abraham: "But the birds divided he not."

Chapter 18. —27. On the question of baptism, then, I think that I have argued at sufficient length; and since this is a most manifest schism which is called by the name of the Donatists, it only remains that about baptism we should believe with pious faith what the universal Church maintains, apart from the sacrilege of schism. And yet, if within the Church different men still held different opinions on the point, without meanwhile violating peace, then till someone clear and simple decree should have been passed by a universal Council, it would have been right for the charity which seeks for unity to throw a veil over the error of human infirmity, as it is written "For charity shall cover the multitude of sins." For, seeing that its absence causes the presence of all other things to be of no avail, we may well suppose that in its presence there is found pardon for the absence of some missing things.

28. There are great proofs of this existing on the part of the blessed martyr Cyprian, in his letters, —to come at last to him of whose authority they carnally flatter themselves they are possessed, whilst by his love they are spiritually overthrown. For at that time, before

the consent of the whole Church had declared authoritatively, by the decree of a plenary Council, what practice should be followed in this matter, it seemed to him, in common with about eighty of his fellow bishops of the African churches, that every man who had been baptized outside the communion of the Catholic Church should, on joining the Church, be baptized anew. And I take it, that the reason why the Lord did not reveal the error in this to a man of such eminence, was, that his pious humility and charity in guarding the peace and health of the Church might be made manifest, and might be noticed, so as to serve as an example of healing power, so to speak, not only to Christians of that age, but also to those who should come after. For when a bishop of so important a Church, himself a man of so great merit and virtue, endowed with such excellence of heart and power of eloquence, entertained an opinion about baptism different from that which was to be confirmed by a more diligent searching into the truth; though many of his colleagues held what was not yet made manifest by authority, but was sanctioned by the past custom of the Church, and afterwards embraced by the whole Catholic world; yet under these circumstances he did not sever himself, by refusal of communion, from the others who thought differently, and indeed never ceased to urge on the others that they should "forbear one another in love, endeavoring to keep the unity of the Spirit in the bond of peace." For so, while the framework of the body remained whole, if any infirmity occurred in certain of its members, it might rather regain its health from their general soundness, than be deprived of the chance of any healing care by their death in severance from the body. And if he had severed himself, how many were there to follow! what a name was he likely to make for himself among men! how much more widely would the name of Cyprianist have spread than that of Donatist! But he was not a son of perdition, one of those of whom it is said, "Thou casted them down while they were elevated;" but he was the son of the peace of the Church, who in the clear illumination of his mind failed to see one thing, only that through him another thing might be more excellently seen. "And yet," says the apostle, "show I unto you a more excellent way: though I speak with the tongues of men and of angels, and have not charity, I am become as sounding brass, or a tinkling cymbal." He had therefore imperfect insight into the hidden mystery of the sacrament. But if he had known the mysteries of all sacraments, without having charity, it would have been nothing. But as he, with imperfect insight into the mystery, was careful to preserve charity with all courage and humility and faith, he deserved to come to the crown of martyrdom; so that, if any cloud had crept over the clearness of his intellect from his infirmity as man, it might be dispelled by the glorious brightness of his blood. For it was not in vain that our Lord Jesus Christ, when He declared Himself to be the vine, and His disciples, as it were, the branches in the vine, gave command that those which bare no fruit should be cut off, and removed from the vine as useless branches. But what is really fruit, save that new offspring, of which He further says, "A new commandment I give unto you, that ye love one another?" This is that very charity, without which the rest profited nothing. The apostle also says: "But the fruit of the Spirit is love, joy, peace, longsuffering, gentleness, goodness, faith, meekness, temperance;" which all begin with charity, and with the rest of the combination forms one unity in a kind of wondrous cluster. Nor is it again in vain that our Lord added, "And every branch that bears fruit, my Father purges it, that it may bring forth more fruit," but because those who are strong in the fruit of charity may yet have something which requires purging, which the Husbandman will not leave untended. Whilst then, that holy man entertained about baptism an opinion at variance with the true view, which was afterwards thoroughly examined and confirmed after most diligent consideration, his error was compensated by his remaining in catholic unity, and by the abundance of his charity; and finally, it was cleared away by the pruning-hook of martyrdom.

Chapter 19. —29. But that I may not seem to be uttering these praises of the blessed martyr (which, indeed, are not his, but rather those of Him by whose grace he showed himself what he was), in order to escape the burden of proof, let us now bring forward from his letters the testimony by which the mouths of the Donatists may most of all be stopped. For they advance his authority before the unlearned, to show that in a manner they do well when they baptize afresh the faithful who come to them. Too wretched are they—and, unless they correct themselves, even by themselves are they utterly condemned—who choose in the example set them by so great a man to imitate just that fault, which only did not injure him, because he walked with constant steps even to the end in that from which they have strayed who "have not known the way of peace." It is true that Christ's baptism is holy; and although it may exist among heretics or schismatics, yet it does not belong to the heresy or schism; and therefore, even those who come from thence to the Catholic Church herself ought not to be baptized afresh. Yet to err on this point is one thing; it is another thing that those who are straying from the peace of the Church, and have fallen headlong into the pit of schism, should go on to decide that any who join them ought to be baptized again. For the former is a speck on the brightness of a holy soul which abundance of charity would fain have covered; the latter is a stain in their nether foulness which the hatred of peace in their countenance ostentatiously brings to light. But the subject for our further consideration, relating to the authority of the blessed Cyprian, we will commence from a fresh beginning.

Book II.

In which Augustin proves that it is to no purpose that the Donatists bring forward the authority of Cyprian, bishop and martyr, since it is really more opposed to them than to the Catholics. For that he held that the view of his predecessor Agrippinus, about baptizing heretics in the Catholic Church when they join its communion, should only be received on condition that peace should be maintained with those who entertained the opposite view, and that the unity of the Church should never be broken by any kind of schism.

Chapter 1. —1. How much the arguments make for us, that is, for catholic peace, which the party of Donatus profess to bring forward against us from the authority of the blessed Cyprian, and how much they prove against those who bring them forward, it is my intention, with the help of God, to show in the ensuing book. If, therefore, in the course of my argument, I am obliged to repeat what I have already said in other treatises (although I will do so as little as I can,) yet this ought not to be objected to by those who have already read them and agree with them; since it is not only right that those things which are necessary for instruction should be frequently instilled into men of dull intelligence, but even in the case of those who are endowed with larger understanding, it contributes very much both to make their learning easier and their powers of teaching readier, where the same points are handled and discussed in many various ways. For I know how much it discourages a reader, when he comes upon any knotty question in the book which he has in hand, to find himself presently referred for its solution to another which he happens not to have. Wherefore, if I am compelled, by the urgency of the present questions, to repeat what I have already said in other books, I would seek forgiveness from those who know those books already, that those who are ignorant may have their difficulties removed; for it is better to give to one who has already, than to abstain from satisfying anyone who is in want.

2. What, then, do they venture to say, when their mouth is closed by the force of truth, with which they will not agree? "Cyprian," say they, "whose great merits and vast learning we all know, decreed in a Council, with many of his fellow-bishops contributing their several opinions, that all heretics and schismatics, that is, all who are severed from the communion of the one Church, are without baptism; and therefore, whosoever has joined the communion of the Church after being baptized by them must be baptized in the Church." The authority of

Cyprian does not alarm me, because I am reassured by his humility. We know, indeed, the great merit of the bishop and martyr Cyprian; but is it in any way greater than that of the apostle and martyr Peter, of whom the said Cyprian speaks as follows in his epistle to Quintus? "For neither did Peter, whom the Lord chose first, and on whom He built His Church, when Paul afterwards disputed with him about circumcision, claim or assume anything insolently and arrogantly to himself, so as to say that he held the primacy, and should rather be obeyed of those who were late and newly come. Nor did he despise Paul because he had before been a persecutor of the Church, but he admitted the counsel of truth, and readily assented to the legitimate grounds which Paul maintained; giving us thereby a pattern of concord and patience, that we should not pertinaciously love our own opinions, but should rather account as our own any true and rightful suggestions of our brethren and colleagues for the common health and weal." Here is a passage in which Cyprian records what we also learn in holy Scripture, that the Apostle Peter, in whom the primacy of the apostles shines with such exceeding grace, was corrected by the later Apostle Paul, when he adopted a custom in the matter of circumcision at variance with the demands of truth. If it was therefore possible for Peter in some point to walk not uprightly according to the truth of the gospel, so as to compel the Gentiles to Judaize, as Paul writes in that epistle in which he calls God to witness that he does not lie; for he says, "Now the things which I write unto you, behold, before God, I lie not;" and, after this sacred and awful calling of God to witness, he told the whole tale, saying in the course of it, "But when I saw that they walked not uprightly, according to the truth of the gospel,

I said unto Peter before them all, If thou, being a Jew, lives after the manner of the Gentiles, and not as do the Jews, why compels thou the Gentiles to live as do the Jews?"—if Peter, I say, could compel the Gentiles to live after the manner of the Jews, contrary to the rule of truth which the Church afterwards held, why might not Cyprian, in opposition to the rule of faith which the whole Church afterwards held, compel heretics and schismatics to be baptized afresh? I suppose that there is no slight to Cyprian in comparing him with Peter in respect to his crown of martyrdom; rather I ought to be afraid lest I am showing disrespect towards Peter. For who can be ignorant that the primacy of his apostleship is to be preferred to any episcopate whatever? But, granting the difference in the dignity of their sees, yet they have the same glory in their martyrdom. And whether it may be the case that the hearts of those who confess and die for the true faith in the unity of charity take precedence of each other in different points, the Lord Himself will know, by the hidden and wondrous dispensation of whose grace the thief hanging on the cross once for all confesses Him, and is sent on the selfsame day to paradise, while Peter, the follower of our Lord, denies Him thrice, and has his crown postponed: for us it were rash to form a judgment from the evidence. But if anyone were now found compelling a man to be circumcised after the Jewish fashion, as a necessary preliminary for baptism, this would meet with much more general repudiation by mankind, than if a man should be compelled to be baptized again. Wherefore, if Peter, on doing this, is corrected by his later colleague Paul, and is yet preserved by the bond of peace and unity till he is promoted to martyrdom, how much more readily and constantly should we prefer, either to the authority of a single bishop, or to the Council of a single province, the rule that has been established by the statutes of the universal Church? For this same Cyprian, in urging his view of the question, was still anxious to remain in the unity of peace even with those who differed from him on this point, as is shown by his own opening address at the beginning of the very Council which is quoted by the Donatists. For it is as follows:

Chapter 2. —3. "When, on the calends of September, very many bishops from the provinces of Africa, Numidia, and Mauritania, with their presbyters and deacons, had met together at Carthage, a great part of the laity also being present; and when the letter addressed by Jubaianus to Cyprian, as also the answer of Cyprian to Jubaianus, on the subject of baptizing heretics, had been read, Cyprian said: 'Ye have heard, most beloved colleagues, what Jubaianus, our fellow-bishop, has written to me, consulting my moderate ability concerning the unlawful and profane baptism of heretics, and what answer I gave him,—giving a judgment which we have once and again and often given, that heretics coming to the Church ought to be baptized, and sanctified with the baptism of the Church. Another letter of Jubaianus has likewise been read to you, in which, agreeably to his sincere and religious devotion, in answer to our epistle, he not only expressed his assent, but returned thanks also, acknowledging that he had received instruction. It remains that we severally declare our opinion on this subject, judging no one, nor depriving any one of the right of communion if he differs from us. For no one of us sets himself up as a bishop of bishops, or, by tyrannical terror, forces his colleagues to a necessity of obeying, inasmuch as every bishop, in the free use of his liberty and power, has the right of forming his own judgment, and can no more be judged by another than he can himself judge another. But we must all await the judgment of our Lord Jesus Christ, who alone has the power both of setting us in the government of His Church, and of judging of our acts therein.'"

Chapter 3. —4. Now let the proud and swelling necks of the heretics raise themselves, if they dare, against the holy humility of this address. Ye mad Donatists, whom we desire earnestly to return to the peace and unity of the holy Church, that ye may receive health therein, what have ye to say in answer to this? You are wont, indeed, to bring up against us the letters of Cyprian, his opinion, his Council; why do ye claim the authority of Cyprian for your schism, and reject his example when it makes for the peace of the Church? But who can fail to be aware that the sacred canon of Scripture, both of the Old and New Testament, is confined within its own limits, and that it stands so absolutely in a superior position to all later letters of the bishops, that about it we can hold no manner of doubt or disputation whether what is confessedly contained in it is right and true; but that all the letters of bishops which have been written, or are being written, since the closing of the canon, are liable to be refuted if there be anything contained in them which strays from the truth, either by the discourse of someone who happens to be wiser in the matter than themselves, or by the weightier authority and more learned experience of other bishops, by the authority of Councils; and further, that the Councils themselves, which are held in the several districts and provinces, must yield, beyond all possibility of doubt, to the authority of plenary Councils which are formed for the whole Christian world; and that even of the plenary Councils, the earlier are often corrected by those which follow them, when, by some actual experiment, things are brought to light which were before concealed, and that is known which previously lay hid, and this without any whirlwind of sacrilegious pride, without any puffing of the neck through arrogance, without any strife of envious hatred, simply with holy humility, catholic peace, and Christian charity?

Chapter 4. —5. Wherefore the holy Cyprian, whose dignity is only increased by his humility, who so loved the pattern set by Peter as to use the words, "Giving us thereby a pattern of concord and patience, that we should not pertinaciously love our own opinions, but should rather account as our own any true and rightful suggestions of our brethren and colleagues, for the common health and weal,"—he, I say, abundantly shows that he was most willing to correct his own opinion, if anyone should prove to him that it is as certain that the baptism of Christ can be given by those who have strayed from the fold, as that it could not be lost when they strayed; on which subject we have already said much. Nor should we ourselves venture to assert anything of the kind, were we not supported by the unanimous authority of the whole Church, to which he himself would unquestionably have yielded, if at that time the truth of this question had been placed beyond dispute by the investigation and decree of a plenary Council. For if he quotes Peter as an example for his allowing himself quietly and peacefully to be corrected by one junior colleague, how much more readily would he himself, with the Council of his province, have yielded to the authority of the whole world, when the truth had been thus brought to light? For, indeed, so holy and peaceful a soul would have been most ready to assent to the arguments of any single person who could prove to him the truth; and perhaps he even did so, though we have no knowledge of the fact. For it was neither possible that all the proceedings which took place between the bishops at that time should have been committed to writing, nor are we acquainted with all that was so committed. For how could a matter which was involved in such mists of disputation even have been brought to the full illumination and authoritative decision of a plenary Council, had it not first been known to be discussed for some considerable time in the various districts of the world, with many discussions and comparisons of the views of the bishop on every side? But this is one effect of the soundness of peace, that when any doubtful points are long under investigation, and when, because the difficulty of arriving at the truth, they produce difference of opinion during brotherly disputation, till men at last arrive at the unalloyed truth; yet the bond of unity remains, lest in the part that is cut away there should be found the incurable wound of deadly error.

Chapter 5. —6. And so, it is that often something is imperfectly revealed to the more learned, that their patient and humble charity, from which proceeds the greater fruit, may be proved, either in the way in which they preserve unity, when they hold different opinions on matters of comparative obscurity, or in the temper with which they receive the truth, when they learn that it has been declared to be contrary to what they thought. And of these two we have a manifestation in the blessed Cyprian of the one, viz., of the way in which he preserved unity with those from whom he differed in opinion. For he says, "Judging no one nor depriving any one of the right of communion if he differ from us." And the other, viz., in what temper he could receive the truth when found to be different from what he thought it, though his letters are silent on the point, is yet proclaimed by his merits. If there is no letter extant to prove it, it is witnessed by his crown of martyrdom; if the Council of bishops declare it not, it is declared by the host of angels. For it is no small proof of a most peaceful soul, that he won the crown of martyrdom in that unity from which he would not separate, even though he differed from it. For we are but men; and it is therefore a temptation incident to men that we should hold views at variance with the truth on any point. But to come through too great love for our own opinion, or through jealousy of our betters, even to the sacrilege of dividing the communion of the Church, and of founding heresy or schism, is a presumption worthy of the devil. But never in any point to entertain an opinion at variance with the truth is perfection found only in the angels. Since then we are men, yet forasmuch as in hope we are angels, whose equals we shall be in the resurrection, at any rate, so long as we are wanting in the perfection of angels, let us at least be without the presumption of the devil. Accordingly the apostle says, "There hath no temptation taken you but such as is common to man." It is therefore part of man's nature to be sometimes wrong. Wherefore he says in another place, "Let us therefore, as many as be perfect, be thus minded: and if in anything ye be otherwise minded, God shall reveal even this unto you." But to whom does He reveal it when it is His will (be it in this life or in the life to come), save to those who walk in the way of peace, and stray not aside into any schism? Not to such as those who have not known the way of peace, or for some other cause have broken the bond of unity. And so, when the apostle said, "And if in anything ye be otherwise minded, God shall reveal even this unto you," lest they should think that besides the way of peace their own wrong views might be revealed to them, he immediately added, "Nevertheless, whereto we have already attained, let us walk by the same rule." And Cyprian, walking by this rule, by the most persistent tolerance, not simply by the shedding of his blood, but because it was shed in unity (for if he gave his body to be burned, and had not charity, it would profit him nothing), came by the confession of martyrdom to the light of the angels, and if not before, at least then, acknowledged the revelation of the truth on that point on which, while yet in error, he did not prefer the maintenance of a wrong opinion to the bond of unity.

Chapter 6. —7. What then, ye Donatists, what have ye to say to this? If our opinion about baptism is true, yet all who thought differently in the time of Cyprian were not cut off from the unity of the Church, till God revealed to them the truth of the point on which they were in error, why then have ye by your sacrilegious separation broken the bond of peace? But if yours is the true opinion about baptism, Cyprian and the others, in conjunction with whom ye set forth that he held such a Council, remained in unity with those who thought otherwise; why, therefore, have ye broken the bond of peace? Choose which alternative ye will, ye are compelled to pronounce an opinion against your schism. Answer me, wherefore have ye separated yourselves? Wherefore have ye erected an altar in opposition to the whole world? Wherefore do ye not communicate with the Churches to which apostolic epistles have been sent, which you yourselves read and acknowledge, in accordance with whose tenor you say that you order your lives? Answer me, wherefore have ye separated yourselves? I suppose in order that ye might not perish by communion with wicked men. How then was it that Cyprian, and so many of his colleagues, did not perish? For though they believed that heretics and schismatics did not possess baptism, yet they chose rather to hold communion with them when they had been received into the Church without baptism, although they believed that their flagrant and sacrilegious sins were yet upon their heads, than to be separated from the unity of the Church, according to the words of Cyprian, "Judging no one, nor depriving any one of the right of communion if he differ from us."

8. If, therefore, by such communion with the wicked the just cannot but perish, the Church had already perished in the time of Cyprian. Whence then sprang the origin of Donatus? where was he taught, where was he baptized, where was he ordained, since the Church had been already destroyed by the contagion of communion with the wicked? But if the Church still existed, the wicked could do no harm to the good in one communion with them. Wherefore did ye separate yourselves? Behold, I see in unity Cyprian and others, his colleagues, who, on holding a council, decided that those who have been baptized without the communion of the Church have no true baptism, and that therefore it must be given them when they join the Church. But again, behold I see in the

same unity that certain men think differently in this matter, and that, recognizing in those who come from heretics and schismatics the baptism of Christ, they do not venture to baptize them afresh. All of these catholic unity embraces in her motherly breast, bearing each other's burdens by turns, and endeavoring to keep the unity of the Spirit in the bond of peace, till God should reveal to one or other of them any error in their views. If the one party held the truth, were they infected by the others, or no? If the others held the truth, were they infected by the first, or no? Choose which ye will. If there was contamination, the Church even then ceased to exist; answer me, therefore, whence came ye forth hither? But if the Church remained, the good are in no wise contaminated by the bad in such communion; answer me, therefore, why did ye break the bond?

9. Or is it perhaps that schismatics, when received without baptism, bring no infection, but that it is brought by those who deliver up the sacred books? For that there were traditors of your number is proved by the clearest testimony of history. And if you had then brought true evidence against those whom you were accusing, you would have proved your cause before the unity of the whole world, so that you would have been retained whilst they were shut out. And if you endeavored to do this, and failed, the world is not to blame, which trusted the judges of the Church rather than the beaten parties in the suit; whilst, if you would not urge your suit, the world again is not to blame, which could not condemn men without their cause being heard. Why, then, did you separate yourselves from the innocent? You cannot defend the sacrilege of your schism. But this I pass over. But so much I say, that if the traditors could have defiled you,

who were not convicted by you, and by whom, on the contrary, you were beaten, much more could the sacrilege of schismatics and heretics, received into the Church, as you maintain, without baptism, have defiled Cyprian. Yet he did not separate himself. And inasmuch as the Church continued to exist, it is clear that it could not be defiled. Wherefore, then, did you separate yourselves, I do not say from the innocent, as the facts proved them, but from the traditors, as they were never proved to be? Are the sins of traditors, as I began to say, heavier than those of schismatics? Let us not bring in deceitful balances, to which we may hang what weights we will and how we will, saying to suit ourselves, "This is heavy and this is light;" but let us bring forward the sacred balance out of holy Scripture, as out of the Lord's treasure-house, and let us weigh them by it, to see which is the heavier; or rather, let us not weigh them for ourselves, but read the weights as declared by the Lord. At the time when the Lord showed, by the example of recent punishment, that there was need to guard against the sins of olden days, and an idol was made and worshipped, and the prophetic book was burned by the wrath of a scoffing king, and schism was attempted, the idolatry was punished with the sword, the burning of the book by slaughter in war and captivity in a foreign land, schism by the earth opening, and swallowing up alive the leaders of the schism while the rest were consumed with fire from heaven. Who will now doubt that that was the worse crime which received the heavier punishment? If men coming from such sacrilegious company, without baptism, as you maintain, could not defile Cyprian, how could those defile you who were not convicted but supposed betrayers of the sacred books? For if they had not only given up the books to be burned, but had actually burned them with their own hands, they would have been guilty of a less sin than if they had committed schism; for schism is visited with the heavier, the other with the lighter punishment, not at man's discretion, but by the judgment of God.

Chapter 7. —10. Wherefore, then, have ye severed yourselves? If there is any sense left in you, you must surely see that you can find no possible answer to these arguments. "We are not left," they say, "so utterly without resource, but that we can still answer, It is our will. 'Who art thou that judges another man's servant? to his own master he stands or falls.'" They do not understand that this was said to men who were wishing to judge, not of open facts, but of the hearts of other men. For how does the apostle himself come to say so much about the sins of schisms and heresies? Or how comes that verse in the Psalms,

"If of a truth ye love justice, judge uprightly, O ye sons of men?" But why does the Lord Himself say, "Judge not according to the appearance, but judge righteous judgment," if we may not judge any man? Lastly, why, in the case of those traditors, whom they have judged unrighteously, have they themselves ventured to pass any judgments at all on another man's servants? To their own master they were standing or falling. Or why, in the case of the recent followers of Maximianus, have they not hesitated to bring forward the judgment delivered with the infallible voice, as they aver, of a plenary Council, in such terms as to compare them with those first schismatics whom the earth swallowed up alive? And yet some of them, as they cannot deny, they either condemned though innocent, or received back again in their guilt. But when a truth is urged which they cannot gainsay, they mutter a truly wholesome murmuring: "It is our will: 'Who art thou that judges another man's servant? to his own master he stands or falls.'" But when a weak sheep is espied in the desert, and the pastor who should reclaim it to the fold is nowhere to be seen, then there is setting of teeth, and breaking of the weak neck: "Thou wouldst be a good man, wert thou not a traditor. Consult the welfare of thy soul; be a Christian." What unconscionable madness! When it is said to a Christian, "Be a Christian," what other lesson is taught, save a denial that he is a Christian? Was it not the same lesson which those persecutors of the Christians wished to teach, by resisting whom the crown of martyrdom was gained? Or must we even look on crime as lighter when committed with threatening of the sword than with treachery of the tongue?

11. Answer me this, ye ravening wolves, who, seeking to be clad in sheep's clothing, think that the letters of the blessed Cyprian are in your favor. Did the sacrilege of schismatics defile Cyprian, or did it not? If it did, the Church perished from that instant, and there remained no source from which ye might spring. If it did not, then by what offense on the part of others can the guiltless possibly be defiled, if the sacrilege of schism cannot defile them? Wherefore, then, have ye severed yourselves? Wherefore, while shunning the lighter offenses, which are inventions of your own, have ye committed the heaviest offense of all, the sacrilege of schism? Will ye now perchance confess that those men were no longer schismatics or heretics who had been baptized without the communion of the Church, or in some heresy or schism, because by coming over to the

Church, and renouncing their former errors, they had ceased to be what formerly they were? How then was it, that though they were not baptized, their sins remained not on their heads? Was it that the baptism was Christ's, but that it could not profit them without the communion of the Church; yet when they came over, and, renouncing their past error, were received into the communion of the Church by the laying on of hands, then, being now rooted and founded in charity, without which all other things are profitless, they began to receive profit for the remission of sins and the sanctification of their lives from that sacrament, which, while without the pale of the Church, they possessed in vain?

12. Cease, then, to bring forward against us the authority of Cyprian in favor of repeating baptism, but cling with us to the example of Cyprian for the preservation of unity. For this question of baptism had not been as yet completely worked out, but yet the Church observed the most wholesome custom of correcting what was wrong, not repeating what was already given, even in the case of schismatics and heretics: she healed the wounded part, but did not meddle with what was whole. And this custom, coming, I suppose, from apostolical tradition (like many other things which are held to have been handed down under their actual sanction, because they are preserved throughout the whole Church, though they are not found either in their letters, or in the Councils of their successors), —this most wholesome custom, I say, according to the holy Cyprian, began to be what is called amended by his predecessor Agrippinus. But, according to the teaching which springs from a more careful investigation into the truth, which, after great doubt and fluctuation, was brought at last to the decision

of a plenary Council, we ought to believe that it rather began to be corrupted than to receive correction at the hands of Agrippinus. Accordingly, when so great a question forced itself upon him, and it was difficult to decide the point, whether remission of sins and man's spiritual regeneration could take place among heretics or schismatics, and the authority of Agrippinus was there to guide him, with that of some few men who shared in his misapprehension of this question, having preferred attempting something new to maintaining a custom which they did not understand how to defend; under these circumstances considerations of probability forced themselves into the eyes of his soul, and barred the way to the thorough investigation of the truth.

Chapter 8. —13. Nor do I think that the blessed Cyprian had any other motive in the free expression and earlier utterance of what he thought in opposition to the custom of the Church, save that he should thankfully receive any one that could be found with a fuller revelation of the truth, and that he should show forth a pattern for imitation, not only of diligence in teaching, but also of modesty in learning; but that, if no one should be found to bring forward any argument by which those considerations of probability should be refuted, then he should abide by his opinion, with the full consciousness that he had neither concealed what he conceived to be the truth, nor violated the unity which he loved. For so he understood the words of the apostle: "Let the prophets speak two or three, and let the other judge. If anything be revealed to another that sits by, let the first hold his peace." "In which passage he has taught and shown, that many things are revealed to individuals for the better, and that we ought not each to strive pertinaciously for what he has once imbibed and held, but if anything has appeared better and more useful, he should willingly embrace it." At any rate, in these words he not only advised those to agree with him who saw no better course, but also exhorted any who could to bring forward arguments by which the maintenance of the former custom might rather be established; that if they should be of such a nature as not to admit of refutation, he might show in his own person with what sincerity he said "that we ought not each to strive pertinaciously for what he has once imbibed and held, but that, if anything has appeared better and more useful, he should willingly embrace it." But inasmuch as none appeared, except such as simply urged the custom against him, and the arguments which they produced in its favor were not of a kind to bring conviction to a soul like his, this mighty reasoner was not content to give up his opinions, which, though they were not true, as he was himself unable to see, were at any rate not confuted, in favor of a custom which had truth on its side, but had not yet been confirmed. And yet, had not his predecessor Agrippinus, and some of his fellow-bishops throughout Africa, first tempted him to desert this custom, even by the decision of a Council, he certainly would not have dared to argue against it. But, amid the perplexities of so obscure a question, and seeing everywhere around him a strong universal custom, he would rather have put restraint upon himself by prayer and stretching forth his mind towards God, so as to have perceived or taught that for truth which was afterwards decided by a plenary Council. But when he had found relief amid his weariness in the authority of the former Council which was held by Agrippinus, he preferred maintaining what was in a manner the discovery of his predecessors, to expending further toil in investigation. For, at the end of his letter to Quintus, he thus shows how he has sought repose, if one may use the expression, for his weariness, in what might be termed the resting-place of authority.

Chapter 9. —14. "This, moreover," says he, "Agrippinus, a man of excellent memory, with the rest, bishops with him, who at that time governed the Church of the Lord in the province of Africa and Numidia, did establish and, after the investigation of a mutual Council had weighed it, confirm; whose sentence, being both religious and legitimate and salutary in accordance with the Catholic faith and Church, we also have followed."
By this witness he gives sufficient proof how much more ready he would have been to bear his testimony, had any Council been held to discuss this matter which either embraced the whole Church, or at least represented our brethren beyond the sea. But such a Council had not yet been held, because the whole world was bound together by the powerful bond of custom; and this was deemed sufficient to oppose to those who wished to introduce what was new, because they could not comprehend the truth. Afterwards, however, while the question became matter for discussion and investigation amongst many on either side, the new practice was not only invented, but even submitted to the authority and power of a plenary Council, —after the martyrdom of Cyprian, it is true, but before we were born. But that this was indeed the custom of the Church, which afterwards was confirmed by a plenary Council, in which the truth was brought to light, and many difficulties cleared away, is plain enough from the words of the blessed Cyprian himself in that same

letter to Jubaianus, which was quoted as being read in the Council. For he says, "But someone asks, What then will be done in the case of those who, coming out of heresy to the Church, have already been admitted without baptism?" where certainly he shows plainly enough what was usually done, though he would have wished it otherwise; and in the very fact of his quoting the Council of Agrippinus, he clearly proves that the custom of the Church was different. Nor indeed was it requisite that he should seek to establish the practice by this Council, if it was already sanctioned by custom; and in the Council itself some of the speakers expressly declare, in giving their opinion, that they went against the custom of the Church in deciding what they thought was right. Wherefore let the Donatists consider this one point, which surely none can fail to see, that if the authority of Cyprian is to be followed, it is to be followed rather in maintaining unity than in altering the custom of the Church; but if respect is paid to his Council, it must at any rate yield place to the later Council of the universal Church, of which he rejoiced to be a member, often warning his associates that they should all follow his example in upholding the coherence of the whole body. For both later Councils are preferred among later generations to those of earlier date; and the whole is always, with good reason, looked upon as superior to the parts.

Chapter 10. —15. But what attitude do they assume, when it is shown that the holy Cyprian, though he did not himself admit as members of the Church those who had been baptized in heresy or schism, yet held communion with those who did admit them, according to his express declaration, "Judging no one, nor depriving any one of the right of communion if he differ from us?" If he was polluted by communion with persons of this kind, why do they follow his authority in the question of baptism? But if he was not polluted by communion with them, why do they not follow his example in maintaining unity? Have they anything to urge in their defense except the plea, "We choose to have it so?" What other answer have any sinful or wicked men to the discourse of truth or justice, —the voluptuous, for instance, the drunkards, adulterers, and those who are impure in any way, thieves, robbers, murderers, plunderers, evil-doers, idolaters, — what other answer can they make when convicted by the voice of truth, except "I choose to do it;" "It is my pleasure so"? And if they have in them a tinge of Christianity, they say further, "Who art thou that judges another man's servant?" Yet these have so much more remains of modesty, that when, in accordance with divine and human law, they meet with punishment for their abandoned life and deeds, they do not style themselves martyrs; while the Donatists wish at once to lead a sacrilegious life and enjoy a blameless reputation, to suffer no punishment for their wicked deeds, and to gain a martyr's glory in their just punishment. As if they were not experiencing the greater mercy and patience of God, in proportion as "executing His judgments upon them by little and little, He giveth them place of repentance," and ceases not to redouble His scourgings in this life; that, considering what they suffer, and why they suffer it, they may in time grow wise; and that those who have received the baptism of the party of Maximianus in order to preserve the unity of Donatus, may the more readily embrace the baptism of the whole world in order to preserve the peace of Christ; that they may be restored to the root, may be reconciled to the unity of the Church, may see that they have nothing left for them to say, though something yet remains for them to do; that for their former deeds the sacrifice of loving-kindness may be offered to a long-suffering God, whose unity they have broken by their wicked sin, on whose sacraments they have inflicted such a lasting wrong. For "the Lord is merciful and gracious, slow to anger, plenteous in mercy and truth." Let them embrace His mercy and long-suffering in this life, and fear His truth in the next. For He wills not the death of a sinner, but rather that he should turn from his way and live; because He bends His judgment against the wrongs that have been inflicted on Him. This is our exhortation.

Chapter 11. —16. For this reason, then, we hold them to be enemies, because we speak the truth, because we are afraid to be silent, because we fear to shrink from pressing our point with all the force that lies within our power, because we obey the apostle when he says, "Preach the word; be instant in season out of season; reprove, rebuke, exhort." But, as the gospel says, "They love the praise of men more than the praise of God;" and while they fear to incur blame for a time, they do not fear to incur damnation forever. They see, too, themselves what wrong they are doing; they see that they have no answer which they can make, but they overspread the inexperienced with mists, whilst they themselves are being swallowed up alive, —that is, are perishing knowingly and willfully. They see that men are amazed, and look with abhorrence on the fact that they have divided themselves into many schisms, especially in Carthage, the capital and most noted city of all Africa;

they have endeavored to patch up the disgrace of their rags. Thinking that they could annihilate the followers of Maximianus, they pressed heavily on them through the agency of Optatus the Gildonian; they inflicted on them many wrongs amid the cruelest of persecutions. Then they received back some, thinking that all could be converted under the influence of the same terror; but they were unwilling to do those whom they received the wrong of baptizing afresh those who had been baptized by them in their schism, or rather of causing them to be baptized again within their communion by the very same men by whom they had been baptized outside, and thus they at once made an exception to their own impious custom. They feel how wickedly they are acting in assailing the baptism of the whole world, when they have received the baptism of the followers of Maximianus. But they fear those whom they have themselves rebaptized, lest they should receive no mercy from them, when they have shown it to others; lest these should call them to account for their souls when they have ceased to destroy those of other men.

Chapter 12. —17. What answer they can give about the followers of Maximianus whom they have received, they cannot divine. If they say, "Those we received were innocent," the answer is obvious, "Then you had condemned the innocent." If they say, "We did it in ignorance," then you judged rashly (just as you passed a rash judgment on the traditors), and your declaration was false that "you must know that they were condemned by the truthful voice of a plenary Council." For indeed the innocent could never be condemned by a voice of truth. If they say, "We did not condemn them," it is only necessary to cite the Council, to cite the names of bishops and states alike. If they say, "The Council itself is none of ours," then we cite the records of the proconsular province, where more than once they quoted the same Council to justify the exclusion of the followers of Maximianus from the basilicas, and to confound them by the din of the judges and the force of their allies. If they say that Felicianus of Musti, and Prætextatus of Assavæ, whom they afterwards received, were not of the party of Maximianus, then we cite the records in which they demanded, in the courts of law, that these persons should be excluded from the Council which they held against the party of Maximianus. If they say, "They were received for the sake of peace," our answer is, "Why then do ye not acknowledge the only true and full peace? Who urged you, who compelled you to receive a schismatic whom you had condemned, to preserve the peace of Donatus, and to condemn the world unheard, in violation of the peace of Christ?" Truth hems them in on every side. They see that there is no answer left for them to make, and they think that there is nothing left for them to do; they cannot find out what to say. They are not allowed to be silent. They had rather strive with perverse utterance against truth, than be restored to peace by a confession of their faults.

Chapter 13. —18. But who can fail to understand what they may be saying in their hearts? "What then are we to do," say they, "with those whom we have already rebaptized?" Return with them to the Church. Bring those whom you have wounded to be healed by the medicine of peace: bring those whom you have slain to be brought to life again by the life of charity. Brotherly union has great power in propitiating God. "If two of you," says our Lord, "shall agree on earth as touching anything that they shall ask, it shall be done for them." If for two men who agree, how much more for two communities? Let us throw ourselves together on our knees before the Lord. Do you share with us our unity; let us share with you your contrition and let charity cover the multitude of sins. Seek counsel from the blessed Cyprian himself. See how much he considered to depend upon the blessing of unity, from which he did not sever himself to avoid the communion of those who disagreed with him; how, though he considered that those who were baptized outside the communion of the Church had no true baptism, he was yet willing to believe that, by simple admission into the Church, they might, merely in virtue of the bond of unity, be admitted to a share in pardon. For thus he solved the question which he proposed to himself in writing as follows to Jubaianus: "But some will say, 'What then will become of those who, in times past, coming to the Church from heresy, were admitted without baptism?' The Lord is able of His mercy to grant pardon, and not to sever from the gifts of His Church those who, being out of simplicity admitted to the Church, have in the Church fallen asleep."

Chapter 14. —19. But which is the worse, not to be baptized at all, or to be twice baptized, it is difficult to decide. I see, indeed, which is more repugnant and abhorrent to men's feelings; but when I have recourse to that divine balance, in which the weight of things is determined, not by man's feelings, but by the authority of God, I find a statement by our Lord on either side. For He said to Peter, "He who is washed has no need of washing a second time;" and to Nicodemus, "Except a man be born of water and of the Spirit, he cannot enter into the kingdom of God." What is the purport of the more secret determination of God, it is perhaps difficult for men like us to learn; but as far as the mere words are concerned, any one may see what a difference there is between "has no need of washing," and "cannot enter into the kingdom of heaven." The Church, lastly, herself holds as her tradition, that without baptism she cannot admit a man to her altar at all; but since it is allowed that one who has been rebaptized may be admitted after penance, surely this plainly proves that his baptism is considered valid. If, therefore, Cyprian thought that those whom he considered to be unbaptized yet had some share in pardon, in virtue of the bond of unity, the Lord has power to be reconciled even to the rebaptized by means of the simple bond of unity and peace, and by this same compensating power of peace to mitigate His displeasure against those by whom they were rebaptized, and to pardon all the errors which they had committed while in error, on their offering the sacrifice of charity, which covered the multitude of sins; so that He looks not to the number of those who have been wounded by their separation, but to the greater number who have been delivered from bondage by their return. For in the same bond of peace in which Cyprian conceived that, through the mercy of God, those whom he considered to have been admitted to the Church without baptism, were yet not severed from the gifts of the Church, we also believe that through the same mercy of God the rebaptized can earn their pardon at His hands.

Chapter 15. —20. Since the Catholic Church, both in the time of the blessed Cyprian and in the older time before him, contained within her bosom either some that were rebaptized or some that were unbaptized, either the one section or the other must have won their salvation only by the force of simple unity. For if those who came over from the heretics were not baptized, as Cyprian asserts, they were not rightly admitted into the Church; and yet he himself did not despair of their obtaining pardon from the mercy of God in virtue of the unity of the Church. So again, if they were already baptized, it was not right to rebaptize them. What, therefore, was there to aid the other section, save the same charity that delighted in unity, so that what was hidden from man's weakness, in the consideration of the sacrament, might not be reckoned, by the mercy of God, as a fault in those who were lovers of peace? Why, then, while ye fear those whom ye have rebaptized, do ye grudge yourselves and them the entrance to salvation? There was at one time a doubt upon the subject of baptism; those who held different opinions yet remained in unity. In course of time, owing to the certain discovery of the truth, that doubt was taken away. The question which, unsolved, did not frighten Cyprian into separation from the Church, invites you, now that it is solved, to return once more within the fold. Come to the Catholic Church in its agreement, which Cyprian did not desert while yet disturbed with doubt; or if now you are dissatisfied with the example of Cyprian, who held communion with those who were received with the baptism of heretics, declaring openly that we should "neither judge any one, nor deprive any one of the right of communion if he differ from us," whither are ye going, ye wretched men? What are ye doing? You are bound to fly even from yourselves, because you have advanced beyond the position where he abodes. But if neither his own sins nor those of others could stand in his way, because the abundance of his charity and his love of brotherly kindness and the bond of peace, do you return to us, where you will find much less hindrance in the way of either us or you from the fictions which your party have invented.

Book III.

Augustin undertakes the refutation of the arguments which might be derived from the epistle of Cyprian to Jubaianus, to give color to the view that the baptism of Christ could not be conferred by heretics.

Chapter 1. —1. I think that it may now be considered clear to everyone, that the authority of the blessed Cyprian for the maintenance of the bond of peace, and the avoiding of any violation of that most wholesome charity which preserves unity in the Church, may be urged on our side rather than on the side of the Donatists. For if they have chosen to act upon his example in rebaptizing Catholics, because he thought that heretics ought to be baptized on joining the Catholic Church, shall not we rather follow his example, whereby he laid down a manifest rule that one ought in no wise, by the establishment of a separate communion, to secede from the Catholic communion, that is, from the body of Christians dispersed throughout the world, even on the admission of evil and sacrilegious men, since he was unwilling even to remove from the right of communion those whom he considered to have received sacrilegious men without baptism into the Catholic communion, saying, "Judging no one, nor depriving any of the right of communion if he differ from us?"

Chapter 2. —2. Nevertheless, I see what may still be required of me, viz., that I should answer those plausible arguments, by which, in even earlier times, Agrippinus, or Cyprian himself, or those in Africa who agreed with them, or any others in far distant lands beyond the sea, were moved, not indeed by the authority of any plenary or even regionary Council, but by a mere epistolary correspondence, to think that they ought to adopt a custom which had no sanction from the ancient custom of the Church, and which was expressly forbidden by the most unanimous resolution of the Catholic world in order that an error which had begun to creep into the minds of some men, through discussions of this kind, might be cured by the more powerful truth and universal healing power of unity coming on the side of safety. And so, they may see with what security I approach this discourse. If I am unable to gain my point, and show how those arguments may be refuted which they bring forward from the Council and the epistles of Cyprian, to the effect that Christ's baptism may not be given by the hands of heretics, I shall still remain safely in the Church, in whose communion Cyprian himself remained with those who differed from him.

3. But if they say that the Catholic Church existed then, because there were a few, or, if they prefer it, even a considerable number, who denied the validity of any baptism conferred in a heretical body, and baptized all who came from thence, what then? Did the Church not exist at all before Agrippinus, with whom that new kind of system began, at variance with all previous custom?

Or how, again after the time of Agrippinus, when, unless there had been a return to the primitive custom, there would have been no need for Cyprian to set on foot another Council? Was there no Church then, because such a custom as this prevailed everywhere, that the baptism of Christ should be considered nothing but the baptism of Christ, even though it were proved to have been conferred in a body of heretics or schismatics? But if the Church existed even then, and had not perished through a breach of its continuity, but was, on the contrary, holding its ground, and receiving increase in every nation, surely it is the safest plan to abide by this same custom, which then embraced good and bad alike in unity. But if there was then no Church in existence, because sacrilegious heretics were received without baptism, and this prevailed by universal custom, whence has Donatus made his appearance? From what land did he spring? or from what sea did he emerge? or from what sky did he fall? And so we, as I had begun to say, are safe in the communion of that Church, throughout the whole extent of which the custom now prevails, which prevailed in like manner through its whole extent before the time of Agrippinus, and in the interval between Agrippinus and Cyprian, and whose unity neither Agrippinus nor Cyprian ever deserted, nor those who agreed with them, although they entertained different views from the rest of their brethren—all of them remaining in the same communion of unity with the very men from whom they differed in opinion. But let the Donatists themselves consider what their true position is, if they neither can say whence they derived their origin, if the Church had already been destroyed by the plague-spot of communion with heretics and schismatics received into her bosom without baptism; nor again agree with Cyprian himself, for he declared that he remained in communion with those who received heretics and schismatics, and so also with those who were received as well: while they have separated themselves from the communion of the whole world, on account of the charge of having delivered up the sacred books, which they brought against the men whom they maligned in Africa, but failed to convict when brought to trial beyond the sea; although, even had the crimes which they alleged been true, they were much less heinous than the sins of heresy and schism; and yet these could not defile Cyprian in the persons of those who came from them without baptism, as he conceived, and were admitted without baptism into the Catholic communion. Nor, in the very point in which they say that they imitate Cyprian, can they find any answer to make about acknowledging the baptism of the followers of Maximianus, together with those whom, though they belonged to the party that they had first condemned in their own plenary Council, and then gone on to prosecute even at the tribunal of the secular power, they yet received back into their communion, in the episcopate of the very same bishop under whom they had been condemned. Wherefore, if the communion of wicked men destroyed the Church in the time of Cyprian, they have no source from which they can derive their own communion; and if the Church was not destroyed, they have no excuse for their separation from it. Moreover, they are neither following the example of Cyprian, since they have burst the bond of unity, nor abiding by their own Council, since they have recognized the baptism of the followers of Maximianus.

Chapter 3. —4. Let us therefore, seeing that we adhere to the example of Cyprian, go on now to consider Cyprian's Council. What says Cyprian? "Ye have heard," he says, "most beloved colleagues, what Jubaianus our fellow-bishop has written to me, consulting my moderate ability concerning the unlawful and profane baptism of heretics, and what answer I gave him, — giving a judgment which we have once and again and often given, that heretics coming to the Church ought to be baptized and sanctified with the baptism of the Church. Another letter of Jubaianus has likewise been read to you, in which, agreeably to his sincere and religious devotion, in answer to our epistle, he not only expressed his assent, but returned thanks also, acknowledging that he had received instruction." In these words of the blessed Cyprian, we find that he had been consulted by Jubaianus, and what answer he had given to his questions, and how Jubaianus acknowledged with gratitude that he had received instruction. Ought we then to be thought unreasonably persistent if we desire to consider this same epistle by which Jubaianus was convinced? For till such time as we are also convinced (if there are any arguments of truth whereby this can be done), Cyprian himself has established our security by the right of Catholic communion.

5. For he goes on to say: "It remains that we severally declare our opinion on this same subject, judging no one, nor depriving any one of the right of communion if he differs from us." He allows me, therefore, without losing the right of communion, not only to continue inquiring into the truth, but even to hold opinions differing from his own. "For no one of us," he

says, "sets himself up as a bishop of bishops, or by tyrannical terror forces his colleagues to a necessity of obeying." What could be more kind? what humbler? Surely there is here no authority restraining us from inquiry into what is truth. "Inasmuch as every bishop," he says, "in the free use of his liberty and power, has the right of forming his own judgment, and can no more be judged by another than he can himself judge another,"— that is, I suppose, in those questions which have not yet been brought to perfect clearness of solution; for he knew what a deep question about the sacrament was then occupying the whole Church with every kind of disputation, and gave free liberty of inquiry to every man, that the truth might be made known by investigation. For he was surely not uttering what was false, and trying to catch his simpler colleagues in their speech, so that, when they should have betrayed that they held opinions at variance with his, he might then propose, in violation of his promise, that they should be excommunicated. Far be it from a soul so holy to entertain such accursed treachery; indeed, they who hold such a view about such a man, thinking that it conduces to his praise, do but show that it would be in accordance with their own nature. I for my part will in no wise believe that Cyprian, a Catholic bishop, a Catholic martyr, whose greatness only made him proportionately humble in all things, so as to find favor before the Lord,1267should ever, especially in the sacred Council of his colleagues, have uttered with his mouth what was not echoed in his heart, especially as he further adds, "But we must all await the judgment of our Lord Jesus Christ, who alone has the power both of setting us in the government of His Church, and of judging of our acts therein."1268 When, then, he called to their remembrance so solemn a judgment, hoping to hear the truth from his colleagues, would he first set them the example of lying? May God avert such madness from every Christian man, and how much more from Cyprian! We have therefore the free liberty of inquiry granted to us by the most moderate and most truthful speech of Cyprian.

Chapter 4. —6. Next his colleagues proceed to deliver their several opinions. But first they listened to the letter written to Jubaianus; for it was read, as was mentioned in the preamble. Let it therefore be read among ourselves also, that we too, with the help of God, may discover from it what we ought to think. "What!" I think I hear someone saying, "do you proceed to tell us what Cyprian wrote to Jubaianus?" I have read the letter, I confess, and should certainly have been a convert to his views, had I not been induced to consider the matter more carefully by the vast weight of authority, originating in those whom the Church, distributed throughout the world amid so many nations, of Latins, Greeks, barbarians, not to mention the Jewish race itself, has been able to produce,—that same Church which gave birth to Cyprian himself,—men whom I could in no wise bring myself to think had been unwilling without reason to hold this view,—not because it was impossible that in so difficult a question the opinion of one or of a few might not have been more near the truth than that of more, but because one must not lightly, without full consideration and investigation of the matter to the best of his abilities, decide in favor of a single individual, or even of a few, against the decision of so very many men of the same religion and communion, all endowed with great talent and abundant learning. And so how much was suggested to me on more diligent inquiry, even by the letter of Cyprian himself, in favor of the view which is now held by the Catholic Church, that the baptism of Christ is to be recognized and approved, not by the standard of their merits by whom it is administered, but by His alone of whom it is said, "The same is He which baptizes," will be shown naturally during our argument. Let us therefore suppose that the letter which was written by Cyprian to Jubaianus has been read among us, as it was read in the Council. And I would have everyone read it who means to read what I am going to say, lest he might possibly think that I have suppressed some things of consequence. For it would take too much time, and be irrelevant to the elucidation of the matter in hand, were we at this moment to quote all the words of this epistle.

Chapter 5. —7. But if anyone should ask what I hold in the meantime, while discussing this question, I answer that, in the first place, the letter of Cyprian suggested to me what I should hold till I should see clearly the nature of the question which next begins to be discussed. For Cyprian himself says: "But some will say, 'What then will become of those who in times past, coming to the Church from heresy, were admitted without baptism?'" Whether they were really without baptism, or whether they were admitted because those who admitted them conceived that they had partaken of baptism, is a matter for our future consideration. At any rate, Cyprian himself shows plainly enough what was the ordinary custom of the Church, when he says that in past time those who came to the Church from heresy were admitted without baptism.

8. For in the Council itself Castus of Sicca says: "He who, despising truth, presumes to follow custom, is either envious or evil-disposed towards the brethren to whom the truth is revealed, or is ungrateful towards God, by whose inspiration His Church is instructed." Whether the truth had been revealed, we shall investigate hereafter; at any rate, he acknowledges that the custom of the Church was different.

Chapter 6. —9. Libosus also of Vaga says: "The Lord says in the gospel, 'I am the Truth.' He does not say, 'I am custom.' Therefore, when the truth is made manifest, custom must give way to truth." Clearly, no one could doubt that custom must give way to truth where it is made manifest. But we shall see presently about the manifestation of the truth. Meanwhile he also makes it clear that custom was on the other side.

Chapter 7. —10. Zosimus also of Tharassa said: "When a revelation of the truth has been made, error must give way to truth; for even Peter, who at the first circumcised, afterwards gave way to Paul when he declared the truth." He indeed chose to say error, not custom; but in saying "for even Peter, who at the first circumcised, afterwards gave way to Paul when he declared the truth," he shows plainly enough that there was a custom also about baptism at variance with his views. At the same time, also, he warns us that it was not impossible that Cyprian might have held an opinion about baptism at variance with that required by the truth, as held by the Church both before and after him, if even Peter could hold a view at variance with the truth as taught us by the Apostle Paul.

Chapter 8. —11. Likewise, Felix of Buslacene said: "In admitting heretics without the baptism of the Church, let no one prefer custom to reason and truth; because reason and truth always prevail to the exclusion of custom." Nothing could be better, if it be reason, and if it be truth; but this we shall see presently. Meanwhile, it is clear from the words of this man also that the custom was the other way.

Chapter 9. —12. Likewise, Honoratus of Tucca said: "Since Christ is the Truth, we ought to follow truth rather than custom." By all these declarations it is proved that we are not excluded from the communion of the Church, till it shall have been clearly shown what is the nature of the truth, which they say must be preferred to our custom. But if the truth has made it clear that the very regulation ought to be maintained which the said custom had prescribed, then it is evident both that this custom was not established or confirmed in vain, and also that, in consequence of the discussions in question, the most wholesome observance of so great a sacrament, which could never, indeed, have been changed in the Catholic Church, was even more watchfully guarded with the most scrupulous caution, when it had received the further corroboration of Councils.

Chapter 10. —13. Therefore, Cyprian writes to Jubaianus as follows, "concerning the baptism of heretics, who, being placed without, and set down out of the Church," seem to him to "claim to themselves a matter over which they have neither right nor power. Which we," he says, "cannot account valid or lawful, since it is clear that among them it is unlawful." Neither, indeed, do we deny that a man who is baptized among heretics, or in any schism outside the Church, derives no profit from it so far as he is partner in the perverseness of the heretics and schismatics; nor do we hold that those who baptize, although they confer the real true sacrament of baptism, are yet acting rightly, in gathering adherents outside the Church, and entertaining opinions contrary to the Church. But it is one thing to be without a sacrament, another thing to be in possession of it wrongly, and to usurp it unlawfully. Therefore, they do not cease to be sacraments of Christ and the Church, merely because they are unlawfully used, not only by heretics, but by all kinds of wicked and impious persons. These, indeed, ought to be corrected and punished, but the sacraments should be acknowledged and revered.

14. Cyprian, indeed, says that on this subject not one, but two or more Councils were held; always, however, in Africa. For indeed in one he mentions that seventy-one bishops had been assembled, —to all whose authority we do not hesitate, with all due deference to Cyprian, to prefer the authority, supported by many more bishops, of the whole Church spread throughout the whole world, of which Cyprian himself rejoiced that he was an inseparable member.

15. Nor is the water "profane and adulterous" over which the name of God is invoked, even though it be invoked by profane and adulterous persons; because neither the creature itself of water, nor the name invoked, is adulterous. But the baptism of Christ, consecrated by the words of the gospel, is necessarily holy, however polluted and unclean its ministers may be; because its inherent sanctity cannot be polluted, and the divine

excellence abides in its sacrament, whether to the salvation of those who use it aright, or to the destruction of those who use it wrong. Would you indeed maintain that, while the light of the sun or of a candle, diffused through unclean places, contracts no foulness in itself therefrom, yet the baptism of Christ can be defiled by the sins of any man, whatsoever he may be? For if we turn our thoughts to the visible materials themselves, which are to us the medium of the sacraments, everyone must know that they admit of corruption. But if we think on that which they convey to us, who can fail to see that it is incorruptible, however much the men through whose ministry it is conveyed are either being rewarded or punished for the character of their lives?

Chapter 11. —16. But Cyprian was right in not being moved by what Jubaianus wrote, that "the followers of Novatian rebaptize those who come to them from the Catholic Church." For, in the first place, it does not follow that whatever heretics have done in a perverse spirit of mimicry, Catholics are therefore to abstain from doing, because the heretics do the same. And again, the reasons are different for which heretics and the Catholic Church ought respectively to abstain from rebaptizing. For it would not be right for heretics to do so, even if it were fitting in the Catholic Church; because their argument is, that among the Catholics is wanting that which they themselves received whilst still within the pale, and took away with them when they departed. Whereas the reason why the Catholic Church should not administer again the baptism which was given among heretics, is that it may not seem to decide that a power which is Christ's alone belongs to its members, or to pronounce that to be wanting in the heretics which they have received within her pale, and certainly could not lose by straying outside. For thus much Cyprian himself, with all the rest, established, that if any should return from heresy to the Church, they should be received back, not by baptism, but by the discipline of penitence; whence it is clear that they cannot be held to lose by their secession what is not restored to them when they return. Nor ought it for a moment to be said that, as their heresy is their own, as their error is their own, as the sacrilege of disunion is their own, so also the baptism is their own, which is really Christ's. Accordingly, while the evils which are their own are corrected when they return, so in that which is not theirs His presence should be recognized, from whom it is.

Chapter 12. —17. But the blessed Cyprian shows that it was no new or sudden thing that he decided, because the practice had already begun under Agrippinus. "Many years," he says, "and much time has passed away since, under Agrippinus of honored memory, a large assembly of bishops determined this point." Accordingly, under Agrippinus, at any rate, the thing was new. But I cannot understand what Cyprian means by saying, "And thenceforward to the present day, so many thousand heretics in our provinces, having been converted to our Church, showed no hesitation or dislike, but rather with full consent of reason and will, have embraced the opportunity of the grace of the laver of life and the baptism unto salvation," unless indeed he says, "thenceforward to the present day," because from the time when they were baptized in the Church, in accordance with the Council of Agrippinus, no question of excommunication had arisen in the case of any of the rebaptized. Yet if the custom of baptizing those who came over from heretics remained in force from the time of Agrippinus to that of Cyprian, why should new Councils have been held by Cyprian on this point? Why does he say to this same Jubaianus that he is not doing anything new or sudden, but only what had been established by Agrippinus? For why should Jubaianus be disturbed by the question of novelty, so as to require to be satisfied by the authority of Agrippinus, if this was the continuous practice of the Church from Agrippinus till Cyprian? Why, lastly, did so many of his colleagues urge that reason and truth must be preferred to custom, instead of saying that those who wished to act otherwise were acting contrary to truth and custom alike?

Chapter 13. —18. But about the remission of sins, whether it is granted through baptism at the hands of the heretics, I have already expressed my opinion on this point in a former book; but I will shortly recapitulate it here. If remission of sins is there conferred by the sacredness of baptism, the sins return again through obstinate perseverance in heresy or schism; and therefore, such men must need return to the peace of the Catholic Church, that they may cease to be heretics and schismatics, and deserve that those sins which had returned on them should be cleansed away by love working in the bond of unity. But if, although among heretics and schismatics it be still the same baptism of Christ, it yet cannot work remission of sins owing to this same foulness of discord and wickedness of dissent, then the same baptism begins to be of avail for the remission of sins when they come to the peace of the Church,—

[not] that what has been already truly remitted should not be retained; nor that heretical baptism should be repudiated as belonging to a different religion, or as being different from our own, so that a second baptism should be administered; but that the very same baptism, which was working death by reason of discord outside the Church, may work salvation by reason of the peace within. It was, in fact, the same savor of which the apostle says, "We are a sweet savor of Christ in every place;" and yet, says he, "both in them that are saved and in them that perish. To the one we are the savor of life unto life; and to the other the savor of death unto death." And although he used these words with reference to another subject, I have applied them to this, that men may understand that what is good may not only work life to those who use it aright, but also death to those who use it wrong.

Chapter 14. —19. Nor is it material, when we are considering the question of the genuineness and holiness of the sacrament, "what the recipient of the sacrament believes, and with what faith he is imbued." It is of the very highest consequence about the entrance into salvation, but is wholly immaterial about the question of the sacrament. For it is quite possible that a man may be possessed of the genuine sacrament and a corrupted faith, as it is possible that he may hold the words of the creed in their integrity, and yet entertain an erroneous belief about the Trinity, or the resurrection, or any other point. For it is no slight matter, even within the Catholic Church itself, to hold a faith entirely consistent with the truth about even God Himself, to say nothing of any of His creatures. Is it then to be maintained, that if anyone who has been baptized within the Catholic Church itself should afterwards, during reading, or by listening to instruction, or by quiet argument, find out, through God's own revelation, that he had before believed otherwise than he ought, it is requisite that he should therefore be baptized afresh? But what carnal and natural man is there who does not stray through the vain conceits of his own heart, and picture God's nature to himself to be such as he has imagined out of his carnal sense, and differ from the true conception of God as far as vanity from truth? Most truly, indeed, speaks the apostle, filled with the light of truth: "The natural man," says he, "received not the things of the Spirit of God." And yet herein he was speaking of men whom he himself shows to have been baptized. For he says to them, "Was Paul crucified for you? or were ye baptized in the name of Paul?" These men had therefore the sacrament of baptism; and yet, inasmuch as their wisdom was of the flesh, what could they believe about God otherwise than according to the perception of their flesh, according to which "the natural man received not the things of the Spirit of God?" To such he says: "I could not speak unto you as unto spiritual, but as unto carnal, even as unto babes in Christ. I have fed you with milk, and not with meat: for hitherto ye were not able to bear it, neither yet now are ye able. For ye are yet carnal." For such are carried about with every wind of doctrine, of which kind he says, "That we be no more children, tossed to and fro, and carried about with every wind of doctrine." It is then true that, if these men shall have advanced even to the spiritual age of the inner man, and in the integrity of understanding shall have learned how far different from the requirements of the truth has been the belief which they have been led by the fallacious character of their conceits to entertain of God, they are therefore to be baptized again? For, on this principle, it would be possible for a Catholic catechumen to light upon the writings of some heretic, and, not having the knowledge requisite for discerning truth from error, he might entertain some belief contrary to the Catholic faith, yet not condemned by the words of the creed, just as, under color of the same words, innumerable heretical errors have sprung up. Supposing, then, that the catechumen was under the impression that he was studying the work of some great and learned Catholic, and was baptized with that belief in the Catholic Church, and by subsequent research should discover what he ought to believe, so that, embracing the Catholic faith, he should reject his former error, ought he, on confessing this, to be baptized again? Or supposing that, before learning and confessing this for himself, he should be found to entertain such an opinion, and should be taught what he ought to reject and what he should believe, and it were to become clear that he had held this false belief when he was baptized, ought he therefore to be baptized again? Why should we maintain the contrary? Because the sanctity of the sacrament, consecrated in the words of the gospel, remains upon him in its integrity, just as he received it from the hands of the minister, although he, being firmly rooted in the vanity of his carnal mind entertained a belief other than was right at the time when he was baptized. Wherefore it is manifest that it is possible that, with defective faith, the sacrament of baptism may yet remain without defect in any man; and therefore, all that is said about the diversity of the several heretics is beside the question. For in each person that is to be corrected which is found to be amiss by the man who undertakes his correction. That is to be made whole which is unsound; that is to be given which is wanting, and, above all, the peace of Christian charity, without which the rest is profitless. Yet, as the rest is there, we must not administer it as though it were wanting, only take care that its possession be to the profit, not the hurt of him who has it, through the very bond of peace and excellence of charity.

Chapter 15. —20. Accordingly, if Marcion consecrated the sacrament of baptism with the words of the gospel, "In the name of the Father, and of the Son, and of the Holy Ghost," the sacrament was complete, although his faith expressed under the same words, seeing that he held opinions not taught by the Catholic truth, was not complete, but stained with the falsity of fables. For under these same words, "In the name of the Father, and of the Son, and of the Holy Ghost," not Marcion only, or Valentinus, or Arius, or Eunomius, but the carnal babes of the Church themselves (to whom the apostle said, "I could not speak unto you as unto spiritual, but as unto carnal"), if they could be individually asked for an accurate exposition of their opinions, would probably show a diversity of opinions as numerous as the persons who held them, "for the natural man received not the things of the Spirit of God." Can it, however, be said on this account that they do not receive the complete sacrament? or that, if they shall advance, and correct the vanity of their carnal opinions, they must seek again what they had received? Each man receives after the fashion of his own faith; yet how much does he obtain under the guidance of that mercy of God, in the confident assurance of which the same apostle says, "If in anything ye be otherwise minded, God shall reveal even this unto you"?1296 Yet the snares of heretics and schismatics prove for this reason only too pernicious to the carnally-minded, because their very progress is intercepted when their vain opinions are confirmed in opposition to the Catholic truth, and the perversity of their dissension is strengthened against the Catholic peace. Yet if the sacraments are the same, they are everywhere complete, even when they are wrongly understood, and perverted to be instruments of discord, just as the very writings of the gospel, if they are only the same, are everywhere complete, even though quoted with a boundless variety of false opinions. For as to what Jeremiah says: —"Why do those who grieve me prevail against me? My wound is stubborn, whence shall I be healed? In its origin it became unto me as lying water, having no certainty,"—if the term "water" were never used figuratively and in the allegorical language of prophecy except to signify baptism, we should have trouble in discovering what these words of Jeremiah meant; but as it is, when "waters" are expressly used in the Apocalypse to signify "peoples," I do not see why, by "lying water having no certainty," I should not understand, a "lying people, whom I cannot trust."

Chapter 16. —21. But when it is said that "the Holy Spirit is given by the imposition of hands in the Catholic Church only, I suppose that our ancestors meant that we should understand thereby what the apostle says, "Because the love of God is shed abroad in our hearts by the Holy Ghost which is given unto us." For this is that very love which is wanting in all who are cut off from the communion of the Catholic Church; and for lack of this, "though they speak with the tongues of men and of angels, though they understand all mysteries and all knowledge, and though they have the gift of prophecy, and all faith, so that they could remove mountains, and though they bestow all their goods to feed the poor, and though they give their bodies to be burned, it profited them nothing." But those are wanting in God's love who do not care for the unity of the Church; and consequently, we are right in understanding that the Holy Spirit may be said not to be received except in the Catholic Church. For the Holy Spirit is not only given by the laying on of hands amid the testimony of temporal sensible miracles, as He was given in former days to be the credentials of a rudimentary faith, and for the extension of the first beginnings of the Church. For who expects in these days that those on whom hands are laid that they may receive the Holy Spirit should forthwith begin to speak with tongues? but it is understood that invisibly and imperceptibly, because the bond of peace, divine love is breathed into their hearts, so that they may be able to say, "Because the love of God is shed abroad in our hearts by the Holy Ghost which is given unto us." But there are many operations of the Holy Spirit, which the same apostle commemorates in a certain passage at such length as he thinks sufficient, and then concludes: "But all these worketh that one and the selfsame Spirit, dividing to every man severally as He will." Since, then, the sacrament is one thing, which even Simon Magus could have; and the operation of the Spirit is another thing, which is even often found in wicked men, as Saul had the gift of prophecy; and that operation of the same Spirit is a third thing, which only the good can have, as "the end of the commandment is charity out of a pure heart, and of a good conscience, and of faith unfeigned:" whatever, therefore, may be received by heretics and schismatics, the charity which covered the multitude of sins is the especial gift of Catholic unity and peace; nor is it found in all that are within that bond, since not all that are within it are of it, as we shall see in the proper place. At any rate, outside the bond that love cannot exist, without which all the other requisites, even if they can be recognized and approved, cannot profit or release from sin. But the laying on of hands in reconciliation to the Church is not, like baptism, incapable of repetition; for what is it more than a prayer offered over a man?

Chapter 17. —22. "For about the fact that to preserve the figure of unity the Lord gave the power to Peter that whatsoever he should loose on earth should be loosed," it is clear that that unity is also described as one dove without fault. Can it be said, then, that to this same dove belong all those greedy ones, whose existence in the same Catholic Church Cyprian himself so grievously bewailed? For birds of prey, I believe, cannot be called doves, but rather hawks. How then did they baptize those who used to plunder estates by treacherous deceit, and increase their profits by compound usury,1308if baptism is only given by that indivisible and chaste and perfect dove, that unity which can only be understood as existing among the good? Is it possible that, by the prayers of the saints who are spiritual within the Church, as though by the frequent lamentations of the dove, a great sacrament is dispensed, with a secret administration of the mercy of God, so that their sins also are loosed who are baptized, not by the dove but by the hawk, if they come to that sacrament in the peace of Catholic unity? But if this be so, why should it not also be the case that, as each man comes from heresy or schism to the Catholic peace, his sins should be loosed through their prayers? But the integrity of the sacrament is everywhere recognized, though it will not avail for the irrevocable remission of sins outside the unity of the Church. Nor will the prayers of the saints, or, in other words, the groanings of that one dove, be able to help one who is set in heresy or schism; just as they are not able to help one who is placed within the Church, if by a wicked life he himself retain the debts of his sins against himself, and that though he be baptized, not by this hawk, but by the pious ministry of the dove herself.

Chapter 18—23. "As my Father hath sent me," says our Lord, "even so send I you. And what He had said this, He breathed on them, and saith unto them, Receive ye the Holy Ghost. Whose soever sins ye remit, they are remitted unto them; and whose soever sins ye retain, they are retained." Therefore, if they represented the Church, and this was said to them as to the Church herself, it follows that the peace of the Church looses sins, and estrangement from the Church retains them, not according to the will of men, but according to the will of God and the prayers of the saints who are spiritual, who "judge all things, but themselves are judged of no man." For the rock retains, the rock remits; the dove retains, the dove remits; unity retains, unity remits. But the peace of this unity exists only in the good, in those who are either already spiritual, or are advancing by the obedience of concord to spiritual things; it exists not in the bad, whether they make disturbances abroad, or are endured within the Church with lamentations, baptizing and being baptized. But just as those who are tolerated with groanings within the Church, although they do not belong to the same unity of the dove, and to that "glorious Church, not having spot or wrinkle, or any such thing," yet if they are corrected, and confess that they approached to baptism most unworthily, are not baptized again, but begin to belong to the dove, through whose groans those sins are remitted which were retained in them who were estranged from her peace; so those also who are more openly without the Church, if they have received the same sacraments, are not freed from their sins on coming, after correction, to the unity of the Church, by a repetition of baptism, but by the same law of charity and bond of unity. For if "those only may baptize who are set over the Church, and established by the law of the gospel and ordination as appointed by the Lord," were they in any wise of this kind who seized on estates by treacherous frauds, and increased their gains by compound interest? I trow not, since those are established by ordination as appointed of the Lord, of whom the apostle, in giving them a standard, says, "Not greedy, not given to filthy lucre." Yet men of this kind used to baptize in the time of Cyprian himself; and he confesses with many lamentations that they were his fellow-bishops, and endures them with the great reward of tolerance. Yet did they not confer remission of sins, which is granted through the prayers of the saints, that is, the groans of the dove, whoever it be that baptizes, if those to whom it is given belong to her peace. For the Lord would not say to robbers and usurers, "Whose soever sins ye remit, they shall be remitted to him; and whose soever sins ye retain, they shall be retained." "Outside the Church, indeed, nothing can be either bound or loosed, since there is no one who can either bind or loose;" but he is loosed who has made peace with the dove, and he is bound who is not at peace with the dove, whether he is openly without, or appears to be within.

24. But we know that Dathan, Korah, and Abiram, who tried to usurp to themselves the right of sacrificing, contrary to the unity of the people of God, and also the sons of Aaron who offered strange fire upon the altar, did not escape punishment. Nor do we say that such offenses remain unpunished, unless those guilty of them correct themselves, if the patience of God leading them to repentance give them time for correction.

Chapter 19. —25. They indeed who say that baptism is not to be repeated, because only hands were laid on those whom Philip the deacon had baptized, are saying what is quite beside the point; and far be it from us, in seeking the truth, to use such arguments as this. Wherefore we are all the further from "yielding to heretics," if we deny that what they possess of Christ's Church is their own property, and do not refuse to acknowledge the standard of our General because of the crimes of deserters; nay, even more because "the Lord our God is a jealous God," let us refuse, whenever we see anything of His with an alien, to allow him to consider it his own. For of a truth the jealous God Himself rebukes the woman who commits fornication against Him, as the type of an erring people, and says that she gave to her lovers what belonged to Him, and again received from them what was not theirs but His. In the hands of the adulterous woman and the adulterous lovers, God in His wrath, as a jealous God, recognizes His gifts; and do we say that baptism, consecrated in the words of the gospel, belongs to heretics? and are we willing, from consideration of their deeds, to attribute to them even what belongs to God, as though they had the power to pollute it, or as though they could make what is God's to be their own, because they themselves have refused to belong to God?

26. Who is that adulterous woman whom the prophet Hosea points out, who said, "I will go after my lovers, that give me my bread and my water, my wool and my flax, and everything that befits me?" Let us grant that we may understand this also of the people of the Jews that went astray; yet whom else are the false Christians (such as are all heretics and schismatics) want to imitate, except false Israelites? For there were also true Israelites, as the Lord Himself bears witness to Nathanael, "Behold an Israelite indeed, in whom is no guile." But who are true Christians, save those of whom the same Lord said, "He that hath my commandments, and kept them, he it is that loveth me?" But what is it to keep His commandments, except to abide in love? Whence also He says, "A new commandment I give unto you, that ye love one another;" and again, "By this shall all men know that ye are my disciples, if ye have love one to another." But who can doubt that this was spoken not only to those who heard His words with their fleshly ears when He was present with them, but also to those who learn His words through the gospel, when He is sitting on His throne in heaven? For He came not to destroy the law, but to fulfill. But the fulfilling of the law is love. And in this Cyprian abounded greatly, insomuch that though he held a different view concerning baptism, he yet did not forsake the unity of the Church, and was in the Lord's vine a branch firmly rooted, bearing fruit, which the heavenly Husbandman purged with the knife of suffering, that it

should bear more fruit. But the enemies of this brotherly love, whether they are openly without, or appear to be within, are false Christians, and antichrists. For when they have found an opportunity, they go out, as it is written: "A man wishing to separate himself from his friends, seeks opportunities." But even if occasions are wanting, while they seem to be within, they are severed from that invisible bond of love. Whence St. John says, "They went out from us, but they were not of us; for had they been of us, they would no doubt have continued with us." He does not say that they ceased to be of us by going out, but that they went out because they were not of us. The Apostle Paul also speaks of certain men who had erred concerning the truth, and were overthrowing the faith of some; whose word was eating as a canker. Yet in saying that they should be avoided, he nevertheless intimates that they were all in one great house, but as vessels to dishonor, —I suppose because they had not as yet gone out. Or if they had already gone out, how can he say that they were in the same great house with the honorable vessels, unless it was in virtue of the sacraments themselves, which even in the severed meetings of heretics are not changed, that he speaks of all as belonging to the same great house, though in different degrees of esteem, some to honor and some to dishonor? For thus he speaks in his Epistle to Timothy: "But shun profane and vain babblings; for they will increase unto more ungodliness. And their word will eat as doth a canker; of whom is Hymenæus and Philetus; who concerning the truth have erred, saying that the resurrection is past already; and overthrow the faith of some. Nevertheless, the foundation of God stands firm, having this seal, The Lord knows them that are His. And,

Let everyone that names the name of Christ depart from iniquity. But in a great house there are not only vessels of gold and of silver, but also of wood and of earth; and some to honor, and some to dishonor. If a man therefore purge himself from these, he shall be a vessel unto honor, sanctified, and meet for the master's use, and prepared unto every good work." But what is it to purge oneself from such as these, except what he said just before, "Let everyone that names the name of Christ depart from iniquity." And lest anyone should think that, as being in one great house with them, he might perish with such as these, he has most carefully forewarned them, "The Lord knows them that are His,"—those, namely, who, by departing from iniquity, purge themselves from the vessels made to dishonor, lest they should perish with them whom they are compelled to tolerate in the great house.

27. They, therefore, who are wicked, evildoers, carnal, fleshly, devilish, think that they receive at the hands of their seducers what are the gifts of God alone, whether sacraments, or any spiritual workings about present salvation. But these men have not love towards God, but are busied about those by whose pride they are led astray, and are compared to the adulterous woman, whom the prophet introduces as saying, "I will go after my lovers, that give me my bread and my water, my wool and my flax, and my oil, and everything that befits me." For thus arise heresies and schisms, when the fleshly people which is not founded on the love of God says, "I will go after my lovers," with whom, either by corruption of her faith, or by the puffing up of her pride, she shamefully commits adultery. But for the sake of those who, having undergone the difficulties, and straits, and

barriers of the empty reasoning of those by whom they are led astray, afterwards feel the prickings of fear, and return to the way of peace, to seeking God in all sincerity, —for their sake He goes on to say, "Therefore, behold, I will hedge up thy way with thorns, and make a wall, that she shall not find her paths. And she shall follow after her lovers, but she shall not overtake them: and she shall seek them, but she shall not find them: then shall she say, I will go and return to my first husband; for then was it better with me than now." Then, that they may not attribute to their seducers what they have that is sound, and derived from the doctrine of truth, by which they lead them astray to the falseness of their own dogmas and dissensions; that they may not think that what is sound in them belongs to them, he immediately added, "And she did not know that I gave her corn, and wine, and oil, and multiplied her money; but she made vessels of gold and silver for Baal." For she had said above, "I will go after my lovers, that give me my bread," etc., not at all understanding that all this, which was held soundly and lawfully by her seducers, was of God, and not of men. Nor would even they themselves claim these things for themselves, and as it were assert a right in them, had not they in turn been led astray by a people which had gone astray, when faith is reposed in them, and such honors are paid to them, that they should be enabled thereby to say such things, and claim such things for themselves, that their error should be called truth, and their iniquity be thought righteousness, in virtue of the sacraments and Scriptures, which they hold, not for salvation, but only in appearance. Accordingly, the same adulterous woman is addressed by the mouth of Ezekiel: "Thou hast also taken thy fair jewels of my gold and of my silver, which I had given thee, and made to thyself images of men, and didst commit whoredom with them; and took my broidered garments, and covered them: and thou hast set mine oil and mine incense before them. My meat also which I gave thee, fine flour, and oil, and honey, wherewith I fed thee, thou hast even set it before thine idols for a sweet savor: and this thou hast done." For she turns all the sacraments, and the words of the sacred books, to the images of her own idols, with which her carnal mind delights to wallow. Nor yet, because those images are false, and the doctrines of devils, speaking lies in hypocrisy, are those sacraments and divine utterances therefore so to lose their due honor, as to be thought to belong to such as these; seeing that the Lord says," Of my gold, and my silver, and my broidered garments, and mine oil, and mine incense, and my meat," and so forth. Ought we, because those erring ones think that these things belong to their seducers, therefore not to recognize whose they really are, when He Himself says, "And she did not know that I gave her corn, and wine, and oil, and multiplied her money"? For He did not say that she did not have these things because she was an adulteress; but she is said to have had them, and that not as belonging to herself or her lovers, but to God, whose alone they are. Although, therefore, she had her fornication, yet those things wherewith she adorned it, whether as seduced or in her turn seducing, belonged not to her, but to God. If these things were spoken in a figure of the Jewish nation, when the scribes and Pharisees were rejecting the commandment of God in order to set up their own traditions, so that they were in a manner committing whoredom with a people which was abandoning their God; and yet for all that, whoredom at that time among the people, such as the Lord brought to light by convicting it, did not cause that the mysteries should belong to them, which were not theirs but God's, who, in speaking to the adulteress, says that all these things were His; whence the Lord Himself also sent those whom He cleansed from leprosy to the same mysteries, that they should offer sacrifice for themselves before the priests, because that sacrifice had not become efficacious for them, which He Himself afterwards wished to be commemorated in the Church for all of them, because He Himself proclaimed the tidings to them all;—if this be so, how much the more ought we, when we find the sacraments of the New Testament among certain heretics or schismatics, not to attribute them to these men, nor to condemn them, as though we could not recognize them? We ought to recognize the gifts of the true husband, though in the possession of an adulteress, and to amend, by the word of truth, that whoredom which is the true possession of the unchaste woman, instead of finding fault with the gifts, which belong entirely to the pitying Lord.

28. From these considerations, and such as these, our forefathers, not only before the time of Cyprian and Agrippinus, but even afterwards, maintained a most wholesome custom, that whenever they found anything divine and lawful remaining in its integrity even amid any heresy or schism, they approved rather than repudiated it; but whatever they found that was alien, and peculiar to that false doctrine or division, this they convicted in the light of the truth, and healed. The points, however, which remain to be considered in the letter written by Jubaianus, must, I think, when looking at the size of this book, be taken in hand and treated with a fresh beginning.

Book IV.

In which he treats of what follows in the same epistle of Cyprian to Jubaianus.

Chapter 1. —1. The comparison of the Church with Paradise shows us that men may indeed receive her baptism outside her pale, but that no one outside can either receive or retain the salvation of eternal happiness. For, as the words of Scripture testify, the streams from the fountain of Paradise flowed copiously even beyond its bounds. Record indeed is made of their names; and through what countries they flow, and that they are situated beyond the limits of Paradise, is known to all; and yet in Mesopotamia, and in Egypt, to which countries those rivers extended, there is not found that blessedness of life which is recorded in Paradise. Accordingly, though the waters of Paradise are found beyond its boundaries, yet its happiness is in Paradise alone. So, therefore, the baptism of the Church may exist outside, but the gift of the life of happiness is found alone within the Church, which has been founded on a rock, which has received the keys of binding and loosing. "She it is alone who holds as her privilege the whole power of her Bridegroom and Lord;" by virtue of which power as bride, she can bring forth sons even of handmaids. And these, if they be not high-minded, shall be called into the lot of the inheritance; but if they be high-minded, they shall remain outside.

Chapter 2. —2. Even more, then, because "we are fighting for the honor and unity" of the Church, let us beware of giving to heretics the credit of whatever we acknowledged among them as belonging to the Church; but let us teach them by argument, that what they possess that is derived from unity is of no efficacy to their salvation, unless they shall return to that same unity. For "the water of the Church is full of faith, and salvation, and holiness" to those who use it rightly. No one, however, can use it well outside the Church. But to those who use it perversely, whether within or without the Church, it is employed to work punishment, and does not conduce to their reward. And so baptism "cannot be corrupted and polluted," though it be handled by the corrupt or by adulterers, just as also "the Church herself is uncorrupt, and pure, and chaste." And so no share in it belongs to the avaricious, or thieves, or usurers, —many of whom, by the testimony of Cyprian himself in many places of his letters, exist not only without, but actually within the Church, —and yet they both are baptized and do baptize, with no change in their hearts.

3. For this, too, he says, in one of his epistles to the clergy about prayer to God, in which, after the fashion of the holy Daniel, he represents the sins of his people as falling upon himself. For among many other evils of which he makes mention, he speaks of them also as "renouncing the world in words only and not in deeds;" as the apostle says of certain men, "They profess that they know God, but in works they deny Him." These, therefore, the blessed Cyprian shows to be contained within the Church herself, who are baptized without their hearts being changed for the better, seeing that they renounce the world in words and not in deeds, as the Apostle Peter says, "The like figure whereunto even baptism doth also now save us, (not the putting away of the filth of the flesh, but the answer of a good

conscience)," which certainly they had not of whom it is said that they "renounced the world in words only, and not in deeds;" and yet he does his utmost, by chiding and convincing them, to make them at length walk in the way of Christ, and be His friends rather than friends of the world.

Chapter 3. —4. And if they would have obeyed him, and begun to live rightly, not as false but as true Christians, would he have ordered them to be baptized anew? Surely not; but their true conversion would have gained this for them, that the sacrament which availed for their destruction while they were yet unchanged, should begin when they changed to avail for their salvation.

5. For neither are they "devoted to the Church" who seem to be within and live contrary to Christ, that is, act against His commandments; nor can they be considered in any way to belong to that Church, which He so purifies by the washing of water, "that He may present to Himself a glorious Church, not having spot or wrinkle, or any such thing." But if they are not in that Church to whose members they do not belong, they are not in the Church of which it is said, "My dove is but one; she is the only one of her mother;" for she herself is without spot or wrinkle. Or else let him who can assert that those are members of this dove who renounce the world in words but not in deeds. Meantime there is one thing which we see, from which I think it was said, "He that regarded the day, regarded it unto the Lord," for God judges every day. For, according to His foreknowledge, who knows whom He has foreordained before the foundation of the world to be made like to the image of His Son, many who are even openly outside, and are called heretics, are better

than many good Catholics. For we see what they are to-day, what they shall be to-morrow we know not. And with God, with whom the future is already present, they already are what they shall hereafter be. But we, according to what each man is at present, inquire whether they are to be to-day reckoned among the members of the Church which is called the one dove, and the Bride of Christ without a spot or wrinkle, of whom Cyprian says in the letter which I have quoted above, that "they did not keep in the way of the Lord, nor observe the commandments given unto them for their salvation; that they did not fulfill the will of their Lord, being eager about their property and gains, following the dictates of pride, giving way to envy and dissension, careless about single-mindedness and faith, renouncing the world in words only and not in deeds, pleasing each himself, and displeasing all men." But if the dove does not acknowledge them among her members, and if the Lord shall say to them, supposing that they continue in the same perversity, "I never knew you: depart from me, ye that work iniquity;" then they seem indeed to be in the Church, but are not; "nay, they even act against the Church. How then can they baptize with the baptism of the Church," which is of avail neither to themselves, nor to those who receive it from them, unless they are changed in heart with a true conversion, so that the sacrament itself, which did not avail them when they received it whilst they were renouncing the world in words and not in deeds, may begin to profit them when they shall begin to renounce it in deeds also? And so too in the case of those whose separation from the Church is open; for neither these nor those are as yet among the members of the dove, but some of them perhaps will be at some future time.

Chapter 4. —6. We do not, therefore, "acknowledge the baptism of heretics," when we refuse to baptize after them; but because we acknowledge the ordinance to be of Christ even among evil men, whether openly separated from us, or secretly severed whilst within our body, we receive it with due respect, having corrected those who were wrong in the points wherein they went astray. However, as I seem to be hard pressed when it is said to me, "Does then a heretic confer remission of sins?" so I in turn press hard when I say, Does then he who violates the commands of Heaven, the avaricious man, the robber, the usurer, the envious man, does he who renounces the world in words and not in deeds, confer such remission? If you mean by the force of God's sacrament, then both the one and the other; if by his own merit, neither of them. For that sacrament, even in the hands of wicked men, is known to be of Christ; but neither the one nor the other of these men is found in the body of the one uncorrupt, holy, chaste dove, which has neither spot nor wrinkle. And just as baptism is of no profit to the man who renounces the world in words and not in deeds, so it is of no profit to him who is baptized in heresy or schism; but each of them, when he amends his ways, begins to receive profit from that which before was not profitable, but was yet already in him.

7. "He therefore that is baptized in heresy does not become the temple of God; but does it therefore follow that he is not to be considered as baptized? For neither does the avaricious man, baptized within the Church, become the temple of God unless he departs from his avarice; for they who become the temple of God

certainly inherit the kingdom of God. But the apostle says, among many other things, "Neither the covetous, nor extortioners, shall inherit the kingdom of God." For in another place the same apostle compares covetousness to the worship of idols: "Nor covetous man," he says, "who is an idolater;" which meaning the same Cyprian has so far extended in a letter to Antonianus, that he did not hesitate to compare the sin of covetousness with that of men who in time of persecution had declared in writing that they would offer incense. The man, then, who is baptized in heresy in the name of the Holy Trinity, yet does not become the temple of God unless he abandons his heresy, just as the covetous man who has been baptized in the same name does not become the temple of God unless he abandons his covetousness, which is idolatry. For this, too, the same apostle says: "What agreement hath the temple of God with idols?" Let it not, then, be asked of us "of what God he is made the temple" when we say that he is not made the temple of God at all. Yet he is not therefore unbaptized, nor does his foul error cause that what he has received, consecrated in the words of the gospel, should not be the holy sacrament; just as the other man's covetousness (which is idolatry) and great uncleanness cannot prevent what he receives from being holy baptism, even though he be baptized with the same words of the gospel by another man covetous like himself.

Chapter 5. —8. "Further," Cyprian goes on to say, "in vain do some, who are overcome by reason, oppose to us custom, as though custom were superior to truth, or that were not to be followed in spiritual things which has been revealed by the Holy Spirit, as the better way." This is clearly true, since reason and truth are to be preferred to custom. But when truth supports custom, nothing should be more strongly maintained. Then he proceeds as follows: "For one may pardon a man who merely errs, as the Apostle Paul says of himself, 'Who was before a blasphemer, a persecutor, and injurious; but I obtained mercy, because I did it ignorantly;' but he who, after inspiration and revelation given, perseveres advisedly and knowingly in his former error, sins without hope of pardon on the ground of ignorance. For he rests on a kind of presumption and obstinacy, when he is overcome by reason." This is most true, that his sin is much more grievous who has sinned wittingly than his who has sinned through ignorance. And so in the case of the holy Cyprian, who was not only learned, but also patient of instruction, which he so fully himself understood to be a part of the praise of the bishop whom the apostle describes, that he said, "This also should be approved in a bishop, that he not only teaches with knowledge, but also learn with patience." I do not doubt that if he had had the opportunity of discussing this question, which has been so long and so much disputed in the Church, with the pious and learned men to whom we owe it that subsequently that ancient custom was confirmed by the authority of a plenary Council, he would have shown, without hesitation, not only how learned he was in those things which he had grasped with all the security of truth, but also how ready he was to receive instruction in what he had failed to perceive. And yet, since it is so clear that it is much more grievous to sin wittingly than in ignorance, I should be glad if anyone would tell me which is the worse, —the man who falls into heresy, not knowing how great a sin it is, or the man who refuses to abandon his covetousness, knowing its enormity? I might even put the question thus: If one man unwittingly fall into heresy, and another knowingly refuse to depart from idolatry, since the apostle himself says, "The covetous man, which is an idolater;" and Cyprian too understood the same passage in just the same way, when he says, in his letter to Antonianus, "Nor let the new heretics flatter themselves in this, that they say they do not communicate with idolaters, whereas there are amongst them both adulterers and covetous persons, who are held guilty of the sin of idolatry; 'for know this, and understand, that no whoremonger, nor unclean person, nor covetous man, who is an idolater, hath any inheritance in the kingdom of Christ and of God;' and again, 'Mortify therefore your members which are upon the earth; fornication, uncleanness, inordinate affection, evil concupiscence, and covetousness, which is idolatry.'" I ask, therefore, which sins more deeply, —he who ignorantly has fallen into heresy, or he who wittingly has refused to abandon covetousness, that is idolatry? According to that rule by which the sins of those who sin wittingly are placed before those of the ignorant, the man who is covetous with knowledge takes the first place in sin. But as it is possible that the greatness of the actual sin should produce the same effect in the case of heresy that the witting commission of the sin produces in that of covetousness, let us suppose the ignorant heretic to be on a par in guilt with the consciously covetous man, although the evidence which Cyprian himself has advanced from the apostle does not seem to prove this. For what is it that we abominate in heretics except their blasphemies? But when he wished to show that ignorance of the sin may conduce to ease in obtaining pardon, he advanced a proof from the case of the apostle, when he says, "Who was before a blasphemer, and a persecutor, and injurious; but I obtained mercy, because I did it ignorantly." But if possible, as I said before, let the sins of the two men—the blasphemy of the unconscious, and the idolatry of the conscious sinner—be esteemed of equal weight; and let them be judged by the same sentence,—he who, in seeking for Christ, falls into a truth-like setting forth of what is false, and he who wittingly resists Christ speaking through His apostle, "seeing that no whoremonger, nor unclean person, nor covetous man, which is an idolater, hath any inheritance in the kingdom of Christ and of God,"—and then I would ask why baptism and the words of the gospel are held as naught in the former case, and accounted valid in the latter, when each is alike found to be estranged from the members of the dove. Is it because the former is an open combatant outside, that he should not be admitted, the latter a cunning assenter within the fold, that he may not be expelled?

Chapter 6. —9. But as regards his saying, "Nor let anyone affirm that what they have received from the apostles, that they follow; for the apostles handed down only one Church and one baptism, and that appointed only in the same Church:" this does not so much move me to venture to condemn the baptism of Christ when found amongst heretics (just as it is necessary to recognize the gospel itself when I find it with them, though I abominate their error), as it warns me that there were some even in the times of the holy Cyprian who traced to the authority of the apostles that custom against which the African Councils were held, and in respect of which he himself said a little above, "In vain do those who are beaten by reason oppose to us the authority of custom." Nor do I find the reason why the same Cyprian found this very custom, which after his time was confirmed by nothing less than a plenary Council of the whole world, already so strong before his time, that when with all his learning he sought an authority worth following for changing it, he found nothing but a Council of Agrippinus held in Africa a very few years before his own time. And seeing that this was not enough for him, as against the custom of the whole world, he laid hold on these reasons which we just now, considering them with great care, and being confirmed by the antiquity of the custom itself, and by the subsequent authority of a plenary Council, found to be truth-like rather than true; which, however, seemed to him true, as he toiled in a question of the greatest obscurity, and was in doubt about the remission of sins,—whether it could fail to be given in the baptism of Christ, and whether it could be given among heretics. In which matter, if an imperfect revelation of the truth was given to Cyprian, that the greatness of his love in not deserting the unity of the Church might be made manifest, there is yet not any reason why anyone should venture to claim superiority over the strong defenses and excellence of his virtues, and the abundance of graces which were found in him, merely because, with the instruction derived from the strength of a general Council, he sees something which Cyprian did not see, because the Church had not yet held a plenary Council on the matter. Just as no one is so insane as to set himself up as surpassing the merits of the Apostle Peter, because, taught by the epistles of the Apostle Paul, and confirmed by the custom of the Church herself, he does not compel the Gentiles to Judaize, as Peter once had done.

10. We do not then "find that anyone, after being

baptized among heretics, was afterwards admitted by the apostles with the same baptism, and communicated;" but neither do we find this, that anyone coming from the society of heretics, who had been baptized among them, was baptized anew by the apostles. But this custom, which even then those who looked back to past ages could not find to have been invented by men of a later time, is rightly believed to have been handed down from the apostles. And there are many other things of the same kind, which it would be tedious to recount. Wherefore, if they had something to say for themselves to whom Cyprian, wishing to persuade them of the truth of his own view, says, "Let no one say, What we have received from the apostles, that we follow," with how much more force we now say, What the custom of the Church has always held, what this argument has failed to prove false, and what a plenary Council has confirmed, this we follow! To this we may add that it may also be said, after a careful inquiry into the reasoning on both sides of the discussion, and into the evidence of Scripture, What truth has declared, that we follow.

Chapter 7. —11. For in fact, as to what some opposed to the reasoning of Cyprian, that the apostle says, "Notwithstanding every way, whether in pretense or in truth, let Christ be preached;" Cyprian rightly exposed their error, showing that it has nothing to do with the case of heretics, since the apostle was speaking of those who were acting within the Church, with malicious envy seeking their own profit. They announced Christ, indeed, according to the truth whereby we believe in Christ, but not in the spirit in which He was announced by the good evangelists to the sons of the dove. "For Paul," he says, "in his epistle was not speaking of heretics, or of their baptism, so that it could be shown that he had laid down anything concerning this matter. He was speaking of brethren, whether as walking disorderly and contrary to the discipline of the Church, or as keeping the discipline of the Church in the fear of God. And he declared that some of them spoke the word of God steadfastly and fearlessly, but that some were acting in envy and strife; that some had kept themselves encompassed with kindly Christian love, but that others entertained malice and strife: but yet that he patiently endured all things, with the view that, whether in truth or in pretense, the name of Christ, which Paul preached, might come to the knowledge of the greatest number, and that the sowing of the word, which was as yet a new and unaccustomed work, might spread more widely by the preaching of those that spoke. Furthermore, it is one thing for those who are within the Church to speak in the name of Christ, another thing for those who are without, acting against the Church, to baptize in the name of Christ." These words of Cyprian seem to warn us that we must distinguish between those who are bad outside, and those who are bad within the Church. And those whom he says that the apostle represents as preaching the gospel impurely and of envy, he says truly were within. This much, however, I think I may say without rashness, if no one outside can have anything which is of Christ, neither can anyone within have anything which is of the devil. For if that closed garden can contain the thorns of the devil, why cannot the fountain of Christ equally flow beyond the garden's bounds? But if it cannot contain them, whence, even in the time of the Apostle Paul himself, did there arise amongst those who were within so great an evil of envy and malicious strife? For these are the words of Cyprian. Can it be that envy and malicious strife are a small evil? How then were those in unity who were not at peace? For it is not my voice, nor that of any man, but of the Lord Himself; nor did the sound go forth from men, but from angels, at the birth of Christ, "Glory to God in the highest, and on earth peace to men of good will." And this certainly would not have been proclaimed by the voice of angels when Christ was born upon the earth, unless God wished this to be understood, that those are in the unity of the body of Christ who are united in the peace of Christ, and those are in the peace of Christ who are of good will. Furthermore, as good will is shown in kindliness, so is bad will show in malice.

Chapter 8. —12. In short, we may see how great an evil in itself is envy, which cannot be other than malicious. Let us not look for other testimony. Cyprian himself is sufficient for us, through whose mouth the Lord poured forth so many thunders in most perfect truth, and uttered so many useful precepts about envy and malignity. Let us therefore read the letter of Cyprian about envy and malignity, and see how great an evil it is to envy those better than ourselves, —an evil whose origin he shows in memorable words to have sprung from the devil himself. "To feel jealousy," he says, "of what you regard as good, and to envy those who are better than yourselves, to some, dearest brethren, seems a light and minute offense." And again, a little later, when he was inquiring into the source and origin of the evil, he says, "From this the devil, in the very beginning of the world, perished first himself, and led others to destruction." And further on in the same chapter: "What an evil, dearest brethren, is that by which an angel fell! by which that exalted and illustrious loftiness was able to be deceived and overthrown! by which he was deceived who was the deceiver! From that time envy stalks upon the earth, when man, about to perish through malignity, submits himself to the teacher of perdition, —when he who envies imitates the devil, as it is written, 'Through envy of the devil came death into the world, and they that do hold of his side do find it.'" How true, how forcible are these words of Cyprian, in an epistle known throughout the world, we cannot fail to recognize. It was truly fitting for Cyprian to argue and warn most forcibly about envy and malignity, from which most deadly evil he proved his own heart to be so far removed by the abundance of his Christian love; by carefully guarding which he remained in the unity of communion with his colleagues, who without ill-feeling entertained different views about baptism, whilst he himself differed in opinion from them, not through any contention of ill will, but through human infirmity, erring in a point which God, in His own good time, would reveal to him by reason of his perseverance in love. For he says openly, "Judging no one, nor depriving any of the right of communion if he differ from us. For no one of us sets himself up as a bishop of bishops, or by tyrannical terror forces his colleagues to a necessity of obeying." And in the end of the epistle before us he says, "These things I have written to you briefly, dearest brother, according to my poor ability, prescribing to or prejudging no one, so as to prevent each bishop from doing what he thinks right in the free exercise of his own judgment. We, so far as in us lies, do not strive on behalf of heretics with our colleges and fellow-bishops, with whom we hold the harmony that

God enjoins, and the peace of our Lord, especially as the apostle says, 'If any man seem to be contentious, we have no such custom, neither the churches of God.' Christian love in our souls, the honor of our fraternity, the bond of faith, the harmony of the priesthood, all these are maintained by us with patience and gentleness. For this cause we have also, so far as our poor ability admitted, by the permission and inspiration of the Lord, written now a treatise on the benefit of patience, which we have sent to you in consideration of our mutual affection."

Chapter 9. —13. By this patience of Christian love he not only endured the difference of opinion manifested in all kindliness by his good colleagues on an obscure point, as he also himself received toleration, till, in process of time, when it so pleased God, what had always been a most wholesome custom was further confirmed by a declaration of the truth in a plenary Council, but he even put up with those who were manifestly bad, as was very well known to himself, who did not entertain a different view in consequence of the obscurity of the question, but acted contrary to their preaching in the evil practices of an abandoned life, as the apostle says of them, "Thou that preaches a man should not steal, dost thou steal?" For Cyprian says in his letter of such bishops of his own time, his own colleagues, and remaining in communion with him, "While they had brethren starving in the Church, they tried to amass large sums of money, they took possession of estates by fraudulent proceedings, they multiplied their gains by accumulated usuries." For here there is no obscure question. Scripture declares openly, "Neither covetous nor extortioners shall inherit the kingdom of God;" and

"He that putts out his money to usury," and "No whoremonger, nor unclean person, nor covetous man, who is an idolater, hath any inheritance in the kingdom of Christ and of God." He therefore certainly would not, without knowledge, have brought accusations of such covetousness, that men not only greedily treasured up their own goods, but also fraudulently appropriated the goods of others, or of idolatry existing in such enormity as he understands and proves it to exist; nor assuredly would he bear false witness against his fellow-bishops. And yet with the bowels of fatherly and motherly love he endured them, lest that, by rooting out the tares before their time, the wheat should also have been rooted up, imitating assuredly the Apostle Paul, who, with the same love towards the Church, endured those who were ill-disposed and envious towards him.

14. But yet because "by the envy of the devil death entered into the world, and they that do hold of his side do find it," not because they are created by God, but because they go astray of themselves, as Cyprian also says himself, seeing that the devil, before he was a devil, was an angel, and good, how can it be that they who are of the devil's side are in the unity of Christ? Beyond all doubt, as the Lord Himself says, "an enemy hath done this," who "sowed tares among the wheat." As therefore what is of the devil within the fold must be convicted, so what is of Christ without must be recognized. Has the devil what is his within the unity of the Church, and shall Christ not have what is His without? This, perhaps, might be said of individual men, that as the devil has none that are his among the holy angels, so God has none that are His outside the communion of the Church. But though it may be allowed to the devil to mingle tares, that is,

wicked men, with this Church which still wears the mortal nature of flesh, so long as it is wandering far from God, he being allowed this just because of the pilgrimage of the Church herself, that men may desire more ardently the rest of that country which the angels enjoy, yet this cannot be said of the sacraments. For, as the tares within the Church can have and handle them, though not for salvation, but for the destruction to which they are destined in the fire, so also can the tares without, which received them from seceders from within; for they did not lose them by seceding. This, indeed, is made plain from the fact that baptism is not conferred again on their return, when any of the very men who seceded happen to come back again. And let not anyone say, Why, what fruit hath the tares? For if this be so, their condition is the same, so far as this goes, both inside and without. For it surely cannot be that grains of corn are found in the tares inside, and not in those without. But when the question is of the sacrament, we do not consider whether the tares bear any fruit, but whether they have any share of heaven; for the tares, both within and without, share the rain with the wheat itself, which rain is in itself heavenly and sweet, even though under its influence the tares grow up in barrenness. And so the sacrament, according to the gospel of Christ, is divine and pleasant; nor is it to be esteemed as naught because of the barrenness of those on whom its dew falls even without.

Chapter 10. —15. But someone may say that the tares within may more easily be converted into wheat. I grant that it is so; but what has this to do with the question of repeating baptism? You surely do not maintain that if a man converted from heresy, through the occasion and opportunity given by his conversion, should bear fruit before another who, being within the Church, is slower to be washed from his iniquity, and so corrected and changed, the former therefore needs not to be baptized again, but the churchman to be baptized again, who was outstripped by him who came from the heretics, because of the greater slowness of his amendment. It has nothing, therefore, to do with the question now at issue who is later or slower in being converted from his especial waywardness to the straight path of faith, or hope, or charity. For although the bad within the fold are more easily made good yet it will sometimes happen that certain of the number of those outside will outstrip in their conversion certain of those within; and while these remain in barrenness, the former, being restored to unity and communion, will bear fruit with patience, thirtyfold, or sixty-fold, or a hundred-fold. Or if those only are to be called tares who remain in perverse error to the end, there are many ears of corn outside, and many tares within.

16. But it will be urged that the bad outside are worse than those within. It is indeed a weighty question, whether Nicolaus, being already severed from the Church, or Simon, who was still within it, was the worse, —the one being a heretic, the other a sorcerer. But if the mere fact of division, as being the clearest token of violated charity, is held to be the worse evil, I grant that it is so. Yet many, though they have lost all feelings of charity, yet do not secede from considerations of worldly profit; and as they seek their own, not the things which are Jesus Christ's, what they are unwilling to secede from is not the unity of Christ, but their own temporal advantage. Whence it is said in praise of charity, that she "seeks not her own."

17. Now, therefore, the question is, how could men of the party of the devil belong to the Church, which has no spot, or wrinkle, or any such thing, of which also it is said, "My dove is one?" But if they cannot, it is clear that she groans among those who are not of her, some treacherously laying wait within, some barking at her gate without. Such men, however, even within, both receive baptism, and possess it, and transmit it holy in itself; nor is it in any way defiled by their wickedness, in which they persevere even to the end. Wherefore the same blessed Cyprian teaches us that baptism is to be considered as consecrated in itself by the words of the gospel, as the Church has received, without joining to it or mingling with it any consideration of waywardness and wickedness on the part of either minister or recipients; since he himself points out to us both truths,—both that there have been some within the Church who did not cherish kindly Christian love, but practiced envy and unkind dissension, of whom the Apostle Paul spoke; and also that the envious belong to the devil's party, as he testifies in the most open way in the epistle which he wrote about envy and malignity. Wherefore, since it is clearly possible that in those who belong to the devil's party, Christ's sacrament may yet be holy,—not, indeed, to their salvation, but to their condemnation, and that not only if they are led astray after they have been baptized, but even if they were such in heart when they received the sacrament, renouncing the world (as the same Cyprian shows) in words only and not in deeds; and since even if afterwards they be brought into the right way, the sacrament is not to be again administered which they received when they were astray; so far as I can see, the case is already clear and evident, that in the question of

baptism we have to consider, not who gives, but what he gives; not who receives, but what he receives; not who has, but what he has. For if men of the party of the devil, and therefore in no way belonging to the one dove, can yet receive, and have, and give baptism in all its holiness, in no way defiled by their waywardness, as we are taught by the letters of Cyprian himself, how are we ascribing to heretics what does not belong to them? how are we saying that what is really Christ's is theirs, and not rather recognizing in them the signs of our Sovereign, and correcting the deeds of deserters from Him? Wherefore it is one thing, as the holy Cyprian says, "for those within in the Church, to speak in the name of Christ, another thing for those without, who are acting against the Church, to baptize in His name." But both many who are within act against the Church by evil living, and by enticing weak souls to copy their lives; and some who are without speak in Christ's name, and are not forbidden to work the works of Christ, but only to be without, since for the healing of their souls we grasp at them, or reason with them, or exhort them. For he, too, was without who did not follow Christ with His disciples, and yet in Christ's name was casting out devils, which the Lord enjoined that he should not be prevented from doing; although, certainly, in the point where he was imperfect he was to be made whole, in accordance with the words of the Lord, in which He says, "He that is not with me is against me; and he that gathered not with me scattered abroad." Therefore, both some things are done outside in the name of Christ not against the Church, and some things are done inside on the devil's part which are against the Church.

Chapter 11. —18. What shall we say of what is also wonderful, that he who carefully observes may find that it is possible that certain persons, without violating Christian charity, may yet teach what is useless, as Peter wished to compel the Gentiles to observe Jewish customs, as Cyprian himself would force heretics to be baptized anew? whence the apostle says to such good members, who are rooted in charity, and yet walk not rightly in some points, "If in anything ye be otherwise minded, God shall reveal even this unto you;" and that some again, though devoid of charity, may teach something wholesome? of whom the Lord says, "The scribes and the Pharisees sit in Moses' seat: all therefore whatsoever they bid you observe, that observe and do; but do not ye after their works: for they say and do not." Whence the apostle also says of those envious and malicious ones who yet preach salvation through Christ, "Whether in pretense, or in truth, let Christ be preached." Wherefore, both within and without, the waywardness of man is to be corrected, but the divine sacraments and utterances are not to be attributed to men. He is not, therefore, a "patron of heretics" who refuses to attribute to them what he knows not to belong to them, even though it be found among them. We do not grant baptism to be theirs; but we recognize His baptism of whom it is said, "The same is He which baptizes," wheresoever we find it. But if "the treacherous and blasphemous man" continue in his treachery and blasphemy, he receives no "remission of sins either without" or within the Church; or if, by the power of the sacrament, he receives it for the moment, the same force operates both without and within, as the power of the name of Christ used to work the expulsion of devils even without the Church.

Chapter 12.—19. But he urges that "we find that the apostles, in all their epistles, execrated and abhorred the sacrilegious wickedness of heretics, so as to say that 'their word does spread as a canker.'" What then? Does not Paul also show that those who said, "Let us eat and drink, for to-morrow we die," were corrupters of good manners by their evil communications, adding immediately afterwards, "Evil communications corrupt good manners;" and yet he intimated that these were within the Church when he says, "How say some among you that there is no resurrection of the dead?" But when does he fail to express his abhorrence of the covetous? Or could anything be said in stronger terms, than that covetousness should be called idolatry, as the same apostle declared? Nor did Cyprian understand his language otherwise, inserting it when need required in his letters; though he confesses that in his time there were in the Church not covetous men of an ordinary type, but robbers and usurers, and these found not among the masses, but among the bishops. And yet I should be willing to understand that those of whom the apostle says, "Their word does spread as a canker," were without the Church, but Cyprian himself will not allow me. For, when showing, in his letter to Antonianus, that no man ought to sever himself from the unity of the Church before the time of the final separation of the just and unjust, merely because of the admixture of evil men in the Church, when he makes it manifest how holy he was, and deserving of the illustrious martyrdom which he won, he says, "What swelling of arrogance it is, what forgetfulness of humility and gentleness, that anyone should dare or believe that he can do what the Lord did not grant even to the apostles,—to think that he can distinguish the tares from the wheat, or, as if it were granted to him to carry the fan and purge the floor, to endeavor to separate the chaff from the grain! And whereas the apostle says, 'But in a great house there are not only vessels of gold and of silver, but also of wood and of earth,' that he should seem to choose those of gold and of silver, and despise and cast away and condemn those of wood and of earth, when really the vessels of wood are only to be burned in the day of the Lord by the burning of the divine conflagration, and those of earth are to be broken by Him to whom the 'rod of iron has been given.'" By this argument, therefore, against those who, under the pretext of avoiding the society of wicked men, had severed themselves from the unity of the Church, Cyprian shows that by the great house of which the apostle spoke, in which there were not only vessels of gold and of silver, but also of wood and of earth, he understood nothing else but the Church, in which there should be good and bad, till at the last day it should be cleansed as a threshing-floor by the winnowing-fan. And if this be so, in the Church herself, that is, in the great house itself, there were vessels to dishonor, whose word did spread like a canker. For the apostle, speaking of them, taught as follows: "And their word," he says, "will spread as doth a canker; of whom is Hymenæus and Philetus; who concerning the truth have erred, saying that the resurrection is past already; and overthrow the faith of some. Nevertheless, the foundation of God stands sure, having this seal, The Lord knows them that are His. And, Let everyone that names the name of Christ depart from iniquity. But in a great house there are not only vessels of gold and of silver, but also of wood and of earth." If, therefore, they whose words did spread as doth a canker were as it were vessels to dishonor in the great house, and by that "great house" Cyprian understands the unity of the Church itself, surely it cannot be that their canker polluted the baptism of Christ. Accordingly, neither without, any more than within, can anyone who is of the devil's party, either in himself or in any other person, stain the sacrament which is of Christ. It is not, therefore, the case that "the word which spreads as a canker to the ears of those who hear it gives remission of sins;" but when baptism is given in the words of the gospel, however great be the perverseness of understanding on the part either of him through whom, or of him to whom it is given, the sacrament itself is holy because Him whose sacrament it is. And if anyone, receiving it at the hands of a misguided man, yet does not receive the perversity of the minister, but only the holiness of the mystery, being closely bound to the unity of the Church in good faith and hope and charity, he receives remission of his sins, —not by the words which do eat as doth a canker, but by the sacraments of the gospel flowing from a heavenly source. But if the recipient himself be misguided, on the one hand, what is given is of no avail for the salvation of the misguided man; and yet, on the other hand, that which is received remains holy in the recipient, and is not renewed to him if he be brought to the right way.

Chapter13. —20. There is therefore "no fellowship between righteousness and unrighteousness," not only without, but also within the Church; for "the Lord knows them that are His," and "Let everyone that names the name of Christ depart from iniquity." There is also "no communion between light and darkness," not only without, but also within the Church; for "he that hated his brother is still in darkness." And they at any rate hated Paul, who, preaching Christ of envy and malicious strife, supposed that they added affliction to his bonds; and yet the same Cyprian understands these still to have been within the Church. Since, therefore, "neither darkness can enlighten, nor unrighteousness justify," as Cyprian again says, I ask, how could those men baptize within the very Church herself? I ask, how could those vessels which the large house contains not to honor, but to dishonor, administer what is holy for the sanctifying of men within the great house itself, unless because that holiness of the sacrament cannot be polluted even by the unclean, either when it is given at their hands, or when it is received by those who in heart and life are not changed for the better? of whom, as situated within the Church, Cyprian himself says, "Renouncing the world in word only, and not in deed."

21. There are therefore also within the Church "enemies of God, whose hearts the spirit of Antichrist has possessed;" and yet they, "deal with spiritual and divine things," which cannot profit for their salvation so long as they remain such as they are; and yet neither can they pollute them by their own uncleanness. About what he says, therefore, "that they have no part given them in the saving grace of the Church, who, scattering and fighting against the Church of Christ, are called adversaries by Christ Himself, and antichrists by His apostles, this must be received under the consideration that there are men of this kind both within and without. But the separation of those that are within from the perfection and unity of the dove is not only known in the case of some men to God, but even in the case of some to their fellow-men; for, by regarding their openly abandoned life and confirmed wickedness, and comparing it with the rules of God's

commandments, they understand to what a multitude of tares and chaff, situated now some within and some without, but destined to be most manifestly separated at the last day, the Lord will then say, "Depart from me, ye that work iniquity," and "Depart into everlasting fire, prepared for the devil and his angels."

Chapter 14. —22. But we must not despair of the conversion of any man, whether situated within or without, so long as "the goodness of God leaded him to repentance," and "visits their transgressions with the rod, and their inquiry with stripes." For in this way "He does not utterly take from them His loving-kindness," if they will themselves sometimes "love their own soul, pleasing God." But as the good man "that shall endure unto the end, the same shall be saved," so the bad man, whether within or without, who shall persevere in his wickedness to the end, shall not be saved. Nor do we say that "all, wheresoever and howsoever baptized, obtain the grace of baptism," if by the grace of baptism is understood the actual salvation which is conferred by the celebration of the sacrament; but many fail to obtain this salvation even within the Church, although it is clear that they possess the sacrament, which is holy in itself. Well, therefore, does the Lord warn us in the gospel that we should not company with ill-advisers, who walk under the pretense of Christ's name; but these are found both within and without, as, in fact, they do not proceed without unless they have first been ill-disposed within. And we know that the apostle said of the vessels placed in the great house, "If a man therefore purge himself from these, he shall be a vessel unto honor, sanctified, and meet for the Master's use, and prepared unto every good work." But in what manner each man ought to purge himself from these he shows a little above, saying, "Let everyone that names the name of Christ depart from iniquity," that he may not in the last day, with the chaff, whether with that which has already been driven from the threshing-floor, or with that which is to be separated at the last, hear the command, "Depart from me, ye that work iniquity." Whence it appears, indeed, as Cyprian says, that "we are not at once to admit and adopt whatsoever is professed in the name of Christ, but only what is done in the truth of Christ." But it is not an action done in the truth of Christ that men should "seize on estates by fraudulent pretenses, and increase their gains by accumulated usury," or that they should "renounce the world in word only;" and yet, that all this is done within the Church, Cyprian himself bears sufficient testimony.

Chapter 15. —23. To go on to the point which he pursues at great length, that "they who blaspheme the Father of Christ cannot be baptized in Christ," since it is clear that they blaspheme through error (for he who comes to the baptism of Christ will not openly blaspheme the Father of Christ, but he is led to blaspheme by holding a view contrary to the teaching of the truth about the Father of Christ), we have already shown at sufficient length that baptism, consecrated in the words of the gospel, is not affected by the error of any man, whether ministrant or recipient, whether he hold views contrary to the revelation of divine teaching on the subject of the Father, or the Son, or the Holy Ghost. For many carnal and natural men are baptized even within the Church, as the apostle expressly says: "The natural man received not the things of the Spirit of God;" and after they had received baptism, he says that they "are yet carnal." But according to it carnal sense, a soul given up to fleshly appetites cannot entertain but fleshly wisdom about God. Wherefore many, progressing after baptism, and especially those who have been baptized in infancy or early youth, in proportion as their intellect becomes clearer and brighter, while "the inward man is renewed day by day," throw away their former opinions which they held about God while they were mocked with vain imaginings, with scorn and horror and confession of their mistake. And yet they are not therefore considered not to have received baptism, or to have received baptism of a kind corresponding to their error; but in them both the perfection of the sacrament is honored and the delusion of their mind is corrected, even though it had become inveterate through long confirmation, or been, perhaps, maintained in many controversies. Wherefore even the heretic, who is manifestly without, if he has there received baptism as ordained in the gospel, has certainly not received baptism of a kind corresponding to the error which blinds him. And therefore, in returning into the way of wisdom he perceives that he ought to relinquish what he has held amiss, he must not at the same time give up the good which he had received; nor because his error is to be condemned, is the baptism of Christ in him to be therefore extinguished. For it is already sufficiently clear, from the case of those who happen to be baptized within the Church with false views about God, that the truth of the sacrament is to be distinguished from the error of him who believes amiss, although both may be found in the same man. And therefore, when any one grounded in any error, even outside the Church, has yet been baptized with the true sacrament, when he is restored to the unity of the

Church, a true baptism cannot take the place of a true baptism, as a true faith takes the place of a false one, because a thing cannot take the place of itself, since neither can it give place. Heretics therefore join the Catholic Church to this end, that what they have evil of themselves may be corrected, not that what they have good of God should be repeated.

Chapter 16. —24. Someone says, Does it then make no difference, if two men, rooted in like error and wickedness, be baptized without change of life or heart, one without, the other within the Church? I acknowledge that there is a difference. For he is worse who is baptized without, in addition to his other sin, —not because of his baptism, however, but because he is without; for the evil of division is in itself far from insignificant or trivial. Yet the difference exists only if he who is baptized within has desired to be within not for the sake of any earthly or temporal advantage, but because he has preferred the unity of the Church spread throughout the world to the divisions of schism; otherwise he too must be considered among those who are without. Let us therefore put the two cases in this way. Let us suppose that the one, for the sake of argument, held the same opinions as Photinus about Christ, and was baptized in his heresy outside the communion of the Catholic Church; and that another held the same opinion but was baptized in the Catholic Church, believing that his view was really the Catholic faith. I consider him as not yet a heretic, unless, when the doctrine of the Catholic faith is made clear to him, he chooses to resist it, and prefers that which he already holds; and till this is the case, it is clear that he who was baptized outside is the worse. And so in the one case erroneous opinion alone, in the other the sin of schism also, requires correction; but in neither of them is the truth of the sacrament to be repeated. But if anyone holds the same view as the first, and knows that it is only in heresy severed from the Church that such a view is taught or learned, but yet for the sake of some temporal emolument has desired to be baptized in the Catholic unity, or, having been already baptized in it, is unwilling on account of the said emolument to secede from it, he is not only to be considered as seceding, but his offense is aggravated, in so far as to the error of heresy and the division of unity he adds the deceit of hypocrisy. Wherefore the depravity of each man, in proportion as it is more dangerous and wanting in straightforwardness, must be corrected with the more earnestness and energy; and yet, if he has anything that is good in him, especially if it be not of himself, but from God, we ought not to think it of no value because of his depravity, or to be blamed like it, or to be ascribed to it, rather than to His bountiful goodness, who even to a soul that plays the harlot, and goes after her lovers, yet gives His bread, and His wine, and His oil, and other food or ornaments, which are neither from herself nor from her lovers, but from Him who in compassion for her is even desirous to warn her to whom she should return.

Chapter 17. —25. "Can the power of baptism," says Cyprian, "be greater or better than confession? than martyrdom? that a man should confess Christ before men, and be baptized in his own blood? And yet," he goes on to say, "neither does this baptism profit the heretic, even though for confessing Christ he be put to death outside the Church." This is most true; for, by being put to death outside the Church, he is proved not to have had charity, of which the apostle says, "Though I give my body to be burned, and have not charity, it profited me nothing." But if martyrdom is of no avail for this reason, because it has not charity, neither does it profit those who, as Paul says, and Cyprian further sets forth, are living within the Church without charity in envy and malice; and yet they can both receive and transmit true baptism. "Salvation," he says, "is not without the Church." Who says that it is? And therefore, whatever men have that belongs to the Church, it profits them nothing towards salvation outside the Church. But it is one thing not to have, another to have so as to be of no use. He who has not must be baptized that he may have; but he who has to no avail must be corrected, that what he has may profit him. Nor is the water in the baptism of heretics "adulterous," because neither is the creature itself which God made evil, nor is fault to be found with the words of the gospel in the mouths of any who are astray; but the fault is theirs in whom there is an adulterous spirit, even though it may receive the adornment of the sacrament from a lawful spouse. Baptism therefore can "be common to us, and the heretics," just as the gospel can be common to us, whatever difference there may be between our faith and their error,—whether they think otherwise than the truth about the Father, or the Son, or the Holy Spirit; or, being cut away from unity, do not gather with Christ, but scatter abroad,—seeing that the sacrament of baptism can be common to us, if we are the wheat of the Lord, with the covetous within the Church, and with robbers, and drunkards, and other pestilent persons of the same sort, of whom it is said, "They shall not inherit the kingdom of God," and yet the vices by which they are separated from the kingdom of God are not shared by us.

Chapter 18. —26. Nor indeed, is it of heresies alone that the apostle says, "that they which do such things shall not inherit the kingdom of God." But it may be worthwhile to look for a moment at the things which he groups together. "The works of the flesh," he says "are manifest, which are these; fornication, uncleanness, lasciviousness, idolatry, witchcraft, hatred, variance, emulations, wrath, strife, seditions, heresies, envyings, murders, drunkenness, retellings, and such like: of the which I tell you before, as I have also told you in time past, that they which do such things shall not inherit the kingdom of God." Let us suppose someone, therefore, chaste, continent, free from covetousness, no idolater, hospitable, charitable to the needy, no man's enemy, not contentious, patient, quiet, jealous of none, envying none, sober, frugal, but a heretic; it is of course clear to all that for this one fault only, that he is a heretic, he will fail to inherit the kingdom of God. Let us suppose another, a fornicator, unclean, lascivious, covetous, or even more openly given to idolatry, a student of witchcraft, a lover of strife and contention, envious, hot-tempered, seditious, jealous, drunken, and a reveler, but a Catholic; can it be that for this sole merit, that he is a Catholic, he will inherit the kingdom of God, though his deeds are of the kind of which the apostle thus concludes: "Of the which I tell you before, as I have also told you in time past, that they which do such things shall not inherit the kingdom of God?" If we say this, we lead ourselves astray. For the word of God does not lead us astray, which is neither silent, nor lenient, nor deceptive through any flattery. Indeed, it speaks to the same effect elsewhere: "For this ye know, that no whoremonger, nor unclean person, nor covetous man, which is an idolater, hath any inheritance in the kingdom of Christ and of God. Let no man deceive you with vain words." We have no reason, therefore, to complain of the word of God. It certainly says, and says openly and freely, that those who live a wicked life have no part in the kingdom of God.

Chapter 19. —27. Let us therefore not flatter the Catholic who is hemmed in with all these vices, nor venture, merely because he is a Catholic Christian, to promise him the impunity which holy Scripture does not promise him; nor, if he has any one of the faults above mentioned, ought we to promise him a partnership in that heavenly land. For, in writing to the Corinthians, the apostle enumerates the several sins, under each of which it is implicitly understood that it shall not inherit the kingdom of God: "Be not deceived," he says: "neither fornicators, nor idolaters, nor adulterers, nor effeminate, nor abusers of themselves with mankind, nor thieves, nor covetous, nor drunkards, nor revilers, nor extortioners, shall inherit the kingdom of God." He does not say, those who possess all these vices together shall not inherit the kingdom of God; but neither these nor those: so that, as each is named, you may understand that no one of them shall inherit the kingdom of God. As, therefore, heretics shall not possess the kingdom of God, so the covetous shall not inherit the kingdom of God. Nor can we indeed doubt that the punishments themselves, with which they shall be tortured who do not inherit the kingdom of God, will vary in proportion to the difference of their offences, and that some will be more severe than others; so that in the eternal fire itself there will be different tortures in the punishments, corresponding to the different weights of guilt. For indeed it was not idly that the Lord said, "It shall be more tolerable for the land of Sodom in the day of judgment than for thee." But yet, so far as failing to inherit the kingdom of God is concerned, it is just as certain, if you choose any one of the less heinous of these vices, as if you choose more than one, or someone which you saw was more atrocious; and because those will inherit the kingdom of God whom the Judge shall set on His right hand, and for those who shall not be found worthy to be set at the right hand nothing will remain but to be at the left, no other announcement is left for them to hear like goats from the mouth of the Shepherd, except, "Depart into everlasting fire, prepared for the devil and his angels;" though in that fire, as I said before, it may be that different punishments will be awarded corresponding to the difference of the sins.

Chapter 20. —28. But on the question whether we ought to prefer a Catholic of the most abandoned character to a heretic in whose life, except that he is a heretic, men can find nothing to blame, I do not venture to give a hasty judgment. But if anyone says, because he is a heretic, he cannot be this only without other vices also following,—for he is carnal and natural, and therefore must be also envious, and hot-tempered, and jealous, and hostile to truth itself, and utterly estranged from it,—let him fairly understand, that of those other faults of which he is supposed to have chosen someone less flagrant, a single one cannot exist by itself in any man, because he in turn is carnal and natural; as, to take the case of drunkenness, which people have now become accustomed to talk of not only without horror, but with some degree of merriment, can it possibly exist alone in any one in whom it is found? For what drunkard is not also contentious, and hot-tempered, and jealous, and at variance with all soundness of counsel, and at grievous enmity with those who rebuke him? Further, it is not easy for him to avoid being a fornicator and adulterer, though he may be no heretic; just as a heretic may be no drunkard, nor adulterer, nor fornicator, nor lascivious, nor a lover of money, or given to witchcraft, and cannot well be all these together. Nor indeed is anyone vice followed by all the rest. Supposing, therefore, two men,—one a Catholic with all these vices, the other a heretic free from all from which a heretic can be free,—although they do not both contend against the faith, and yet each lives contrary to the faith, and each is deceived by a vain hope, and each is far removed from charity of spirit, and therefore each is severed from connection with the body of the one dove; why do we recognize in one of them the sacrament of Christ, and not in the other, as though it belonged to this or that man, whilst really it is the same in both, and belongs to God alone, and is good even in the worst of men? And if of the men who have it, one is worse than another, it does not follow that the sacrament which they have is worse in the one than in the other, seeing that neither in the case of two bad Catholics, if one be worse than the other, does he possess a worse baptism, nor, if one of them be good and another bad, is baptism bad in the bad one and good in the good one; but it is good in both. Just as the light of the sun, or even of a lamp, is certainly not less brilliant when displayed to bad eyes than when seen by better ones; but it is the same in the case of both, although it either cheers or hurts them differently according to the difference of their powers.

Chapter 21. —29. With regard to the objection brought against Cyprian, that the catechumens who were seized in martyrdom, and slain for Christ's name's sake, received a crown even without baptism, I do not quite see what it has to do with the matter, unless, indeed, they urged that heretics could much more be admitted with baptism to Christ's kingdom, to which catechumens were admitted without it, since He Himself has said, "Except a man be born of water and of the Spirit, he cannot enter into the kingdom of God." Now, in this matter I do not hesitate for a moment to place the Catholic catechumen, who is burning with love for God, before the baptized heretic; nor yet do we thereby do dishonor to the sacrament of baptism which the latter has already received, the former not as yet; nor do we consider that the sacrament of the catechumen is to be preferred to the sacrament of baptism, when we acknowledge that some catechumens are better and more faithful than some baptized persons. For the centurion Cornelius, before baptism, was better than Simon, who had been baptized. For Cornelius, even before his baptism, was filled with the Holy Spirit; Simon, even after baptism, was puffed up with an unclean spirit. Cornelius, however, would have been convicted of contempt for so holy a sacrament, if, even after he had received the Holy Ghost, he had refused to be baptized. But when he was baptized, he received in no wise a better sacrament than Simon; but the different merits of the men were made manifest under the equal holiness of the same sacrament—so true is it that the good or ill deserving of the recipient does not increase or diminish the holiness of baptism. But as baptism is wanting to a good catechumen to his receiving the kingdom of heaven, so true conversion is wanting to a bad man though baptized. For He who said, "Except a man be born of water and of the Spirit, he cannot enter into the kingdom of God," said also Himself, "except your righteousness shall exceed the righteousness of the scribes and Pharisees, ye shall in no case enter into the kingdom of heaven." For that the righteousness of the catechumens might not feel secure, it is written, "Except a man be born again of water and of the Spirit, he cannot enter into the kingdom of God." And again, that the unrighteousness of the baptized might not feel secure because they had received baptism, it is written, "Except your righteousness shall exceed the righteousness of the scribes and Pharisees, ye shall in no case enter into the kingdom of heaven." The one were too little without the other; the two make perfect the heir of that inheritance. As, then, we ought not to depreciate a man's righteousness, which begins to exist before he is joined to the Church, as the righteousness of Cornelius began to exist before he was in the body of Christian men,—which righteousness was not thought worthless, or the angel would not have said to him, "Thy prayers and thine alms are come up as a memorial before God;" nor did it yet suffice for his obtaining the kingdom of heaven, or he would not have been told to send to Peter,—so neither ought we to depreciate the sacrament of baptism, even though it has been received outside the Church. But since it is of no avail for salvation unless he who has baptism indeed in full perfection be incorporated into the Church, correcting also his own depravity, let us therefore correct the error of the heretics, that we may recognize what in them is not their own but Christ's.

Chapter 22. —30. That the place of baptism is sometimes supplied by martyrdom is supported by an argument by no means trivial, which the blessed Cyprian adduces from the thief, to whom, though he was not baptized, it was yet said, "To-day shall thou be with me in Paradise." On considering which, again and again, I find that not only martyrdom for the sake of Christ may supply what was wanting of baptism, but also faith and conversion of heart, if recourse may not be had to the celebration of the mystery of baptism for want of time. For neither was that thief crucified for the name of Christ, but as the reward of his own deeds; nor did he suffer because he believed, but he believed while suffering. It was shown, therefore, in the case of that thief, how great is the power, even without the visible sacrament of baptism, of what the apostle says, "With the heart man believeth unto righteousness, and with the mouth confession is made unto salvation." But the want is supplied invisibly only when the administration of baptism is prevented, not by contempt for religion, but by the necessity of the moment. For much more in the case of Cornelius and his friends, than in the case of that robber, might it seem superfluous that they should also be baptized with water, seeing that in them the gift of the Holy Spirit, which, according to the testimony of holy Scripture, was received by other men only after baptism, had made itself manifest by every unmistakable sign appropriate to those times when they spoke with tongues. Yet they were baptized, and for this action we have the authority of an apostle as the warrant. So far ought all of us to be from being induced by any imperfection in the inner man, if it so happens that before baptism a person has advanced, through the workings of a pious heart, to spiritual understanding, to despise a sacrament which is applied to the body by the hands of the minister, but which is God's own means for working spiritually a man's dedication to Himself. Nor do I conceive that the function of baptizing was assigned to John, so that it should be called John's baptism, for any other reason except that the Lord Himself, who had appointed it, in not disdaining to receive the baptism of His servant, might consecrate the path of humility, and show most plainly by such an action how high a value was to be placed on His own baptism, with which He Himself was afterwards to baptize. For He saw, like an excellent physician of eternal salvation, that overweening pride would be found in some, who, having made such progress in the understanding of the truth and in uprightness of character that they would not hesitate to place themselves, both in life and knowledge, above many that were baptized, would think it was unnecessary for them to be baptized, since they felt that they had attained a frame of mind to which many that were baptized were still only endeavoring to raise themselves.

Chapter 23. —31. But what is the precise value of the sanctification of the sacrament (which that thief did not receive, not from any want of will on his part, but because it was unavoidably omitted) and what is the effect on a man of its material application, it is not easy to say. Still, had it not been of the greatest value, the Lord would not have received the baptism of a servant. But since we must look at it in itself, without entering upon the question of the salvation of the recipient, which it is intended to work, it shows clearly enough that both in the bad, and in those who renounce the world in word and not in deed, it is itself complete, though they cannot receive salvation unless they amend their lives. But as in the thief, to whom the material administration of the sacrament was necessarily wanting, the salvation was complete, because it was spiritually present through his piety, so, when the sacrament itself is present, salvation is complete, if what the thief possessed be unavoidably wanting. And this is the firm tradition of the universal Church, in respect of the baptism of infants, who certainly are as yet unable "with the heart to believe unto righteousness, and with the mouth to make confession unto salvation," as the thief could do; nay, who even, by crying and moaning when the mystery is performed upon them, raise their voices in opposition to the mysterious words, and yet no Christian will say that they are baptized to no purpose.

Chapter 24. —32. And if anyone seek for divine authority in this matter, though what is held by the whole Church, and that not as instituted by Councils, but as a matter of invariable custom, is rightly held to have been handed down by apostolical authority, still we can form a true conjecture of the value of the sacrament of baptism in the case of infants, from the parallel of circumcision, which was received by God's earlier people, and before receiving which Abraham was justified, as Cornelius also was enriched with the gift of the Holy Spirit before he was baptized. Yet the apostle says of Abraham himself, that "he received the sign of circumcision, a seal of the righteousness of the faith," having already believed in his heart, so that "it was counted unto him for righteousness." Why, therefore, was it commanded him that he should circumcise every male child in order on the eighth day, though it could not yet believe with the heart, that it should be counted unto it for righteousness, because the sacrament in itself was of great avail? And this was made manifest by the message of an angel in the case of Moses' son; for when he was carried by his mother, being yet uncircumcised, it was required, by manifest present peril, that he should be circumcised, and when this was done, the danger of death was removed. As therefore in Abraham the justification of faith came first, and circumcision was added afterwards as the seal of faith; so in Cornelius the spiritual sanctification came first in the gift of the Holy Spirit, and the sacrament of regeneration was added afterwards in the laver of baptism. And as in Isaac, who was circumcised on the eighth day after his birth, the seal of this righteousness of faith was given first, and afterwards, as he imitated the faith of his father, the righteousness itself followed as he grew up, of which the seal had been given before when he was an infant; so in infants, who are baptized, the sacrament of regeneration is given first, and if they maintain a Christian piety, conversion also in the heart will follow, of which the mysterious sign had gone before in the outward body. And as in the thief the gracious goodness of the Almighty supplied what had been wanting in the sacrament of baptism, because it had been missing not from pride or contempt, but from want of opportunity; so in infants who die baptized, we must believe that the same grace of the Almighty supplies the want, that, not from perversity of will, but from insufficiency of age, they can neither believe with the heart unto righteousness, nor make confession with the mouth unto salvation. Therefore, when others take the vows for them, that the celebration of the sacrament may be complete in their behalf, it is unquestionably of avail for their dedication to God, because they cannot answer for themselves. But if another were to answer for one who could answer for himself, it would not be of the same avail. In accordance with which rule, we find in the gospel what strikes everyone as natural when he reads it, "He is of age, he shall speak for himself."

Chapter25. —33. By all these considerations it is proved that the sacrament of baptism is one thing, the conversion of the heart another; but that man's salvation is made complete through the two together. Nor are we to suppose that, if one of these be wanting, it necessarily follows that the other is wanting also; because the sacrament may exist in the infant without the conversion of the heart; and this was found to be possible without the sacrament in the case of the thief, God in either case filling up what was involuntarily wanting. But when either of these requisites is wanting intentionally, then the man is responsible for the omission. And baptism may exist when the conversion of the heart is wanting; but, with respect to such conversion, it may indeed be found when baptism has not been received, but never when it has been despised. Nor can there be said in any way to be a turning of the heart to God when the sacrament of God is treated with contempt. Therefore we are right in censuring, anathematizing, abhorring, and abominating the perversity of heart shown by heretics; yet it does not follow that they have not the sacrament of the gospel, because they have not what makes it of avail. Wherefore, when they come to the true faith, and by penitence seek remission of their sins, we are not flattering or deceiving them, when we instruct them by heavenly discipline for the kingdom of heaven, correcting and reforming in them their errors and perverseness, to the intent that we may by no means do violence to what is sound in them, nor, because of man's fault, declare that anything which he may have in him from God is either valueless or faulty.

Chapter 26. —34. A few things still remain to be noticed in the epistle to Jubaianus; but since these will raise the question both of the past custom of the Church and of the baptism of John, which is wont to excite no small doubt in those who pay slight attention to a matter which is sufficiently obvious, seeing that those who had received the baptism of John were commanded by the apostle to be baptized again they are not to be treated in a hasty manner, and had better be reserved for another book, that the dimensions of this may not be inconveniently large.

Book V.

He examines the last part of the epistle of Cyprian to Jubaianus, together with his epistle to Quintus, the letter of the African synod to the Numidian bishops, and Cyprian's epistle to Pompeius.

Chapter 1. —1. We have the testimony of the blessed Cyprian, that the custom of the Catholic Church is at present retained, when men coming from the side of heretics or schismatics, if they have received baptism as consecrated in the words of the gospel, are not baptized afresh. For he himself proposed to himself the question, and that as coming from the mouth of brethren either seeking the truth or contending for the truth. For in the course of the arguments by which he wished to show that heretics should be baptized again, which we have sufficiently considered for our present purpose in the former books, he says: "But some will say, What then will become of those who in times past, coming to the Church from heresy, were admitted without baptism?" In this question is involved the shipwreck of the whole cause of the Donatists, with whom our contest is on this point. For if those had not really baptism who were thus received on coming from heretics, and their sins were still upon them, then, when such men were admitted to communion, either by those who came before Cyprian or by Cyprian himself, we must acknowledge that one of two things occurred, —either that the Church perished then and there from the pollution of communion with such men, or that anyone abiding in unity is not injured by even the notorious sins of other men. But since they cannot say that the Church then perished through the contamination arising from communion with those who, as Cyprian says, were admitted into it without baptism— for otherwise they cannot maintain the validity of their own origin if the Church then perished, seeing that the list of consuls proves that more than forty years elapsed between the martyrdom of Cyprian and the burning of the sacred books, from which they took occasion to make a schism, spreading abroad the smoke of their calumnies,— it therefore is left for them to acknowledge that the unity of Christ is not polluted by any such communion, even with known offenders. And, after this confession, they will be unable to discover any reason which will justify them in maintaining that they were bound to separate from the churches of the whole world, which, as we read, were equally founded by the apostles, seeing that, while the others could not have perished from any admixture of offenders, of whatsoever kind, they, though they would not have perished if they had remained in unity with them, brought destruction on themselves in schism, by separating themselves from their brethren, and breaking the bond of peace. For the sacrilege of schism is most clearly evident in them, if they had no sufficient cause for separation. And it is clear that there was no sufficient cause for separation, if even the presence of notorious offenders cannot pollute the good while they abide in unity. But that the good, abiding in unity, are not polluted even by notorious offenders, we teach on the testimony of Cyprian, who says that "men in past times, coming to the Church from heresy, were admitted without baptism;" and yet, if the wickedness of their sacrilege, which was still upon them, seeing it had not been purged away by baptism, could not pollute and destroy the holiness of the Church, it cannot perish by any infection from wicked men. Wherefore, if they allow that Cyprian spoke the truth, they are convicted of schism on his testimony; if they maintain that he does not speak truth, let them not use his testimony on the question of baptism.

Chapter 2. —2. But now that we have begun a disputation with a man of peace like Cyprian, let us go on. For when he had brought an objection against himself, which he knew was urged by his brethren, "What then will become of those who in times past, coming to the Church from heresy, were admitted without baptism? The Lord," he answers, "is able of His mercy to grant indulgence, and not to separate from the gifts of His Church those who, being admitted in all honesty to His Church, have fallen asleep within the Church." Well indeed has he assumed that charity can cover the multitude of sins. But if they really had baptism, and this were not rightly perceived by those who thought that they should be baptized again, that error was covered by the charity of unity so long as it contained, not the discord and spirit of the devil, but merely human infirmity, until, as the apostle says, "if they were otherwise minded, the Lord should reveal it to them." But woe unto those who, being torn asunder from unity by a sacrilegious rupture, either rebaptize, if baptism exists with both us and them, or do not baptize at all, if baptism exist in the Catholic Church only. Whether, therefore, they rebaptize, or fail to baptize, they are not in the bond of peace; wherefore let them apply a remedy to which they please of these two wounds. But if we admit to the Church without baptism, we are of the number of those who, as Cyprian has assumed, may receive pardon because they preserved unity. But if (as is, I think, already clear from what has been said in the earlier books) Christian baptism can preserve its integrity even amid the perversity of heretics, then even though any in those times did rebaptize, yet without departing from the bond of unity, they might still attain to pardon in virtue of that same love of peace, through which Cyprian bears witness that those admitted even without baptism might obtain that they should not be separated from the gifts of the Church. Further, if it is true that with heretics and schismatics the baptism of Christ does not exist, how much less could the sins of others hurt those who were fixed in unity, if even men's own sins were forgiven when they came to it even without baptism! For if, according to Cyprian, the bond of unity is of such efficacy, how could they be hurt by other men's sins, who were unwilling to separate themselves from unity, if even the unbaptized, who wished to come to it from heresy, thereby escaped the destruction due to their own sins?

Chapter. 3.—3. But in what Cyprian adds, saying, "Nor yet because men once have erred must there be always error, since it rather befits wise and God-fearing men gladly and unhesitatingly to follow truth, when it is clearly laid before their eyes, than obstinately and persistently to fight for heretics against their brethren and their fellow-priests," he is uttering the most perfect truth; and the man who resists the manifest truth is opposing himself rather than his neighbors. But, so far as I can judge, it is perfectly clear and certain, from the many arguments which I have already adduced, that the baptism of Christ cannot be invalidated even by the perversity of heretics, when it is given or received among them. But, granting that it is not yet certain, at any rate no one who has considered what has been said, even from a hostile point of view, will assert that the question has been decided the other way. Therefore, we are not striving against manifest truth, but either, as I think, we are striving in behalf of what is clearly true, or, at any rate, as those may hold who think that the question has not yet been solved, we are seeking for the truth. And therefore, if the truth be other than we think, yet we are receiving those baptized by heretics with the same honesty of heart with which those received them whom, Cyprian supposed, in virtue of their cleaving to the unity of the Church, to be capable of pardon. But if the baptism of Christ, as is indicated by the many arguments used above, can retain its integrity amid any defect either of life or faith, whether on the part of those who seem to be within, and yet do not belong to the members of the one dove or on the part of those whose severance from her extends to being openly without, then those who sought its repetition in those former days deserved the same pardon for their charity in clinging to unity, which Cyprian thought that those deserved for charity of the same kind whom he believed to have been admitted without baptism. They therefore who, without any cause (since, as Cyprian himself shows, the bad cannot hurt the good in the unity of the Church), have cut themselves off from the charity which is shown in this unity, have lost all place of pardon, and whilst they would incur destruction by the very crime of schism, even though they did not rebaptize those who had been baptized in the Catholic Church, of how bitter punishment are they deserving, who are either endeavoring to give to the Catholics who have it what Cyprian affirms that they themselves have not, or, as is clear from the facts of the case, are bringing as a charge against the Catholic Church that she has not what even they themselves possess?

Chapter 4. —4. But since now, as I said before, we have begun a disputation with the epistles of Cyprian, I think that I should not seem even to him, if he were present, "to be contending obstinately and persistently in defense of heretics against my brethren and my fellow-priests," when he learned the powerful reasons which move us to believe that even among heretics, who are perversely obstinate in their malignant error, the baptism of Christ is yet in itself most holy, and most highly to be reverenced. And seeing that he himself, whose testimony has such weight with us, bears witness that they were wont in past times to be admitted without a second baptism, I would have any one, who is induced by Cyprian's arguments to hold it as certain that heretics ought to be baptized afresh, yet consider that those who, on account of weight of the arguments on the other side, are not as yet persuaded that this should be so, hold the same place as those in past time, who in all honesty admitted men who were baptized in heresy on the simple correction of their individual error, and who were capable of salvation with them in virtue of the bond of unity. And let anyone, who is led by the past custom of the Church, and by the subsequent authority of a plenary Council, and by so many powerful proofs from holy Scripture, and by much evidence from Cyprian himself, and by the clear reasoning of truth, to understand that the baptism of Christ, consecrated in the words of the gospel, cannot be perverted by the error of any man on earth,—let such an one understand, that they who then thought otherwise, but yet preserved their charity, can be saved by the same bond of unity. And herein he should also understand of those who, in the society of the Church dispersed throughout the world, could not have been defiled by any tares, by any chaff, so long as they themselves desired to be fruitful corn, and who therefore severed themselves from the same bond of unity without any cause for the divorce, that at any rate, whichever of the two opinions be true,—that which Cyprian then held, or that which was maintained by the universal voice of the Catholic Church, which Cyprian did not abandon,—in either case they, having most openly placed themselves outside in the plain sacrilege of schism, cannot possibly be saved, and all that they possess of the holy sacraments, and of the free gifts of the one legitimate Bridegroom, is of avail, while they continue what they are, for their confusion rather than the salvation of their souls.

Chapter 5. —5. Wherefore, even if heretics should be truly anxious to correct their error and come to the Church, for the very reason that they believed that they had no baptism unless they received it in the Church, even under these circumstances we should not be bound to yield to their desire for the repetition of baptism; but rather they should be taught, on the one hand, that baptism, though perfect in itself, could in no way profit their perversity if they would not submit to be corrected; and, on the other hand, that the perfection of baptism could not be impaired by their perversity, while refusing to be corrected: and again, that no further perfection is added to baptism in them because they are submitting to correction; but that, while they themselves are quitting their iniquity, that which was before within them to their destruction is now beginning to be of profit for salvation. For, learning this, they will both recognize the need of salvation in Catholic unity, and will cease to claim as their own what is really Christ's, and will not confound the sacrament of truth, although existing in themselves, with their own individual error.

6. To this we may add a further reason, that men, by a sort of hidden inspiration from heaven, shrink from anyone who for the second time receives baptism which he had already received in any quarter whatsoever, insomuch that the very heretics themselves, when their arguments start with that subject, rub their forehead in perplexity, and almost all their laity, even those who have grown old in their body, and have conceived an obstinate animosity against the Catholic Church, confess that this one point in their system displeases them; and many who,

for the sake of gaining some secular advantage, or avoiding some disadvantage, wish to secede to them, strive with many secret efforts that they may have granted to them, as a peculiar and individual privilege, that they should not be rebaptized; and some, who are led to place credence in their other vain delusions and false accusations against the Catholic Church, are recalled to unity by this one consideration, that they are unwilling to associate with them lest they should be compelled to be rebaptized. And the Donatists, through fear of this feeling, which has so thorough possession of all men's hearts, have consented to acknowledge the baptism which was conferred among the followers of Maximianus, whom they had condemned, and so to cut short their own tongues and close their mouths, in preference to baptizing again so many men of the people of Musti, and Assuræ, and other districts, whom they received with Felicianus and Prætextatus, and the others who had been condemned by them and afterwards returned to them.

Chapter 6. —7. For when this is done occasionally in the case of individuals, at great intervals of time and space, the enormity of the deed is not equally felt; but if all were suddenly to be brought together who had been baptized in course of time by the aforesaid followers of Maximianus, either under pressure of the peril of death or at their Easter solemnities, and it were told them that they must be baptized again, because what they had already received in the sacrilege of schism was null and void, they might indeed say what obstinate perseverance in their error would compel them to say, that they might hide the rigor and iciness of their hardness under any kind of false shade of consistency against the warmth of truth. But in fact, because the party of Maximianus could not bear this, and because the very men who would have to enforce it could not endure what must needs have been done in the case of so many men at once, especially as those very men would be rebaptizing them in the party of Primianus who had already baptized them in the party of Maximianus, for these reasons their baptism was received, and the pride of the Donatists was cut short. And this course they would certainly not have chosen to adopt, had they not thought that more harm would have been done to their cause by the offense men would have taken at the repetition of the baptism, than by the reputation lost in abandoning their defense. And this I would not say with any idea that we ought to be restrained by consideration of human feelings, if the truth compelled those who came from heretics to be baptized afresh. But because the holy Cyprian says, "that heretics might have been all the more impelled to the necessity of coming over, if only they were to be rebaptized in the Catholic Church," on this account I have wished to place on record the intensity of the repugnance to this act which is seated deeply in the heart of nearly everyone,—a repugnance which I can believe was inspired by God Himself, that the Church might be fortified by the instinct of repugnance against any possible arguments which the weak cannot dispel.

Chapter 7. —8. Truly, when I look at the actual words of Cyprian, I am warned to say some things which are very necessary for the solution of this question. "For if they were to see," he says, "that it was settled and established by our formal decision and vote, that the baptism with which they are baptized in heresy is considered just and lawful, they will think that they are in just and lawful possession of the Church also, and all its other gifts." He does not say "that they will think they are in possession," but "in just and lawful possession of the gifts of the Church." But we say that we cannot allow that they are in just and lawful possession of baptism. That they are in possession of it we cannot deny, when we recognize the sacrament of the Lord in the words of the gospel. They have therefore lawful baptism, but they do not have it lawfully. For whosoever has it both in Catholic unity, and living worthily of it, both has lawful baptism and has it lawfully; but whosoever has it either within the Catholic Church itself, as chaff mixed with the wheat, or outside, as chaff carried away by the wind, has indeed lawful baptism, but not lawfully. For he has it as he uses it. But the man does not use it lawfully who uses it against the law, —which everyone does, who, being baptized, yet leads an abandoned life, whether inside or without the Church.

Chapter8. —9. Wherefore, as the apostle said of the law, "The law is good, if a man use it lawfully," so we may fairly say of baptism, Baptism is good, if a man use it lawfully. And as they who used the law unlawfully could not in that case cause that it should not be in itself good, or make it null and void, so anyone who uses baptism unlawfully, either because he lives in heresy, or because he lives the worst of lives, yet cannot cause that the baptism should be otherwise than good, or altogether null and void. And so, when he is converted either to Catholic unity, or to a mode of living worthy of so great a sacrament, he begins to have not another and a lawful baptism, but that same baptism in a lawful manner. Nor does the remission of irrevocable sins follow on baptism, unless a man not only have lawful baptism, but have it lawfully; and yet it does not follow that if a man have it not lawfully, so that his sins are either not remitted, or, being remitted, are brought on him again, therefore the sacrament of baptism should be in the baptized person either bad or null and void. For as Judas, to whom the Lord gave a morsel, gave a place within himself of the devil, not by receiving what was bad, but by receiving it badly, so each person, on receiving the sacrament of the Lord, does not cause that it is bad because he is bad himself, or that he has received nothing because he has not received it to salvation. For it was none the less the body of the Lord and the blood of the Lord, even in those to whom the apostle said, "He that eats unworthily, eats and drinks damnation to himself." Let the heretics therefore seek in the Catholic Church not what they have, but what they have not, —that is, the end of the commandment, without which many holy things may be possessed, but they cannot profit. "Now, the end of the commandment is charity out of a pure heart, and of a good conscience, and of faith unfeigned." Let them therefore hasten to the unity and truth of the Catholic Church, not that they may have the sacrament of washing, if they have been already bathed in it, although in heresy, but that they may have it to their health.

Chapter 9. —10. Now we must see what is said of the baptism of John. For "we read in the Acts of the Apostles, that those who had already been baptized with the baptism of John were yet baptized by Paul," simply because the baptism of John was not the baptism of Christ, but a baptism allowed by Christ to John, so as to be called especially John's baptism; as the same John says, "A man can receive nothing, except it be given him from heaven." And that he might not possibly seem to receive this from God the Father in such wise as not to receive it from the Son, speaking presently of Christ Himself, he says, "Of His fullness have all we received." But by the grace of a certain dispensation John received this, which was to last not for long, but only long enough to prepare for the Lord the way in which he must needs be the forerunner. And as our Lord was presently to enter on this way with all humility, and to lead those who humbly followed Him to perfection, as He washed the feet of His servants, so was He willing to be baptized with the baptism of a servant. For as He set Himself to minister to the feet of those whose guide He was Himself, so He submitted Himself to the gift of John which He Himself had given, that all might understand what sacrilegious arrogance they would show in despising the baptism which they ought each of them to receive from the Lord, when the Lord Himself accepted what He Himself had bestowed upon a servant, that he might give it as his own; and that when John, than whom no greater had arisen among them that are born of women, bore such testimony to Christ, as to confess that he was not worthy to unloose the latchet of His shoe, Christ might both, by receiving his baptism, be found to be the humblest among men, and, by taking away the place for the baptism of John, be believed to be the most high God, at once the teacher of humility and the giver of exaltation.

11. For to none of the prophets, to no one at all in holy Scripture, do we read that it was granted to baptize in the water of repentance for the remission of sins, as it was granted to John; that, causing the hearts of the people to

hang upon him through this marvelous grace, he might prepare in them the way for Him whom he declared to be so infinitely greater than himself. But the Lord Jesus Christ cleanses His Church by such a baptism that on receiving it no other is required; while John gave a first washing with such a baptism that on receiving it there was further need of the baptism of the Lord, —not that the first baptism should be repeated, but that the baptism of Christ, for whom he was preparing the way, might be further bestowed on those who had received the baptism of John. For if Christ's humility were not to be commended to our notice, neither would there be any need of the baptism of John; again, if the end were in John, after his baptism there would be no need of the baptism of Christ. But because "Christ is the end of the law for righteousness to everyone that believeth," it was shown by John to whom men should go, and in whom, when they had reached Him, they should rest. The same, John, therefore, set forth both the exalted nature of the Lord, when he placed Him far before himself, and His humility, when he baptized Him as the lowest of the people. But if John had baptized Christ alone, he would be thought to have been the dispenser of a better baptism, in that with which Christ alone was baptized, than the baptism of Christ with which Christians are baptized; and again, if all ought to be baptized first with the baptism of John, and then with that of Christ, the baptism of Christ would deservedly seem to be lacking in fullness and perfection, as not sufficing for salvation. Wherefore the Lord was baptized with the baptism of John, that He might bend the proud necks of men to His own health-giving baptism; and He was not alone baptized with it, lest He should show His own to be inferior to this, with which none but He Himself had deserved to be baptized; and He did not allow it to continue longer, lest the one baptism with which He baptizes might seem to need the other to precede it.

Chapter 10. —12. I ask, therefore, if sins were remitted by the baptism of John, what more could the baptism of Christ confer on those whom the Apostle Paul desired to be baptized with the baptism of Christ after they had received the baptism of John? But if sins were not remitted by the baptism of John, were those men in the days of Cyprian better than John, of whom he says himself that they "used to seize on estates by treacherous frauds, and increase their gains by accumulated usuries," through whose, administration of baptism the remission of sins was yet conferred? Or was it because they were contained within the unity of the Church? What then? Was John not contained within that unity, the friend of the Bridegroom, the preparer of the way of the Lord, the baptizer of the Lord Himself? Who will be mad enough to assert this? Wherefore, although my belief is that John so baptized with the water of repentance for the remission of sins, that those who were baptized by him received the expectation of the remission of their sins, the actual remission taking place in the baptism of the Lord,—just as the resurrection which is expected at the last day is fulfilled in hope in us, as the apostle says, that "He hath raised us up together, and made us sit together in heavenly places in Christ Jesus;" and again, "For we are saved by hope;" or as again John himself, while he says, "I indeed baptize you with water unto repentance, for the remission of your sins," yet says, on seeing our Lord, "Behold the Lamb of God, which taketh away the sin of the world,"—nevertheless I am not disposed to contend vehemently against anyone who maintains that sins were remitted even in the baptism of John, but that some fuller sanctification was conferred by the baptism of Christ on those whom Paul ordered to be baptized anew.

Chapter 11. —13. For we must look at the point which especially concerns the matter before us (whatever be the nature of the baptism of John, since it is clear that he belongs to the unity of Christ), viz., what is the reason for which it was right that men should be baptized again after receiving the baptism of the holy John, and why they ought not to be baptized again after receiving the baptism of the covetous bishops. For no one denies that in the Lord's field John was as wheat, bearing a hundred-fold, if that be the highest rate of increase; also no one doubts that covetousness, which is idolatry, is reckoned in the Lord's harvest among the chaff. Why then is a man baptized again after receiving baptism from the wheat, and not after receiving it from the chaff? If it was because he was better than John that Paul baptized after John, why did not also Cyprian baptize after his usurious colleagues, than whom he was better beyond all comparison? If it was because they were in unity with him that he did not baptize after such colleagues, neither ought Paul to have baptized after John, because they were joined together in the same unity. Can it be that defrauders and extortioners belong to the members of that one dove, and that he does not belong to it to whom the full power of the Lord Jesus Christ was shown by the appearance of the Holy Spirit in the form of a dove? Truly he belongs most closely to it; but the others, who must be separated from it either by the occasion of some scandal, or by the winnowing at the last day, do not by any means belong to it, and yet baptism was repeated after John and not after them. What then is the cause, except that the baptism which Paul ordered them to receive was not the same as that which was given at the hands of John? And so in the same unity of the Church, the baptism of Christ cannot be repeated though it be given by a usurious minister; but those who receive the baptism of John, even from the hands of John Himself, ought to be afterwards baptized with the baptism of Christ.

Chapter 12. —14. Accordingly, I too might use the words of the blessed Cyprian to turn the hearts of those that hear me to the consideration of something truly marvelous, if I were to say "that John, who was accounted greater among the prophets,—he who was filled with divine grace while yet in his mother's womb; he who was upheld in the spirit and power of Elias; who was not the adversary, but a forerunner and herald of the Lord: who not only foretold our Lord in words, but also showed Him to the sight; who baptized Christ Himself, through whom all others are baptized,"—he was not worthy to baptize in such wise that those who were baptized by him should not be baptized again after him; and shall no one think that a man should be baptized in the Church after he had been baptized by the covetous, by defrauders, by extortioners, by usurers? Is not the answer ready to this invidious question, Why do you think this unmeet, as though either John were dishonored, or the covetous man honored? But His baptism ought not to be repeated, of whom John says, "The same is He which baptizes with the Holy Ghost." For whoever be the minister by whose hands it is given, it is His baptism of whom it was said, "The same is He which baptizes." But neither was the baptism of John himself repeated, when the Apostle Paul commanded those who had been baptized by him to be baptized in Christ. For what they had not received from the friend of the Bridegroom, this it was right that they should receive from the Bridegroom Himself, of whom that friend had said, "The same is He which baptizes with the Holy Ghost."

Chapter 13. —15. For the Lord Jesus might, if He had so thought fit, have given the power of His baptism to some one or more of His chief servants, whom He had already made His friends, such as those to whom He says, "Henceforth I call you not servants, but friends;" that, as Aaron was shown to be the priest by the rod that budded, so in His Church, when more and greater miracles are performed, the ministers of more excellent holiness, and the dispensers of His mysteries, might be made manifest by some sign, as those who alone ought to baptize. But if this had been done, then though the power of baptizing were given them by the Lord, yet it would necessarily be called their own baptism, as in the case of the baptism of John. And so Paul gives thanks to God that he baptized none of those men who, as though forgetting in whose name they had been baptized, were for dividing themselves into factions under the names of different individuals. For when baptism is as valid at the hands of a contemptible man as it was when given by an apostle, it is recognized as the baptism neither of this man nor of that, but of Christ; as John bears witness that he learned, in the case of the Lord Himself, through the appearance of the dove. For in what other respect he said, "And I knew

Him not," I cannot clearly see. For if he had not known Him in any sense, he could not have said to Him when He came to his baptism, "I have need to be baptized of Thee." What is it, therefore, that he says, "I saw the Spirit descending from heaven like a dove, and it abode upon Him. And I knew Him not: but He that sent me to baptize with water, the same said unto me, Upon whom thou shall see the Spirit descending, and remaining on Him, the same is He which baptizes with the Holy Ghost?" The dove clearly descended on Him after He was baptized. But while He was yet coming to be baptized, John had said, "I have need to be baptized of Thee." He therefore already knew Him. What does he therefore mean by the words, "I knew Him not: but He that sent me to baptize with water, the same said unto me, Upon whom thou shalt see the Spirit descending, and remaining on Him, the same is He which baptizes with the Holy Ghost," since this took place after He was baptized, unless it were that he knew Him in respect of certain attributes, and in respect of others knew Him not? He knew Him, indeed, as the Son of God, the Bridegroom, of whose fullness all should receive; but whereas of His fullness he himself had so received the power of baptizing that it should be called the baptism of John, he did not know whether He would so give it to others also, or whether He would have His own baptism in such wise, that at whosesoever hands it was given, whether by a man that brought forth fruit a hundredfold, or sixtyfold, or thirtyfold, whether by the wheat or by the chaff, it should be known to be of Him alone; and this he learned through the Spirit descending like a dove, and abiding on Him.

Chapter 14. —16. Accordingly, we find the apostles using the expressions, "My glorying," though it was certainly in the Lord; and "Mine office," and "My knowledge," and "My gospel," although it was confessedly bestowed and given by the Lord; but no one of them ever once said, "My baptism." For neither is the glorying of all of them equal, nor do they all minister with equal powers, nor are they all endowed with equal knowledge, and in preaching the gospel one works more forcibly than another, and so one may be said to be more learned than another in the doctrine of salvation itself; but one cannot be said to be more or less baptized than another, whether he be baptized by a greater or a less worthy minister. So when "the works of the flesh are manifest, which are these, fornication, uncleanness, lasciviousness, idolatry, witchcraft, hatred, variance, emulations, strife, seditions, heresies, envyings, drunkenness, retellings, and such like;" if it be strange that it should be said, "Men were baptized after John, and are not baptized after heretics," why is it not equally strange that it should be said, "Men were baptized after John, and are not baptized after the envious," seeing that Cyprian himself bears witness in his epistle concerning envy and malignity that the covetous are of the party of the devil, and Cyprian himself makes it manifest from the words of the Apostle Paul, as we have shown above, that in the time of the apostles themselves there were envious persons in the Church of Christ among the very preachers of the name of Christ?

Chapter 15. —17. That therefore the baptism of John was not the same as the baptism of Christ, has, I think, been shown with sufficient clearness; and therefore no argument can be drawn from it that baptism should be repeated after heretics because it was repeated after John: since John was not a heretic, and could have a baptism, which, though granted by Christ, was yet not the very baptism of Christ, seeing that he had the love of Christ; while a heretic can have at once the baptism of Christ and the perversity of the devil, as another within the Church may have at once the baptism of Christ and the envy of the devil.

18. But it will be urged that baptism after a heretic is much more required, because John was not a heretic, and yet baptism was repeated after him. On this principle, a man may say, much more must we rebaptize after a drunkard, because John was sober, and yet baptism was repeated after him. And we shall have no answer to make to such a man, save that the baptism of Christ was given to those who were baptized by John, because they had it not; but where men have the baptism of Christ, no iniquity on their part can possibly affect that the baptism of Christ should fail to be in them.

19. It is not therefore true that "by baptizing first, the heretic obtains the right of baptism;" but because he did not baptize with his own baptism, and though he did not possess the right of baptizing, yet that which he gave is Christ's, and he who received it is Christ's. For many things are given wrongfully and yet they are not therefore said to be non-existent or not given at all. For neither does he who renounces the world in word only and not in deed receive baptism lawfully, and yet he does receive it. For both Cyprian records that there were such men in the Church in his day, and we ourselves experience and lament the fact.

20. But it is strange in what sense it can be said

that "baptism and the Church cannot in any way be separated and detached from one another." For if baptism remains inseparably in him who is baptized, how can it be that he can be separated from the Church, and baptism cannot? But it is clear that baptism does remain inseparably in the baptized person; because into whatever depth of evil, and into whatever fearful whirlpool of sin the baptized person may fall, even to the ruin of apostasy, he yet is not bereft of his baptism. And therefore, if through repentance he returns, it is not given again, because it is judged that he could not have been bereft of it. But who can ever doubt that a baptized person can be separated from the Church? For hence all the heresies have proceeded which deceive by the use of Christian terms.

Chapter 16. —Wherefore, since it is manifest that the baptism remains in the baptized person when he is separated from the Church, the baptism which is in him is certainly separated with him. And therefore, not all who retain the baptism retain the Church, just as not all who retain the Church retain eternal life. Or if we say that only those retain the Church who observe the commandments of God, we at once concede that there are many who retain baptism, and do not retain the Church.

21. Therefore the heretic is not "the first to seize baptism," since he has received it from the Church. Nor, though he seceded, could baptism have been lost by him whom we assert no longer to retain the Church, and yet allow to retain baptism. Nor does anyone "yield his birthright, and give it to a heretic," because he says that he took away with him what he could not give lawfully, but what would yet be according to law when given; or that

he no longer has lawfully what yet is in accordance with law in his possession. But the birthright rests only in a holy conversation and good life, to which all belong of whom that bride consists as her members which has no spot or wrinkle, or that dove that groans amid the wickedness of the many crows,—unless it be that, while Esau lost his birthright from his lust after a mess of pottage, we are yet to hold that it is retained by defrauders, robbers, usurers, envious persons, drunkards and the like, over whose existence in the Church of his time Cyprian groaned in his epistles. Wherefore, either it is not the same thing to retain the Church and to retain the birthright in divine things, or, if everyone who retains the Church also retains the birthright, then all those wicked ones do not retain the Church who yet both seem and are allowed by every one of us to give baptism within the Church; for no one, save the man who is wholly ignorant of sacred things, would say that they retain the birthright in sacred things.

Chapter 17. —22. But, having considered and handled all these points, we have now come to that peaceful utterance of Cyprian at the end of the epistle, with which I am never sated, though I read and re-read it again and again, —so great is the pleasantness of brotherly love which breathes forth from it, so great the sweetness of charity in which it abounds. "These things," he says, "we have written unto you, dearest brother, shortly, according to our poor ability, prescribing to or prejudging no one, lest each bishop should not do what he thinks right, in the free exercise of his own will. We, so far as in us lies, do not contend on the subject of heretics with our colleagues and fellow-bishops, with whom we maintain concord and peace in the Lord; especially as the apostle also says, 'If any man seems to be contentious, we have no such custom, neither the churches of God.' We observe patiently and gently charity of spirit, the honor of our brotherhood, the bond of faith, the harmony of the priesthood. For this reason, also, to the best of our poor ability, by the permission and the inspiration of God we have written this treatise on 'The Good of Patience,' which we have sent to you in consideration of our mutual love."

23. There are many things to be considered in these words, wherein the brightness of Christian charity shines forth in this man, who "loved the beauty of the Lord's house, and the place of the tabernacle of His habitation." First, that he did not conceal what he felt; then, that he set it forth so gently and peacefully, in that he maintained the peace of the Church with those who thought otherwise, because he understood how great healthfulness was bound up in the bond of peace, loving it so much, and maintaining it with sobriety, seeing and feeling that even men who think differently may entertain their several sentiments with saving charity. For he would not say that he could maintain divine concord or the peace of the Lord with evil men; for the good man can observe peace towards wicked men, but he cannot be united with them in the peace which they have not. Lastly, that prescribing to no one, and prejudging no one, lest each bishop should not do what he thinks right in the free exercise of his own will, he has left for us also, whatsoever we may be, a place for treating peacefully of those things with him. For he is present, not only in his letters, but by that very charity which existed in so extraordinary a degree in him, and which can never die.

Longing, therefore, with the aid of his prayers, to cling to and be in union with him, if I be not hindered by the unmeetness of my sins, I will learn if I can through his letters with how great peace and comfort the Lord administered His Church through him; and, putting on the bowels of humility through the moving influence of his discourse, if, in common with the Church at large, I entertain any doctrine more true than his, I will not prefer my heart to his, even in the point in which he, though holding different views, was yet not severed from the Church throughout the world. For in that, when that question was yet undecided for want of full discussion, though his sentiments differed from those of many of his colleagues, yet he observed so great moderation, that he would not mutilate the sacred fellowship of the Church of God by any stain of schism, a greater strength of excellence appeared in him than would have been shown if, without that virtue, he had held views on every point not only true, but coinciding with their own. Nor should I be acting as he would wish, if I were to pretend to prefer his talent and his fluency of discourse and copiousness of learning to the holy Council of all nations, whereat he was assuredly present through the unity of his spirit, especially as he is now placed in such full light of truth as to see with perfect certainty what he was here seeking in the spirit of perfect peace. For out of that rich abundance he smiles at all that here seems eloquence in us, as though it were the first essay of infancy; there he sees by what rule of piety he acted here, that nothing should be dearer in the Church to him than unity. There, too, with unspeakable delight he beholds with what prescient and most merciful providence the Lord, that He might heal our swellings, "chose the foolish things of the world to confound the wise," and, in the ordering of the members of His Church, placed all things in such a healthful way, that men should not say that they were chosen to the help of the gospel for their own talent or learning, of whose source they yet were ignorant, and so be puffed up with deadly pride. Oh, how Cyprian rejoices! With how much more perfect calmness does he behold how greatly it conduces to the health of the human race, that in the writings even of Christian and pious orators there should be found what merits blame, and in the writings of the fishermen there should nothing of the sort be found! And so I, being fully assured of this joy of that holy soul, neither in any way venture to think or say that my writings are free from every kind of error, nor, in opposing that opinion of his, wherein it seemed to him that those who came from among heretics were to be received otherwise than either they had been in former days, as he himself bears witness, or are now received, as is the reasonable custom, confirmed by a plenary Council of the whole Christian world, do I set against him my own view, but that of the holy Catholic Church, which he so loved and loves, in which he brought forth such abundant fruit with tolerance, whose entirety he himself was not, but in whose entirety he remained; whose root he never left, but, though he already brought forth fruit from its root, he was purged by the heavenly Husbandman that he should bring forth more fruit; for whose peace and safety, that the wheat might not be rooted out together with the tares, he both reproved with the freedom of truth, and endured with the grace of charity, so many evils on the part of men who were placed in unity with himself.

Chapter 18. —24. Whence Cyprian himself again admonishes us with the greatest fullness, that many who were dead in their trespasses and sins, although they did not belong to the body of Christ, and the members of that innocent and guileless dove (so that if she alone baptized, they certainly could not baptize), yet to all appearance seemed both to be baptized and to baptize within the Church. And among them, however dead they are, their baptism nevertheless lives, which is not dead, and death shall have no more dominion over it. Since, therefore, there be dead men within the Church, nor are they concealed, for else Cyprian would not have spoken of them so much, who either do not belong at all to that living dove, or at least do not as yet belong to her; and since there be dead men without, who yet more clearly do not belong to her at all, or not as yet; and since it is true that "another man cannot be quickened by one who himself lived not,"—it is therefore clear that those who within are baptized by such persons, if they approach the sacrament with true conversion of heart, are quickened by Him whose baptism it is. But if they renounce the world in word and not in deed, as Cyprian declares to be the case with some who are within, it is then manifest that they are not themselves quickened unless they be converted, and yet that they have true baptism even though they be not converted. Whence also it is likewise clear that those who are dead without, although they neither "live themselves, nor quicken others," yet have the living baptism, which would profit them unto life so soon as they should be converted unto peace.

Chapter 19. —25. Wherefore, as regards those who received the persons who came from heresy in the same baptism of Christ with which they had been baptized outside the Church, and said "that they followed ancient custom," as indeed the Church now receives such, it is in vain urged against them "that among the ancients there were as yet only the first beginning of heresy and schisms, so that those were involved in them who were seceders from the Church, and had originally been baptized within the Church, so that it was not necessary that they should be baptized again when they returned and did penance." For so soon as each several heresies existed, and departed from the communion of the Catholic Church, it was possible that, I will not even say the next day, but even on that very day, its votaries might have baptized some who flocked to them. And therefore, if this was the old custom, that they should be so received into the Church (as could not be denied even by those who maintained the contrary part in the discussion), there can be no doubt in the mind of anyone who pays careful attention to the matter, that those also were so received who had been baptized without in heresy.

26. But I cannot see what show of reason there is in this, that the name of "erring sheep" should be denied to one whose lot it has been that, while seeking the salvation which is in Christ, he has fallen into the error of heretics, and been baptized in their body; while he is held to have become a sheep already within the body of the Catholic Church herself, who has renounced the world in words and not in deeds, and has received baptism in such falseness of heart as this. Or if such a one also does not become a sheep unless after turning to God with a true heart, then, as he is not baptized at the time when he

becomes a sheep, if he had been already baptized, but was not yet a sheep; so he too, who comes from the heretics that he may become a sheep, is not then to be baptized if he had been already baptized with the same baptism, though he was not yet a sheep. Wherefore, since even all the bad that are within—the covetous, the envious, the drunkards, and those that live contrary to the discipline of Christ—may be deservedly called liars, and in darkness, and dead, and antichrists, do they yet therefore not baptize, because "there can be nothing common between truth and falsehood, between light and darkness, between death and immortality, between Antichrist and Christ?"

27. He assumes, then, not "of mere custom," but "of the reason of truth itself," when he says that the sacrament of God cannot be turned to error by the error of any men, since it is declared to exist even in those who have erred. Assuredly the Apostle John says most plainly, "He that hated his brother is in darkness even until now;" and again, "Whosoever hated his brother is a murderer;" and why, therefore, do they baptize those within the Church whom Cyprian himself declares to be in the envy of malice?

Chapter 20. —How does a murderer cleanse and sanctify the water? How can darkness bless the oil? But if God is present in His sacraments to confirm His words by whomsoever the sacraments may be administered, then both the sacraments of God are everywhere valid, and evil men whom they profit not are everywhere perverse.

28. But what kind of argument is this, that "a heretic must be considered not to have baptism, because he has not the Church?" And it must be acknowledged that "when he is baptized, he is questioned about the

Church." Just as though the same question about the Church were not put in baptism to him who within the Church renounces the world in word and not in deed. As therefore his false answer does not prevent what he receives from being baptism, so also the false reply of the other about the holy Church does not prevent what he receives from being baptism; and as the former, if he afterwards fulfill with truth what he promised in falsehood, does not receive a second baptism, but only an amended life, so also in the case of the latter, if he come afterwards to the Church about which he gave a false answer to the question put to him, thinking that he had it when he had it not, the Church herself which he did not possess is given him, but what he had received is not repeated. But I cannot tell why it should be, that while God can "sanctify the oil" in answer to the words which proceed out of the mouth of a murderer, "He yet cannot sanctify it on the altar reared by a heretic," unless it be that He who is not hindered by the false conversion of the heart of man within the Church is hindered by the false erection of some wood without from deigning to be present in His sacraments, though no falseness on the part of men can hinder Him. If, therefore, what is said in the gospel, that "God hears not sinners," extends so far that the sacraments cannot be celebrated by a sinner, how then does He hear a murderer praying, either over the water of baptism, or over the oil, or over the eucharist, or over the heads of those on whom his hand is laid? All which things are nevertheless done, and are valid, even at the hands of murderers, that is, at the hands of those who hate their brethren, even within, in the Church itself. Since "no one can give what he does not possess himself," how does a murderer give the Holy Spirit? And yet such a one even baptizes within the Church. It is God, therefore, that gives the Holy Spirit even when a man of this kind is baptizing.

Chapter 21. —29. But as to what he says, that "he who comes to the Church is to be baptized and renewed, that within he may be hallowed through the holy," what will he do, if within also he meets with those who are not holy? Or can it be that the murderer is holy? And if the reason for his being baptized in the Church is that "he should put off this very thing also that he, being a man that sought to come to God, fell, through the deceit of error, on one profane," where is he afterwards to put off this, that he may chance, while seeking a man of God within the Church itself, to have fallen, through the deceit of error, on a murderer? If "there cannot be in a man something that is void and something that is valid," why is it possible that in a murderer the sacrament should be holy and his heart unholy? If "whosoever cannot give the Holy Spirit cannot baptize," why does the murderer baptize within the Church? Or how has the murderer the Holy Spirit, when everyone that has the Holy Spirit is filled with light, but "he who hates his brother is still in darkness?" If because "there is one baptism, and one Spirit," therefore they cannot have the one baptism who have not the one Spirit, why do the innocent man and the murderer within the Church have the one baptism and not have the one Spirit? So therefore, the heretic and the Catholic may have the one baptism, and yet not have the one Church, as in the Catholic Church the innocent man and the murderer may have the one baptism, though they have not the one Spirit; for as there is one baptism, so there is one Spirit and one Church. And so the result is, that in each person we must acknowledge what he already has, and to each person we must give what he has not. If "nothing can be confirmed and ratified with God which has been done by those whom God calls His enemies and foes," why is the baptism confirmed which is given by murderers? Are we not to call murderers the enemies and foes of the Lord? But "he that hated his brother is a murderer." How then did they baptize who hated Paul, the servant of Jesus Christ, and thereby hated Jesus Himself, since He Himself said to Saul, "Why persecutes thou me?" when he was persecuting His servants, and since at the last He Himself shall say, "Inasmuch as ye did it not to one of the least of these that are mine, ye did it not to me?" Wherefore all who go out from us are not of us, but not all who are with us are of us; just as when men thresh, all that flies from the threshing-floor is shown not to be corn, but not all that remains there is therefore corn. And so John too says, "They went out from us, but they were not of us; for if they had been of us, they would no doubt have continued with us." Wherefore God gives the sacrament of grace even through the hands of wicked men, but the grace itself only by Himself or through His saints. And therefore, He gives remission of sins either of Himself, or through the members of that dove to whom He says, "Whosesoever sins ye remit, they are remitted unto them; and whosesoever sins ye retain, they are retained." But since no one can doubt that baptism, which is the sacrament of the remission of sins, is possessed even by murderers, who are yet in darkness because the hatred of their brethren is not excluded from their hearts, therefore either no remission of sins is given to them if their baptism is accompanied by no change of heart for the better, or if the sins are remitted, they at once return on them again. And we learn that the baptism is holy in itself, because it is of God; and whether it be given or whether it be received by men of such like character, it cannot be polluted by any perversity of theirs, either within, or yet outside the Church.

Chapter 22. —30. Accordingly, we agree with Cyprian that "heretics cannot give remission of sins;" but we maintain that they can give baptism, —which indeed in them, both when they give and when they receive it, is profitable only to their destruction, as misusing so great a gift of God; just as also the malicious and envious, whom Cyprian himself acknowledges to be within the Church, cannot give remission of sins, while we all confess that they can give baptism. For if it was said of those who have sinned against us, "If ye forgive not men their trespasses, neither will your Father forgive your trespasses," how much more impossible is it that their sins should be forgiven who hate the brethren by whom they are loved, and are baptized in that very hatred; and yet when they are brought to the right way, baptism is not given them anew, but that very pardon which they did not then deserve is granted them in their true conversion? And so even what Cyprian wrote to Quintus, and what, in conjunction with his colleagues Liberalis, Caldonius, Junius, and the rest, he wrote to Saturninus, Maximus, and others, is all found, on due consideration, to be in no wise meet to be preferred as against the agreement of the whole Catholic Church, of which they rejoiced that they were members, and from which they neither cut themselves away nor allowed others to be cut away who held a contrary opinion, until at length, by the will of the Lord, it was made manifest, by a plenary Council many years afterwards, what was the more perfect way, and that not by the institution of any novelty, but by confirming what was old.

Chapter 23. —31. Cyprian writes also to Pompeius about this selfsame matter, and clearly shows in that letter that Stephen, who, as we learn, was then bishop of the Roman Church, not only did not agree with him upon the points before us, but even wrote and taught the opposite views. But Stephen certainly did not "communicate with heretics," merely because he did not dare to impugn the baptism of Christ, which he knew remained perfect amid their perversity. For if none have baptism who entertain false views about God, it has been proved sufficiently, in my opinion, that this may happen even within the Church. "The apostles," indeed, "gave no injunctions on the point;" but the custom, which is opposed to Cyprian, may be supposed to have had its origin in apostolic tradition, just as there are many things which are observed by the whole Church, and therefore are fairly held to have been enjoined by the apostles, which yet are not mentioned in their writings.

32. But it will be urged that it is written of heretics that "they are condemned of themselves." What then? are they not also condemned of themselves to whom it was said, "For wherein thou judges another, thou condemns thyself?" But to these the apostle says, "Thou that preaches a man should not steal, dost thou steal?" and so forth. And such truly were they who, being bishops and established in Catholic unity with Cyprian himself, used to plunder estates by treacherous frauds, preaching all the time to the people the words of the apostle, who says, "Nor shall extortioners inherit the kingdom of God."

33. Wherefore I will do no more than run shortly through the other sentiments founded on the same rules, which are in the aforesaid letter written to Pompeius. By what authority of holy Scripture is it shown that "it is against the commandment of God that persons coming from the society of heretics, if they have already there received the baptism of Christ, are not baptized again?" But it is clearly shown that many pretended Christians, though they are not joined in the same bond of charity with the saints, without which anything holy that they may have been able to possess is of no profit to them, yet have baptism in common with the saints, as has been already sufficiently proved with the greatest fullness. He says, "that the Church, and the Spirit, and baptism, are mutually incapable of separation from each other, and therefore" he wishes that "those who are separated from the Church and the Holy Spirit should be understood to be separated also from baptism." But if this is the case, then when anyone has received baptism in the Catholic Church, it remains so long in him as he himself remains in the Church, which is not so. For it is not restored to him when he returns, just because he did not lose it when he seceded. But as the disaffected sons have not the Holy Spirit in the same manner as the beloved sons, and yet they have baptism; so heretics also have not the Church as Catholics have, and yet they have baptism. "For the Holy Spirit of discipline will flee deceit," and yet baptism will not flee from it. And so, as baptism can continue in one from whom the Holy Spirit withdraws Himself, so can baptism continue where the Church is not. But if "the laying on of hands" were not "applied to one coming from heresy," he would be as it were judged to be wholly blameless; but for the uniting of love, which is the

greatest gift of the Holy Spirit, without which any other holy thing that there may be in a man is profitless to his salvation, hands are laid on heretics when they are brought to a knowledge of the truth.

Chapter 24. —34. I remember that I have already discussed at sufficient length the question of "the temple of God," and how this saying is to be taken, "As many of you as have been baptized into Christ have put on Christ." For neither are the covetous the temple of God, since it is written, "What agreement hath the temple of God with idols?" And Cyprian has adduced the testimony of Paul to the fact that covetousness is idolatry. But men put on Christ, sometimes so far as to receive the sacrament, sometimes so much further as to receive holiness of life. And the first of these is common to good and bad alike; the second, peculiar to the good and pious. Wherefore, if "baptism cannot be without the Spirit," then heretics have the Spirit also, —but to destruction, not to salvation, just as was the case with Saul. For in the Holy Spirit devils are cast out through the name of Christ, which even he could do who was without the Church, which called forth a suggestion from the disciples to their Lord. Just as the covetous have the Holy Spirit, who yet are not the temple of God. For "what agreement hath the temple of God with idols?" If therefore the covetous have not the Spirit of God, and yet have baptism, it is possible for baptism to exist without the Spirit of God.

35. If therefore heresy is rendered "unable to engender sons to God through Christ, because it is not the bride of Christ," neither can that crowd of evil men established within the Church, since it is also not the bride of Christ; for the bride of Christ is described as being

without spot or wrinkle. Therefore, either not all baptized persons are the sons of God, or even that which is not the bride can engender the sons of God. But as it is asked whether "he is spiritually born who has received the baptism of Christ amid heretics," so it may be asked whether he is spiritually born who has received the baptism of Christ in the Catholic Church, without being turned to God in a true heart, of whom it cannot be said that he has not received baptism.

Chapter 25. —36. I am unwilling to go on to handle again what Cyprian poured forth with signs of irritation against Stephen, as it is, moreover, quite unnecessary. For they are but the selfsame arguments which have already been sufficiently discussed; and it is better to pass over those points which involved the danger of baneful dissension. But Stephen thought that we should even hold aloof from those who endeavored to destroy the primitive custom in the matter of receiving heretics; whereas Cyprian, moved by the difficulty of the question itself, and being most largely endowed with the holy bowels of Christian charity, thought that we ought to remain at unity with those who differed in opinion from ourselves. Therefore, although he was not without excitement, though of a truly brotherly kind, in his indignation, yet the peace of Christ prevailed in their hearts, that in such a dispute no evil of schism should arise between them. But it was not found that "hence grew more abundant heresies and schisms," because what is of Christ in them is approved, and what is of themselves is condemned; for even more those who hold this law of rebaptizing were cut into smaller fragments.

Chapter 26. —37. To go on to what he says, "that a bishop should be 'teachable,'" adding, "But he is teachable who is gentle and meek to learn; for a bishop ought not only to teach, but to learn as well, since he is indeed the better teacher who daily grows and advances by learning better things;"—in these words assuredly the holy man, endowed with pious charity, sufficiently points out that we should not hesitate to read his letters in such a sense, that we should feel no difficulty if the Church should afterwards confirm what had been discovered by further and longer discussions; because, as there were many things which the learned Cyprian might teach, so there was still something which the teachable Cyprian might learn. But the admonition that he gives us, "that we should go back to the fountain, that is, to apostolic tradition, and thence turn the channel of truth to our times," is most excellent, and should be followed without hesitation. It is handed down to us, therefore, as he himself records, by the apostles, that there is "one God, and one Christ, and one hope, and one faith, and one Church, and one baptism." Since then we find that in the times of the apostles themselves there were some who had not the one hope, but had the one baptism, the truth is so brought down to us from the fountain itself, that it is clear to us that it is possible that though there is one Church, as there is one hope, and one baptism, they may yet have the one baptism who have not the one Church; just as even in those early times it was possible that men should have the one baptism who had not the one hope. For how had they one hope with the holy and the just, who used to say, "Let us eat and drink, for tomorrow we die," asserting that there was no resurrection of the dead? And yet they were among the very men to whom the same apostle says,

"Was Paul crucified for you? or were you baptized in the name of Paul?" For he writes most manifestly to them, saying, "How say some among you that there is no resurrection of the dead?"

Chapter 27. —38. And in that the Church is thus described in the Song of Songs, "A garden enclosed is my sister, my spouse; a spring shut up, a fountain sealed, a well of living water; thy plants are an orchard of pomegranates, with pleasant fruits;" I dare not understand this save of the holy and just,—not of the covetous, and defrauders, and robbers, and usurers, and drunkards, and the envious, of whom we yet both learn most fully from Cyprian's letters, as I have often shown, and teach ourselves, that they had baptism in common with the just, in common with whom they certainly had not Christian charity. For I would that someone would tell me how they "crept into the garden enclosed and the fountain sealed," of whom Cyprian bears witness that they renounced the world in word and not in deed, and that yet they were within the Church. For if they both are themselves there, and are themselves the bride of Christ, can she then be as she is described "without spot or wrinkle," and is the fair dove defiled with such a portion of her members? Are these the thorns among which she is a lily, as it is said in the same Song? So far therefore, as the lily extends, so far does "the garden enclosed and the fountain sealed," namely, through all those just persons who are Jews inwardly in the circumcision of the heart (for "the king's daughter is all glorious within"), in whom is the fixed number of the saints predestined before the foundation of the world. But that multitude of thorns, whether in secret or in open separation, is pressing on it from without, above number. "If I would declare them," it is said, "and speak of them, they are more than can be numbered." The number, therefore, of the just persons, "who are the called according to His purpose," of whom it is said, "The Lord knows them that are His," is itself "the garden enclosed, the fountain sealed, a well of living water, the orchard of pomegranates with pleasant fruits." Of this number some live according to the Spirit, and enter on the excellent way of charity; and when they "restore a man that is overtaken in a fault in the spirit of meekness, they consider themselves, lest they also be tempted." And when it happens that they also are themselves overtaken, the affection of charity is but a little checked, and not extinguished; and again rising up and being kindled afresh, it is restored to its former course. For they know how to say, "My soul melted for heaviness: strengthen thou me according unto Thy word." But when "in anything they be otherwise minded, God shall reveal even this unto them," if they abide in the burning flame of charity, and do not break the bond of peace. But some who are yet carnal, and full of fleshly appetites, are instant in working out their progress; and that they may become fit for heavenly food, they are nourished with the milk of the holy mysteries, they avoid in the fear of God whatever is manifestly corrupt even in the opinion of the world, and they strive most watchfully that they may be less and less delighted with worldly and temporal matters. They observe most constantly the rule of faith which has been sought out with diligence; and if in aught they stray from it, they submit to speedy correction under Catholic authority, although, in Cyprian's words, they be tossed about, because of their fleshly appetite, with the various conflicts of phantasies. There are some also who as yet live wickedly, or even lie in heresies or the superstitions of the Gentiles, and yet even then "the Lord knows them that are His." For, in that unspeakable foreknowledge of God, many who seem to be without are in reality within, and many who seem to be within yet really are without. Of all those, therefore, who, if I may so say, are inwardly and secretly within, is that "enclosed garden" composed, "the fountain sealed, a well of living water, the orchard of pomegranates, with pleasant fruits." The divinely imparted gifts of these are partly peculiar to themselves, as in this world the charity that never failed, and in the world to come eternal life; partly they are common with evil and perverse men, as all the other things in which consist the holy mysteries.

Chapter 28. —39. Hence, therefore, we have now set before us an easier and more simple consideration of that ark of which Noah was the builder and pilot. For Peter says that in the ark of Noah, "few, that is, eight souls, were saved by water. The like figure whereunto even baptism doth also now save us, (not the putting away of the filth of the flesh, but the answer of a good conscience towards God)." Wherefore, if those appear to men to be baptized in Catholic unity who renounce the world in words only and not in deeds, how do they belong to the mystery of this ark in whom there is not the answer of a good conscience? Or how are they saved by water, who, making a bad use of holy baptism, though they seem to be within, yet persevere to the end of their days in a wicked and abandoned course of life? Or how can they fail to be saved by water, of whom Cyprian himself records that they were in time past simply admitted to the Church with the baptism which they had received in heresy? For the same unity of the ark saved them, in which no one has been saved except by water. For Cyprian himself says, "The Lord is able of His mercy to grant pardon, and not to sever from the gifts of His Church those who, being in all simplicity admitted to the Church, have fallen asleep within her pale." If not by water, how in the ark? If not in the ark, how in the Church? But if in the Church, certainly in the ark; and if in the ark, certainly by water. It is therefore possible that some who have been baptized without may be considered, through the foreknowledge of God, to have been really baptized within, because within the water begins to be profitable to them unto salvation; nor can they be said to have been otherwise saved in the ark except by water. And again, some who seemed to have been baptized within may be considered, through the same foreknowledge of God, more truly to have been baptized without, since, by making a bad use of baptism, they die by water, which then happened to no one who was not outside the ark. Certainly it is clear that, when we speak of within and without in relation to the Church, it is the position of the heart that we must consider, not that of the body, since all who are within in heart are saved in the unity of the ark through the same water, through which all who are in heart without, whether they are also in body without or not, die as enemies of unity. As therefore it was not another but the same water that saved those who were placed within the ark, and destroyed those who were left without the ark, so it is not by different baptisms, but by the same, that good Catholics are saved, and bad Catholics or heretics perish. But what the most blessed Cyprian thinks of the Catholic Church, and how the heretics are utterly crushed by his authority;

notwithstanding the much I have already said, I have yet determined to set forth by itself, if God will, with somewhat greater fullness and perspicuity, so soon as I shall have first said about his Council what I think is due from me, which, in God's will, I shall attempt in the following book.

Book VI.

In which is considered the Council of Carthage, held under the authority and presidency of Cyprian, to determine the question of the baptism of heretics.

Chapter 1. —1. It might perhaps have been sufficient, that after the reasons have been so often repeated, and considered, and discussed with such variety of treatment, supplemented too, with the addition of proofs from holy Scripture, and the concurrent testimony of so many passages from Cyprian himself, even those who are slow of heart should thus understand, as I believe they do, that the baptism of Christ cannot be rendered void by any perversity on the part of man, whether in administering or receiving it. And when we find that in those times, when the point in question was decided in a manner contrary to ancient custom, after discussions carried on without violation of saving charity and unity, it appeared to some even eminent men who were bishops of Christ, among whom the blessed Cyprian was specially conspicuous, that the baptism of Christ could not exist among heretics or schismatics, this simply arose from their not distinguishing the sacrament from the effect or use of the sacrament; and because its effect and use were not found among heretics in freeing them from their sins and setting their hearts right, the sacrament itself was also thought to be wanting among them. But if we turn our eyes to the multitude of chaff within the Church, since these also who are perverse and lead an abandoned life in unity itself appear to have no power either of giving or retaining remission of sins, seeing that it is not to the wicked but the good sons that it was said, "Whosesoever sins ye remit, they are remitted unto them; and whosesoever sins ye retain, they are retained," yet that such persons both have, and give, and receive the sacrament of baptism, was sufficiently manifest to the pastors of the Catholic Church dispersed over the whole world, through whom the original custom was afterwards confirmed by the authority of a plenary Council; so that even the sheep which was straying outside, and had received the mark of the Lord from false plunderers outside, if it seek the salvation of Christian unity, is purified from error, is freed from captivity, is healed of its wound, and yet the mark of the Lord is recognized rather than rejected in it; since the mark itself is often impressed both by wolves and on wolves, who seem indeed to be within the fold, but yet are proved by the fruits of their conduct, in which they persevere even to the end, not to belong to that sheep which is one in many; because, according to the foreknowledge of God, as many sheep wander outside, so many wolves lurk treacherously within, among whom the Lord yet knows them that are His, which hear only the voice of the Shepherd, even when He calls by the voice of men like the Pharisees, of whom it was said, "Whatsoever they bid you observe that observe and do."

2. For as the spiritual man, keeping "the end of the commandment," that is, "charity out of a pure heart,

and of a good conscience, and of faith unfeigned," can see some things less clearly out of a body which is yet "corruptible and presses down the soul," and is liable to be otherwise minded in some things which God will reveal to him in His own good time if he abide in the same charity, so in a carnal and perverse man something good and useful may be found, which has its origin not in the man himself, but in some other source. For as in the fruitful branch there is found something which must be purged that it may bring forth more fruit, so also a grape is often found to hang on a cane that is barren and dry or fettered. And so, as it is foolish to love the portions which require purging in the fruitful branch, while he acts wisely who does not reject the sweet fruit wherever it may hang, so, if any one cuts himself off from unity by rebaptizing, simply because it seemed to Cyprian that one ought to baptize again those who came from the heretics, such a man turns aside from what merits praise in that great man, and follows what requires correction, and does not even attain to the very thing he follows after. For Cyprian, while grievously abhorring, in his zeal for God, all those who severed themselves from unity, thought that thereby they were separated from baptism itself; while these men, thinking it at most a slight offense that they themselves are severed from the unity of Christ, even maintain that His baptism is not in that unity, but issued forth with them. Therefore, they are so far from the fruitfulness of Cyprian, as not even to be equal to the parts in him which needed purging.

Chapter 2. —3. Again, if anyone not having charity, and walking in the abandoned paths of a most wicked life, seems to be within while he really is without, and at the same time does not seek for the repetition of baptism even in the case of heretics, it in no wise helps his barrenness, because he is not rendered fruitful with his own fruit, but laden with that of others. But it is possible that someone may flourish in the root of charity, and may be most rightly minded in the point in which Cyprian was otherwise minded, and yet there may be more that is fruitful in Cyprian than in him, more that requires purging in him than in Cyprian. Not only, therefore, do we not compare bad Catholics with the blessed Cyprian, but even good Catholics we do not hastily pronounce to be on an equality with him whom our pious mother Church counts among the few rare men of surpassing excellence and grace, although these others may recognize the baptism of Christ even among heretics, while he thought otherwise; so that, by the instance of Cyprian, who saw one point less clearly, and yet remained most firm in the unity of the Church, it might be shown more clearly to heretics what a sacrilegious crime it was to break the bond of peace. For neither were the blind Pharisees, although they sometimes enjoined what was right to be done, to be compared to the Apostle Peter, though he at times enjoined what was not right. But not only is their dryness not to be compared to his greenness, but even the fruit of others may not be deemed equal to his fertility. For no one now compels the Gentiles to Judaize, and yet no one now in the Church, however great his progress in goodness, may be compared with the apostleship of Peter. Wherefore, while rendering due reverence, and paying, so far as I can, the fitting honor to the peaceful bishop and glorious martyr Cyprian, I yet venture to say that his view concerning the baptism of schismatics and heretics was contrary to that which was afterwards brought to light by a decision, not of mine, but of the whole Church, confirmed and strengthened by the authority of a plenary Council: just as, while paying the reverence he deserves to Peter, the first of the apostles and most eminent of martyrs, I yet venture to say that he did not do right in compelling the Gentiles to Judaize; for this also, I say, not of my own teaching, but according to the wholesome doctrine of the Apostle Paul, retained and preserved throughout the whole Church.

4. Therefore, in discussing the opinion of Cyprian, though myself of far inferior merit to Cyprian, I say that good and bad alike can have, can give, can receive the sacrament of baptism,—the good, indeed, to their health and profit; the bad to their destruction and ruin,—while the sacrament itself is of equal perfectness in both of them; and that it is of no consequence to its equal perfectness in all, how much worse the man may be that has it among the bad, just as it makes no difference how much better he may be that has it among the good. And accordingly, it makes no difference either how much worse he may be that confers it, as it makes no difference how much better he may be; and so it makes no difference how much worse he may be that receives it, as it makes no difference how much better he may be. For the sacrament is equally holy, in virtue of its own excellence, both in those who are unequally just, and in those who are unequally unjust.

Chapter 3. —5. But I think that we have sufficiently shown, both from the canon of Scripture, and from the letters of Cyprian himself, that bad men, while by no means converted to a better mind, can have, and confer, and receive baptism, of whom it is most clear that they do not belong to the holy Church of God, though they seem to be within it, inasmuch as they are covetous, robbers, usurers, envious, evil thinkers, and the like; while she is one dove, modest and chaste, a bride without spot or wrinkle, a garden enclosed, a fountain sealed, an orchard of pomegranates with pleasant fruits, with all similar properties which are attributed to her; and all this can only be understood to be in the good, and holy, and just,—following, that is, not only the operations of the gifts of God, which are common to good and bad alike, but also the inner bond of charity conspicuous in those who have the Holy Spirit, to whom the Lord says, "Whosoever sins ye remit, they are remitted unto them; and whosoever sins ye retain, they are retained."

Chapter 4. —6. And so it is clear that no good ground is shown herein why the bad man, who has baptism, may not also confer it; and as he has it to destruction, so he may also confer it to destruction, —not because this is the character of the thing conferred, nor of the person conferring, but because it is the character of him on whom it is conferred. For when a bad man confers it on a good man, that is, on one in the bond of unity, converted with a true conversion, the wickedness of him who confers it makes no severance between the good sacrament which is conferred, and the good member of the Church on whom it is conferred. And when his sins are forgiven him on his true conversion to God, they are forgiven by those to whom he is united by his true conversion. For the same Spirit forgives them, which is given to all the saints that cling to one another in love, whether they know one another in the body or not. Similarly when a man's sins are retained, they are assuredly retained by those from whom he, in whom they are retained, separates himself by dissimilarity of life, and by the turning away of a corrupt heart, whether they know him in the body or not.

Chapter 5. —7. Wherefore all bad men are separated in the spirit from the good; but if they are separated in the body also by a manifest dissension, they are made yet worse. But, as it has been said, it makes no difference to the holiness of baptism how much worse the man may be that has it, or how much worse he that confers it: yet he that is separated may confer it, as he that is separated may have it; but as he has it to destruction, so he may confer it to destruction. But he on whom he confers it may receive it to his soul's health, if he, on his part, receive it not in separation; as it has happened to many that, in a catholic spirit, and with heart not alienated from the unity of peace, they have, under some pressure of impending death, turned hastily to some heretic and received from him the baptism of Christ without any share in his perversity, so that, whether dying or restored to life, they by no means remain in communion with those to whom they never passed in heart. But if the recipient himself has received the baptism in separation, he receives it so much the more to his destruction, in proportion to the greatness of the good which he has not received well; and it tends the more to his destruction in his separation, as it would avail the more to the salvation of one in unity. And so, if, reforming himself from his perverseness and turning from his separation, he should come to the Catholic peace, his sins are remitted through the bond of peace and the same baptism under which his sins were retained through the sacrilege of separation, because that is always holy both in the just and the unjust, which is neither increased by the righteousness nor diminished by the unrighteousness of any man.

8. This being the case, what bearing has it on so clear a truth, that many of his fellow bishops agreed with Cyprian in that opinion, and advanced their own several opinions on the same side, except that his charity towards the unity of Christ might become more and more conspicuous? For if he had been the only one to hold that opinion, with no one to agree with him, he might have been thought, in remaining, to have shrunk from the sin of schism, because he found no companions in his error; but when so many agreed with him, he showed, by remaining in unity with the rest who thought differently from him, that he preserved the most sacred bond of universal catholicity, not from any fear of isolation, but from the love of peace. Wherefore it might indeed seem now to be superfluous to consider the several opinions of the other bishops also in that Council; but since those who are slow in heart think that no answer has been made at all, if to any passage in any discourse the answer which might be brought to bear on the spot be given not there but somewhere else, it is better that by reading much they should be polished into sharpness, than that by understanding little they should have room left for complaining that the argument has not been fairly conducted.

Chapter 6. —9. First, then, let us record for further consideration the case proposed for decision by

Cyprian himself, with which he initiates the proceedings of the Council, and by which he shows a peaceful spirit, abounding in the fruitfulness of Christian charity. "Ye have read," he says, "most beloved colleagues, what Jubaianus, our fellow-bishop, has written to me, consulting my poor ability about the unlawful and profane baptism of heretics, and what I have written back to him, expressing to him the same opinion that I have expressed once and again and often, that heretics coming to the Church ought to be baptized, and sanctified with the baptism of the Church. Another letter also of Jubaianus has been read to you, in which, agreeably to his sincere and religious devotion, in answer to our epistle, he not only expressed his assent to it, but also gratefully acknowledged that he had received instruction. It remains that we should individually express our opinions on this same subject, judging no one, and removing no one from the right of communion if he should entertain a different opinion. For neither does any one of us set himself up as a bishop of bishops, or by tyrannical terror force his colleagues to the necessity of obeying, since every bishop, in the free use of his liberty and power, has the right of free judgment, and can no more be judged by another than he can himself judge another. But we are all awaiting the judgment of our Lord Jesus Christ who alone has the power both of preferring us in the government of His Church, and of judging of our actions."

Chapter 7. —10. I have already, I think, argued to the best of my power, in the preceding books, in the interests of Catholic unanimity and counsel, in whose unity these continued as pious members, in reply not only to the letter which Cyprian wrote to Jubaianus, but also to that which he sent to Quintus, and that which, in conjunction with certain of his colleagues, he sent to certain other colleagues, and that which he sent to Pompeius. Wherefore it seems now to be fitting to consider also what the others severally thought, and that with the liberty of which he himself would not deprive us, as he says, "Judging no one, nor removing any from the right of communion if he entertains different opinions." And that he did not say this with the object of arriving at the hidden thoughts of his colleagues, extracted as it were from their secret lurking-places, but because he really loved peace and unity, is very easily to be seen from other passages of the same sort, where he wrote to individuals as to Jubaianus himself. "These things," he says, "we have written very shortly in answer to you, most beloved brother, according to our poor ability, not preventing any one of the bishops by our writing or judgment, from acting as he thinks right, having a free exercise of his own judgment." And that it might not seem that anyone, because of his entertaining different opinions in this same free exercise of his judgment, should be driven from the society of his brethren, he goes on to say, "We, so far as lies in us, do not strive on behalf of heretics against our colleagues and fellow-bishops, with whom we maintain godly unity and the peace of our Lord;" and a little later he says, "Charity of spirit, respect for our fraternity, the bond of faith, the harmony of the priesthood, are by us maintained with patience and gentleness." And so also in the epistle which he wrote to Magnus, when he was asked whether there was any difference in the efficacy of baptism by sprinkling or by immersion, "In this matter," he says, "I am too modest and diffident to prevent any one by my judgment from thinking as he deems right, and acting as he thinks." By which discourses he clearly shows that these subjects were being handled by them at a time when they were not yet received as decided beyond all question, but were being investigated with great care as being yet unrevealed. We, therefore, maintaining on the subject of the identity of all baptisms what must be acknowledged everywhere to be the custom of the universal Church, and what is confirmed by the decision of general Councils, and taking greater confidence also from the words of Cyprian, which allowed me even then to hold opinions differing from his own without forfeiting the right of communion, seeing that greater importance and praise were attached to unity, such as the blessed Cyprian and his colleagues, with whom he held that Council, maintained with those of different opinions, disturbing and overthrowing thereby the seditious calumnies of heretics and schismatics in the name of the Lord Jesus Christ, who, speaking by His apostle, says, "Forbearing one another in love, endeavoring to keep the unity of the Spirit in the bond of peace;" and again, by the mouth of the same apostle, "If in anything ye be otherwise minded, God shall reveal even this unto you,"—we, I say, propose for consideration and discussion the opinions of the holy bishops, without violating the bond of unity and peace with them, in maintaining which we imitate them so far as we can by the aid of the Lord Himself.

Chapter 8. —11. Cæcilius of Bilta said: "I know of one baptism in the one Church and of none outside the Church. The one will be where there is true hope and sure faith. For so it is written, 'One faith, one hope, one baptism.' Not among heretics, where there is no hope and a false faith; where all things are done by a lie; where one possessed of a devil exorcises; the question of the sacrament is asked by one from whose mouth and words proceeds a cancer; the faithless gives faith; the guilty gives pardon for sins and Antichrist baptizes in the name of Christ; one accursed of God blesses; the dead promises life; the unpeaceful gives peace; the blasphemer calls on God; the profane administers the priesthood; the sacrilegious sets up the altar. To all this is added this further evil that the servant of the devil dares to celebrate the eucharist. If this be not so, let those who stand by them prove that all of it is false concerning heretics. See the kind of things to which the Church is compelled to assent, being forced to communicate without baptism or the remission of sins. This, brethren, we ought to shun and avoid, separating ourselves from so great a sin, and holding to the one baptism which is granted to the Church alone."

12. To this I answer, that all who even within the Church profess that they know God, but deny Him in their deeds, such as are the covetous and envious, and those who, because they hate their brethren, are pronounced to be murderers, not on my testimony, but on that of the holy Apostle John,—all these are both devoid of hope, because they have a bad conscience; and are faithless, because they do not do what they have vowed to God; and liars, because they make false professions; and possessed of devils, because they give place in their heart to the devil and his angels; and their words work corruption, since they corrupt good manners by evil communications; and they are infidels, because they laugh at the threats which God utters against such men; and accursed, because they live wickedly; and antichrists, because their lives are opposed to Christ; and cursed of God, since holy

Scripture everywhere calls down curses on such men; and dead, because they are without the life of righteousness; and unpeaceful, because by their contrary deeds they are at variance with God's behests; and blasphemous, because by their abandoned acts despite is done to the name of Christian; and profane, because they are spiritually shut out from that inner sanctuary of God; and sacrilegious, because by their evil life they defile the temple of God within themselves; and servants of the devil, because they do service to fraud and covetousness, which is idolatry. That of such a kind are some, nay very many, even within the Church, is testified both by Paul the apostle and by Cyprian the bishop. Why, then, do they baptize? Why also are some, who "renounce the world in words and not in deeds," baptized without being converted from a life like this, and not rebaptized when they are converted? And as to what he says with such indignation, "See the kind of things to which the Church is compelled to assent, being forced to communicate without baptism or the remission of sins," he could never have used such expressions had there not been the other bishops who elsewhere forced men to such things. Whence also it is shown that at that time those men held the truer views who did not depart from the primitive custom, which is since confirmed by the consent of a general Council. But what does he mean by adding, "This, brethren, we ought to shun and avoid, separating ourselves from so great a sin?" For if he means that he is not to do nor to approve of this, that is another matter; but if he means to condemn and sever from him those that hold the contrary opinion, he is setting himself against the earlier words of Cyprian, "Judging no man, nor depriving any of the right of communion if he differs from us."

Chapter 9. —13. The elder Felix of Migirpa said: "I think that everyone coming from heresy should be baptized. For in vain does anyone suppose that he has been baptized there, seeing that there is no baptism save the one true baptism in the Church; for there is one Lord, and one faith, and one Church, in which rests the one baptism, and holiness, and the rest. For the things that are practiced without have no power to work salvation."

14. To what Felix of Migirpa said we answer as follows. If the one true baptism did not exist except in the Church, it surely would not exist in those who depart from unity. But it does exist in them, since they do not receive it when they return, simply because they had not lost it when they departed. But about his statement, that "the things that are practiced without have no power to work salvation," I agree with him, and think that it is quite true; for it is one thing that baptism should not be there, and another that it should have no power to work salvation. For when men come to the peace of the Catholic Church, then what was in them before they joined it, but did not profit them, begins at once to profit them.

Chapter 10. —15. To the declaration of Polycarp of Adrumetum, that "those who declare the baptism of heretics to be valid, make ours of none effect," we answer, if that is the baptism of heretics which is given by heretics, then that is the baptism of the covetous and murderers which is given by them within the Church. But if this be not their baptism, neither is the other the baptism of heretics; and so it is Christ's, by whomsoever it be given.

Chapter 11. —16. Novatus of Thamugadis said: "Though we know that all Scripture gives its testimony respecting saving baptism, yet we ought to express our belief that heretics and schismatics, coming to the Church with the semblance of having been baptized, ought to be baptized in the unfailing fountain; and that therefore, according to the testimony of the Scriptures, and according to the decree of those most holy men, our colleagues, all schismatics and heretics who are converted to the Church ought to be baptized; and that, moreover, all that seemed to have received ordination should be admitted as simple laymen."

17. Novatus of Thamugadis has stated what he has done, but he has brought forward no proofs by which to show that he ought to have acted as he did. For he has made mention of the testimony of the Scriptures, and the decree of his colleagues, but he has not adduced out of them anything which we could consider.

Chapter 12. —18. Nemesianus of Tubunæ said: "That the baptism which is given by heretics and schismatics is not true is everywhere declared in the holy Scriptures, inasmuch as their very prelates are false Christs and false prophets, as the Lord declares by the mouth of Solomon, 'Whoso trusted in lies, the same feeds the winds; he also followed flying birds. For he deserted the ways of his own vineyard, and hath strayed from the paths of his own field. For he walked through pathless and dry places, and a land destined to thirst; and he gathered fruitless weeds in his hands.' And again, 'Abstain from strange water, and drink not of a strange fountain, that thou mayest live long, and that years may be added to thy life.' And in the gospel our Lord Jesus Christ spoke with His own voice, saying, 'Except a man be born of water and of the Spirit, he cannot enter into the kingdom of God.' This is the Spirit which from the beginning 'moved upon the face of the waters.' For neither can the Spirit act without the water, nor the water without the Spirit. Ill, therefore, for themselves do some interpret, saying that by imposition of hands they receive the Holy Ghost, and are received into the Church, when it is manifest that they ought to be born again by both sacraments in the Catholic Church. For then indeed will they be able to become the sons of God, as the apostle says, 'Endeavoring to keep the unity of the Spirit in the bond of peace. There is one body, and one Spirit, even as ye are called in one hope of your calling; one Lord, one faith, one baptism, one God.' All this the Catholic Church asserts. And again he says in the gospel, 'That which is born of the flesh is flesh, and that which is born of the Spirit is spirit; for the Spirit is God, and is born of God.' Therefore, all things whatsoever all heretics and schismatics do are carnal, as the apostle says, 'Now the works of the flesh are manifest, which are these: fornication, uncleanness, lasciviousness, idolatry, witchcraft, hatred, variance, emulations, wrath, seditions, heresies, and such like: of the which I tell you before, as I have also told you in time past, that they which do such things shall not inherit the kingdom of God.' The apostle condemns, equally with all the wicked, those also who cause divisions, that is, schismatics and heretics. Unless therefore they receive that saving baptism which is one, and found only in the Catholic Church, they cannot be saved, but will be condemned with the carnal in the judgment of the Lord."

19. Nemesianus of Tubunæ has advanced many passages of Scripture to prove his point; but he has in fact said much on behalf of the view of the Catholic Church, which we have undertaken to set forth and maintain. Unless, indeed, we must suppose that he does not "trust in what is false" who trusts in the hope of things temporal, as do all covetous men and robbers, and those "who renounce the world in words but not in deeds," of whom Cyprian yet bears witness that such men not only baptize, but even are baptized within the Church. For they themselves also "follow flying birds," since they do not attain to what they desire. But not only the heretic, but everyone who leads an evil life "deserted the ways of his own vineyard, and hath strayed from the paths of his own field. And he walked through pathless and dry places, and a land destined to thirst; and he gathered fruitless weeds in his hands;" because all justice is fruitful, and all iniquity is barren. Those, again, who "drink strange water out of a strange fountain," are found not only among heretics, but among all who do not live according to the teaching of God, and do live according to the teaching of the devil. For if he were speaking of baptism, he would not say, "Do not drink of a strange fountain," but, do not wash thyself in a strange fountain. Again, I do not see at all what aid he gets towards proving his point from the words of our Lord, "Except a man be born of water and of the Spirit, he cannot enter into the kingdom of God." For it is one thing to say that everyone who shall enter into the kingdom of heaven is first born again of water and the Spirit, because except a man be born of water and of the Spirit, he shall not enter into the kingdom of heaven, which is the Lord's saying, and is true; another thing to say that everyone who is born of water and the Spirit shall

enter into the kingdom of heaven, which is assuredly false. For Simon Magus also was born of water and of the Spirit, and yet he did not enter into the kingdom of heaven; and this may possibly be the case with heretics as well. Or if only those are born of the Spirit who are changed with a true conversion, all "who renounce the world in word and not in deed" are assuredly not born of the Spirit, but of water only, and yet they are within the Church, according to the testimony of Cyprian. For we must perforce grant one of two things,—either those who renounce the world deceitfully are born of the Spirit, though it is to their destruction, not to salvation, and therefore heretics may be so born; or if what is written, that "the Holy Spirit of discipline will flee deceit," extends to proving as much as this, that those who renounce the world deceitfully are not born of the Spirit, then a man may be baptized with water, and not born of the Spirit, and Nemesianus says in vain that neither the Spirit can work without the water, nor the water without the Spirit. Indeed, it has been already often shown how it is possible that men should have one baptism in common who have not one Church, as it is possible that in the body of the Church herself those who are sanctified by their righteousness, and those who are polluted through their covetousness, may not have the same one Spirit, and yet have the same one baptism. For it is said "one body," that is, the Church, just as it is said "one Spirit" and "one baptism." The other arguments which he has adduced rather favor our position. For he has brought forward a proof from the gospel, in the words, "That which is born of the flesh is flesh, and that which is born of the Spirit is spirit; for the Spirit is God, and born of God;" and he has advanced the argument that therefore all things that are done by any heretic or schismatic are carnal, as the apostle says, "The works of the flesh are manifest, which are these: fornication, uncleanness;" and so he goes through the list which the apostle there enumerates, amongst which he has reckoned heresies, since "they who do such things shall not inherit the kingdom of God." Then he goes on to add, that "therefore the apostle condemns with all wicked men those also who cause division, that is, schismatics and heretics." And in this he does well, that when he enumerates the works of the flesh, among which are also heresies, he found and declared that the apostle condemns them alike. Let him therefore question the holy Cyprian himself, and learn from him how many even within the Church live according to the evil works of the flesh, which the apostle condemns in common with the heresies, and yet these both baptize and are baptized. Why then are heretics alone said to be incapable of possessing baptism, which is possessed by the very partners in their condemnation?

Chapter 13. —20. Januarius of Lambæse said: "Following the authority of the holy Scriptures, I pronounce that all heretics should be baptized, and so admitted into the holy Church."

21. To him we answer, that, following the authority of the holy Scriptures, a universal Council of the whole world decreed that the baptism of Christ was not to be disavowed even when found among heretics. But if he had brought forward any proof from the Scriptures, we should have shown either that they were not against us, or even that they were for us, as we proceed to do with him who follows.

Chapter 14. —22. Lucius of Castra Galbæ said: "Since the Lord hath said in His gospel, 'Ye are the salt of the earth: but if the salt have lost his savor, that which is salted from it shall be thenceforth good for nothing, but to be cast out, and to be trodden under foot of men;' and seeing that again, after His resurrection, when sending forth His apostles, He commanded them, saying, 'All power is given unto me in heaven and in earth: go ye therefore, and teach all nations, baptizing them in the name of the Father, and of the Son, and of the Holy Ghost,'—since then it is plain that heretics, that is, the enemies of Christ, have not the full confession of the sacrament, also that schismatics cannot reason with spiritual wisdom, since they themselves, by withdrawing when they have lost their savor from the Church, which is one, have become contrary to it, let that be done which is written, 'The houses of those that are opposed to the law must needs be cleansed;' and it therefore follows that those who have been polluted by being baptized by men opposed to Christ should first be cleansed, and only then baptized."

23. Lucius of Castra Galbæ has brought forward a proof from the gospel, in the words of the Lord, "Ye are the salt of the earth: but if the salt has lost his savor, that which is salted from it shall be good for nothing, but to be cast out, and to be trodden under foot of men;" just as though we maintained that men when cast out were of any profit for the salvation either of themselves or of anyone else. But those also who, though seeming to be within, are yet of such a kind, not only are without spiritually, but will in the end be separated in the body also. For all such are for nothing. But it does not therefore follow that the sacrament of baptism which is in them is nothing. For

even in the very men who are cast out, if they return to their senses and come back, the salvation which had departed from them returns; but the baptism does not return, because it never had departed. And in what the Lord says, "Go therefore, and teach all nations, baptizing them in the name of the Father, and of the Son, and of the Holy Ghost," He did not permit any to baptize except the good, inasmuch as He did not say to the bad, "Whosoever sins ye remit, they are remitted unto them; and whosoever sins ye retain, they are retained." How then do the wicked baptize within, who cannot remit sins? How also is it that they baptize the wicked whose hearts are not changed, whose sins are yet upon them, as John says, "He that hated his brother is in darkness even until now?" But if the sins of these men are remitted when they join themselves in the close bonds of love to the good and just, through whom sins are remitted in the Church, though they have been baptized by the wicked, so the sins of those also are remitted who come from without and join themselves by the inner bond of peace to the same framework of the body of Christ. Yet the baptism of Christ should be acknowledged in both, and held invalid in none, whether before they are converted, though then it profit them nothing, or after they are converted, that so it may profit them, as he says, "Since they themselves, by withdrawing when they have lost their savor from the Church, which is one, have become contrary to it, let that be done which is written, 'The houses of those that are opposed to the law must need be cleansed.' And it therefore follows," he goes on to say, "that those who have been polluted by being baptized by men opposed to Christ should first be cleansed, and only then baptized." What then? Are thieves and murderers not contrary to the law, which says, "Thou shalt not kill; thou shalt not steal?" "They must therefore needs be cleansed." Who will deny it? And yet not only those who are baptized by such within the Church, but also those who, being such themselves, are baptized without being changed in heart, are nevertheless exempt from further baptism when they are so changed. So great is the force of the sacrament of mere baptism, that though we allow that a man who has been baptized and continues to lead an evil life requires to be cleansed, we yet forbid him to be any more baptized.

Chapter 15. —24. Crescens of Cirta said: "The letters of our most beloved Cyprian to Jubaianus, and also to Stephen, having been read in so large an assembly of our most holy brethren in the priesthood, containing as they do so large a body of sacred testimony derived from the Scriptures that give us our God, that we have every reason to assent to them, being all united by the grace of God, I give my judgment that all heretics or schismatics who wish to come to the Catholic Church should not enter therein unless they have been first exorcised and baptized; with the obvious exception of those who have been originally baptized in the Catholic Church, these being reconciled and admitted to the penance of the Church by the imposition of hands."

25. Here we are warned once more to inquire why he says, "Except, of course, those who have been originally baptized in the Catholic Church." Is it because they had not lost what they had before received? Why then could they not also transmit outside the Church what they were able to possess outside? Is it that outside it is unlawfully transmitted? But neither is it lawfully

possessed outside, and yet it is possessed; so it is unlawfully given outside, but yet it is given. But what is given to the person returning from heresy who had been baptized inside, is given to the person coming to the Church who had been baptized outside, —that is, that he may have lawfully inside what before he had unlawfully outside. But perhaps someone may ask what was said on this point in the letter of the blessed Cyprian to Stephen, which is mentioned in this judgment, though not in the opening address to the Council, —I suppose because it was not considered necessary. For Crescens stated that the letter itself had been read in the assembly, which I have no doubt was done, if I am not mistaken, as is customary, in order that the bishops, being already assembled, might receive some information at the same time on the subject contained in that letter. For it certainly has no bearing on the present subject; and I am more surprised at Crescens having thought fit to mention it at all, than at its having been passed over in the opening address. But if anyone thinks that I have shrunk from bringing forward something which has been urged in it that is essential to the present point, let him read it and see that what I say is true; or if he finds it otherwise, let him convict me of falsehood. For that letter contains nothing whatsoever about baptism administered among heretics or schismatics, which is the subject of our present argument.

Chapter 16. —26. Nicomedes of Segermi said: "My judgment is that heretics coming to the Church should be baptized, because they can obtain no remission of sins among sinners outside."

27. The answer to which is: The judgment of the whole Catholic Church is that heretics, being already

baptized with the baptism of Christ, although in heresy, should not be rebaptized on coming to the Church. For if there is no remission of sins among sinners, neither can sinners within the Church remit sins; and yet those who have been baptized by them are not rebaptized.

Chapter 17. —28. Monnulus of Girba said: "The truth of our mother, the Catholic Church, hath continued, and still continues among us, brethren, especially in the threefold nature of baptism, as our Lord says, 'Go, baptize all nations in the name of the Father, and of the Son, and of the Holy Ghost.' Since, therefore," he goes on to say, "we know clearly that heretics have neither Father, Son, nor Holy Ghost, they ought, on coming to our mother, the Church, to be truly regenerated and baptized, that the cancer which they had, and the wrath of condemnation, and the destructive energy of error may be sanctified by the holy and heavenly laver."

29. To this we answer, That all who are baptized with the baptism that is consecrated in the words of the gospel have the Father, and the Son, and the Holy Ghost in the sacrament alone; but that in heart and in life neither do those have them who live an abandoned and accursed life within.

Chapter 18. —30. Secundinus of Cedias said: "Since our Lord Christ said, 'He that is not with me is against me,' and the Apostle John declares those who go out from the Church to be antichrists, without all doubt the enemies of Christ, and those who are called antichrists, cannot minister the grace of the baptism which gives salvation; and therefore my judgment is that those who take refuge in the Church from the snares of heresy should be baptized by us, who of His condescension are called the friends of God."

31. The answer to which is, That all are the opponents of Christ, to whom, on their saying, "Lord, have we not in Thy name done many wonderful things?" with all the rest that is there recorded, He shall at the last day answer, "I never knew you: depart from me, ye that work iniquity,"—all which kind of chaff is destined for the fire, if it persevere to the last in its wickedness, whether any part of it fly outside before its winnowing, or whether it seem to be within. If, therefore, those heretics who come to the Church are to be again baptized, that they may be baptized by the friends of God, are those covetous men, those robbers, murderers, the friends of God, or must those whom they have baptized be baptized afresh?

Chapter 19. —32. Felix of Bagai said: "As when the blind leads the blind, both fall into the ditch, so when a heretic baptizes a heretic, both fall together into death."

33. This is true, but it does not follow that what he adds is true. "And therefore," he says, "the heretic must be baptized and brought to life, lest we who are alive should hold communion with the dead." Were they not dead who said, "Let us eat and drink, for to-morrow we die?" for they did not believe in the resurrection of the dead. Those then who were corrupted by their evil communications, and followed them, were not they likewise falling with them into the pit? And yet among them there were men to whom the apostle was writing as being already baptized; nor would they, therefore, if they were corrected, be baptized afresh. Does not the same apostle say, "To be carnally-minded is death?" and

certainly the covetous, the deceivers, the robbers, amid whom Cyprian himself was groaning, were carnally-minded. What then? Did the dead hurt him who was living in unity? Or who would say, that because such men had or gave the baptism of Christ, that it was therefore violated by their iniquities?

Chapter 20. —34. Polianus of Mileum said: "It is right that a heretic should be baptized in the holy Church."

35. Nothing, indeed, could be expressed more shortly. But I think this too is short: It is right that the baptism of Christ should not be depreciated in the Church of Christ.

Chapter 21. —36. Theogenes of Hippo Regius said: "According to the sacrament of the heavenly grace of God which we have received, we believe in the one only baptism which is in the holy Church."

37. This may be my own judgment also. For it is so balanced, that it contains nothing contrary to the truth. For we also believe in the one only baptism which is in the holy Church. Had he said, indeed, We believe in that which is in the holy Church alone, the same answer must have been made to him as to the rest. But as it is, since he has expressed himself in this wise, "We believe in the one only baptism which is in the holy Church," so that it is asserted that it exists in the holy Church, but not denied that it may be elsewhere as well, whatever his meaning may have been, there is no need to argue against these words. For if I were questioned on the several points, first, whether there was one baptism, I should answer that there was one. Then if I were asked, whether this was in

the holy Church, I should answer that it was. In the third place, if it were asked whether I believed in this baptism, I should answer that I did so believe; and consequently I should answer that I believed in the one baptism which is in the holy Church. But if it were asked whether it was found in the holy Church alone, and not among heretics and schismatics, I should answer that, in common with the whole Church, I believed the contrary. But since he did not insert this in his judgment, I should consider that it was mere wantonness if I added words which I did not find there, for the sake of arguing against them. For if he were to say, There is one water of the river Euphrates, which is in Paradise, no one could gainsay the truth of what he said. But if he were asked whether that water were in Paradise and nowhere else, and were to say that this was so, he would be saying what was false. For, besides Paradise, it is also in those lands into which it flows from that source. But who is rash enough to say that he would have been likely to assert what is false, when it is quite possible that he was asserting what is true? Wherefore the words of this judgment require no contradiction, because they in no wise run counter to the truth.

Chapter 22. —38. Dativus of Badiæ said "We, so far as lies within our power, refuse to communicate with a heretic, unless he has been baptized in the Church, and received remission of his sins."

39. The answer to this is: If your reason for wishing him to be baptized is that he has not received remission of sins, supposing you find a man within the Church who has been baptized, though entertaining hatred towards his brother, since the Lord cannot lie, who says,

"If ye forgive not men their trespasses, neither will your Father forgive your trespasses," will you bid such a one, when corrected, to be baptized afresh? Assuredly not; so neither should you bid the heretic. It is clear that we must not pass unnoticed why he did not briefly say, "We do not communicate with a heretic," but added, "so far as lies within our power." For he saw that a greater number agreed with this view, from whose communion, however, he and his friends could not separate themselves, lest unity should be impaired, and so he added, "so far as lies within our power,"—showing beyond all doubt that he did not willingly communicate with those whom he held to be without baptism, but that yet all things were to be endured for the sake of peace and unity; just as was done also by those who thought that Dativus and his party were in the wrong, and who held what afterwards was taught by a fuller declaration of the truth, and urged by ancient custom, which received the stronger confirmation of a later Council; yet in turn, with anxious piety, they showed toleration towards each other, though without violation of Christian charity they entertained different opinions, endeavoring to keep the unity of the Spirit in the bond of peace, till God should reveal to one of them, were he otherwise minded, even this error of his ways. And to this I would have those give heed, by whom unity is attacked on the authority of this very Council by which it is declared how much unity should be loved.

Chapter 23. —40. Successus of Abbir Germaniciana said: "Heretics may either do nothing or everything. If they can baptize, they can also give the Holy Spirit; but if they cannot give the Holy Spirit, because they do not possess the Holy Spirit, then can they not either spiritually baptize. Therefore, we give our judgment that heretics should be baptized."

41. To this we may answer almost word for word: Murderers may either do nothing or everything. If they can baptize, they can also give the Holy Spirit; but if they cannot give the Holy Spirit, because they do not possess the Holy Spirit, then can they not either spiritually baptize. Therefore, we give our judgment that persons baptized by murderers, or murderers themselves who have been baptized without being converted, should, when they have corrected themselves, be baptized. Yet this is not true. For "whosoever hated his brother is a murderer;" and Cyprian knew such men within the Church, who certainly baptized. Therefore, it is to no purpose that words of this sort are used concerning heretics.

Chapter 24. —42. Fortunatus of Thuccabori said: "Jesus Christ our Lord and God, the Son of God the Father and Creator, built His Church upon a rock, not upon heresy, and gave the power of baptizing to bishops, not to heretics. Wherefore those who are outside the Church, and stand against Christ, scattering His sheep and flock, cannot baptize outside."

43. He added the word "outside" in order that he might not be answered with a like brevity to Successus. For otherwise he might also have been answered word for word: Jesus Christ our Lord and God, the Son of God the Father and Creator, built His Church upon a rock, not upon iniquity, and gave the power of baptizing to bishops, not to the unrighteous. Wherefore those who do not belong to the rock on which they build, who hear the word of God and do it, but, living contrary to Christ in hearing the word and not doing it, and hereby building on

the sand, in this way scatter His sheep and flock by the example of an abandoned character, cannot baptize. Might not this be said with all the semblance of truth? and yet it is false. For the unrighteous do baptize, since those robbers are unrighteous whom Cyprian maintained to be at unity with himself. But for this reason, says the Donatist, he adds "outside." Why therefore can they not baptize outside? Is it because they are worse from the very fact that they are outside? But it makes no difference, in respect of the validity of baptism, how much worse the minister may be. For there is not so much difference between bad and worse as between good and bad; and yet, when the bad baptizes, he gives the selfsame sacrament as the good. Therefore, also, when the worse baptizes, he gives the selfsame sacrament as the less bad. Or is it that it is not in respect of man's merit, but of the sacrament of baptism itself, that it cannot be given outside? If this were so, neither could it be possessed outside, and it would be necessary that a man should be baptized again so often as he left the Church and again returned to it.

44. Further, if we inquire more carefully what is meant by "outside," especially as he himself makes mention of the rock on which the Church is built, are not they in the Church who are on the rock, and they who are not on the rock, not in the Church either? Now, therefore, let us see whether they build their house upon a rock who hear the words of Christ and do them not. The Lord Himself declares the contrary, saying, "Whosoever hears these sayings of mine, and doeth them, I will liken him unto a wise man, which built his house upon a rock;" and a little later, "Everyone that hears these sayings of mine, and doeth them not, shall be likened unto a foolish man,

which built his house upon the sand." If, therefore, the Church is on a rock, those who are on the sand, because they are outside the rock, are necessarily outside the Church. Let us recollect, therefore, how many Cyprian mentions as placed within who build upon the sand, that is, who hear the words of Christ and do them not. And therefore, because they are on the sand, they are proved to be outside the rock, that is, outside the Church; yet even while they are so situated, and are either not yet or never changed for the better, not only do they baptize and are baptized, but the baptism which they have remains valid in them though they are destined to damnation.

45. Neither can it be said in this place, Yet who is there that doeth all the words of the Lord which are written in the evangelic sermon itself, at the end of which He says, that he who heard the said words and did them built upon a rock, and he who heard them and did them not built upon the sand? For, granting that by certain persons all the words are not accomplished, yet in the same sermon He has appointed the remedy, saying, "Forgive, and ye shall be forgiven." And after the Lord's prayer had been recorded in detail in the same sermon, He says, "For I say unto you, if ye forgive men their trespasses, your heavenly Father will also forgive you: but if ye forgive not men their trespasses, neither will your Father forgive your trespasses." Hence also Peter says, "For charity shall cover the multitude of sins;" which charity they certainly did not have, and on this account they built upon the sand, of whom the same Cyprian says, that within the Church they held conversation, even in the time of the apostles, in unkindly hatred alien from Christian charity; and therefore they seemed indeed to be within, but really were without,

because they were not on that rock by which the Church is signified.

Chapter 25. —46. Sedatus of Tuburbo said: "Inasmuch as water, sanctified by the prayer of the priest in the Church, washes away sins, just so much does it multiply sins when infected, as by a cancer, with the words of heretics. Wherefore one must strive, with all such efforts as conduce to peace, that no one who has been infected and tainted by heretical error should refuse to receive the one true baptism, with which whosoever is not baptized shall not inherit the kingdom of heaven."

47. To this we answer, that if the water is not sanctified, when through want of skill the priest who prays utters some words of error, many, not only of the bad, but of the good brethren in the Church itself, fail to sanctify the water. For the prayers of many are corrected every day on being recited to men of greater learning, and many things are found in them contrary to the Catholic faith. Supposing, then, that it were shown that some persons were baptized when these prayers had been uttered over the water, will they be bidden to be baptized afresh? Why not? Because generally the fault in the prayer is more than counterbalanced by the intent of him who offers it; and those fixed words of the gospel, without which baptism cannot be consecrated, are of such efficacy, that, by their virtue, anything faulty that is uttered in the prayer contrary to the rule of faith is made of no effect, just as the devil is excluded by the name of Christ. For it is clear that if a heretic utters a faulty prayer, he has no good intent of love whereby that want of skill may be compensated, and therefore he is like any envious or spiteful person in the Catholic Church itself,

such as Cyprian proves to exist within the Church. Or one might offer some prayer, as not unfrequently happens, in which he should speak against the rule of faith, since many rush into the use of prayers which are composed not only by unskillful men who love to talk, but even by heretics, and in the simplicity of ignorance, not being able to discern their true character, use them, thinking they are good; and yet what is erroneous in them does not vitiate what is right, but rather it is rendered null thereby, just as in the man of good hope and approved faith, who yet is but a man, if in anything he be otherwise minded, what he holds aright is not thereby vitiated until God reveal to him also that in which he is otherwise minded. But supposing that the man himself is wicked and perverse, then, if he should offer an upright prayer, in no part contrary to the Catholic faith, it does not follow that because the prayer is right the man himself is also right; and if over some he offer an erroneous prayer, God is present to uphold the words of His gospel, without which the baptism of Christ cannot be consecrated, and He Himself consecrates His sacrament, that in the recipient, either before he is baptized, or when he is baptized, or at some future time when he turns in truth to God, that very sacrament may be profitable to salvation, which, were he not to be converted, would be powerful to his destruction. But who is there who does not know that there is no baptism of Christ, if the words of the gospel in which consists the outward visible sign be not forthcoming? But you will more easily find heretics who do not baptize at all, than any who baptize without those words. And therefore we say, not that every baptism (for in many of the blasphemous rites of idols men are said to be baptized), but that the baptism of Christ, that is, every baptism consecrated in the words of the gospel, is everywhere the same, and cannot be vitiated by any perversity on the part of any men.

48. We must certainly not lightly pass over in this judgment that he here inserted a clause, and says, "Wherefore we must strive, with all such efforts as conduce to peace, that no one who has been infected," etc. For he had regard to those words of the blessed Cyprian in his opening speech, "Judging no man, nor depriving any of the right of communion if he entertains a different view." See of what power is the love of unity and peace in the good sons of the Church, that they should choose rather to show tolerance towards those whom they called sacrilegious and profane, being admitted, as they thought, without the sacrament of baptism, if they could not correct them as they thought was right, than on their account to break that holy bond, lest on account of the tares the wheat also should be rooted out,—permitting, so far as rested with them, as in that noblest judgment of Solomon, that the infant body should rather be nourished by the false mother than be cut in pieces. But this was the opinion both of those who held the truer view about the sacrament of baptism, and of those to whom God, in consideration of their great love, was purposing to reveal any point in which they were otherwise minded.

Chapter 26. —49. Privatianus of Sufetula said: "He who says that heretics have the power of baptizing should first say who it was that founded heresy. For if heresy is of God, it may have the divine favor; but if it be not of God, how can it either have or confer on any one the grace of God?"

50. This man may thus be answered word for

word: He who says that malicious and envious persons have the power of baptizing, should first say who was the founder of malice and envy. For if malice and envy are of God, they may have the divine favor; but if they are not of God, how can they either have or confer on any one the grace of God? But as these words are in the same way most manifestly false, so are also those which these were uttered to confute. For the malicious and envious baptize, as even Cyprian himself allows, because he bears testimony that they also are within. So therefore even heretics may baptize, because baptism is the sacrament of Christ; but envy and heresy are the works of the devil. Yet though a man possesses them, he does not thereby cause that if he has the sacrament of Christ, it also should itself be reckoned in the number of the devil's works.

Chapter 27. —51. Privatus of Sufes said: "What can be said of the man who approves the baptism of heretics, save that he communicates with heretics?"

52. To this we answer: It is not the baptism of heretics which we approve in heretics, as it is not the baptism of the covetous, or the treacherous, or deceitful, or of robbers, or of envious men which we approve in them; for all of these are unjust, but Christ is just, whose sacrament existing in them, they do not in its essence violate. Otherwise another man might say: What can be said of the man who approves the baptism of the unjust, save that he communicates with the unjust. And if this objection were brought against the Catholic Church herself, it would be answered just as I have answered the above.

Chapter 28. —53. Hortensianus of Lares said:

"How many baptisms there are, let those who uphold or favor heretics determine. We assert one baptism of the Church, which we only know in the Church. Or how can those baptize anyone in the name of Christ whom Christ Himself declares to be His enemies?"

54. Giving answer to this man in a like tenor of words, we say: Let those who uphold or favor the unrighteous see to it: we recall to the Church when we can the one baptism which we know to be of the Church alone, wherever it be found. Or how can they baptize anyone in the name of Christ whom Christ Himself declares to be His enemies? For He says to all the unrighteous, "I never knew you: depart from me, ye that work iniquity;" and yet, when they baptize, it is not themselves that baptize, but He of whom John says, "The same is He which baptizes."

Chapter 29. —55. Cassius of Macomades said: "Since there cannot be two baptisms, he who grants baptism unto heretics takes it away from himself. I therefore declare my judgment that heretics, those objects for our tears, those masses of corruption, should be baptized when they begin to come to the Church, and that so being washed by the sacred and divine laver, and enlightened with the light of life, they may be received into the Church,—as being now made not enemies, but peaceful; not strangers, but of the household of the faith of the Lord; not bastards, but sons of God; partaking not of error, but of salvation,—with the exception of those who, being believers transplanted from the Church, had gone over to heresy, and that these should be restored by the laying on of hands."

56. Another might say: Since there cannot be

two baptisms, he who grants baptism to the unrighteous takes it away from himself. But even our opponents would join us in resisting such a man when he says that we grant baptism to the unrighteous, which is not of the unrighteous, like their unrighteousness, but of Christ, of whom is righteousness, and whose sacrament, even among the unrighteous, is not unrighteous. What, therefore, they would join us in saying of the unrighteous, that let them say to themselves of heretics. And therefore he should rather have said as follows: I therefore give my judgment that heretics, those objects for our tears, those masses of corruption, should not be baptized when they begin to come to the Church, if they already have the baptism of Christ, but should be corrected from their error. For we may similarly say of the unrighteous, of whom the heretics are a part: I therefore give my judgment that the unrighteous, those objects for our tears, and masses of corruption, if they have been already baptized, should not be baptized again when they begin to come to the Church, that is, to that rock outside which are all who hear the words of Christ and do them not; but being already washed with the sacred and divine laver, and now further enlightened with the light of truth, should be received into the Church no longer as enemies but as peaceful, for the unrighteous have no peace; no longer as strangers, but of the household of the faith of the Lord, for to the unrighteous it is said, "How then art thou turned into the degenerate plant of a strange vine unto me?" no longer as bastards, but the sons of God, for the unrighteous are the sons of the devil, partaking not of error but of salvation, for un-righteousness cannot save. And by the Church I mean that rock, that dove, that garden enclosed and fountain sealed, which is recognized only in the wheat, not in the chaff, whether that be scattered far apart by the wind, or appear to be mingled with the corn even till the last winnowing. In vain, therefore, did Cassius add, "With the exception of those who, being believers transplanted from the Church, had gone over to heresy." For if even they themselves had lost baptism by seceding, to themselves also let it be restored; but if they had not lost it, let what was given by them receive due recognition.

Chapter 30. —57. Another Januarius of Vicus Cæsaris said: "If error does not obey truth, much more does truth refuse assent to error; and therefore we stand by the Church in which we preside, so that, claiming her baptism for herself alone, we baptize those whom the Church has not baptized."

58. We answer: Whom the Church baptizes, those that rock baptizes outside which are all they who hear the words of Christ and do them not. Let all, therefore, be baptized again who have been baptized by such. But if this is not done, then, as we recognize the baptism of Christ in these, so should we recognize it in heretics, though we either condemn or correct their unrighteousness and error.

Chapter 31. —59. Another Secundinus of Carpis said: "Are heretics Christians or not? If they are Christians, why are they not in the Church of God? If they are not Christians, let them be made so. Else what will be the reference in the discourse of the Lord, in which He says, 'He that is not with me is against me; and he that gathered not with me scattered abroad?' Whence it is clear that on strange children and the offspring of

Antichrist the Holy Spirit cannot descend by the laying on of hands alone, since it is clear that heretics have not baptism."

60. To this we answer: Are the unrighteous Christians or not? If they are Christians, why are they not on that rock on which the Church is built? for they hear the words of Christ and do them not. If they are not Christians, let them be made so. Else what will be the reference in the discourse of our Lord, in which He says, "He that is not with me is against me; and he that gathered not with me scattered abroad?" For they scatter His sheep who lead them to the ruin of their lives by a false imitation of the Lord. Whence it is clear that upon strange children (as all the unrighteous are called), and upon the offspring of Antichrist (which all are who oppose themselves to Christ), the Holy Spirit cannot descend by the laying on of hands alone, if there be not added a true conversion of the heart; since it is clear that the unrighteous, so long as they are unrighteous, may indeed have baptism, but cannot have the salvation of which baptism is the sacrament. For let us see whether heretics are described in that psalm where the following words are used of strange children: "Deliver me, O Lord, from the hand of strange children, whose mouth speaks vanity, and their right hand is a right hand of falsehood: whose sons are like young shoots well established, and their daughters polished after the similitude of the temple. Their garners are full, affording all manner of store; their sheep are fruitful, bringing forth plenteously in their streets; their oxen are strong: there is no breaking down of their fence, no opening of a passage out, no complaining in their streets. Men deemed happy the people that is in such a case; rather blessed is the people

whose God is the Lord." If, therefore, those are strange children who place their happiness in temporal things, and in the abundance of earthly prosperity, and despise the commandments of the Lord, let us see whether these are not the very same of whom Cyprian so speaks, transforming them also into himself, that he may show that he is speaking of men with whom he held communion in the sacraments: "In not keeping," he says, "the way of the Lord, nor observing the heavenly commandments given us for our salvation. Our Lord did the will of His Father, and we do not do the will of the Lord, being eager about our patrimony or our gains, following after pride, and so forth." But if these could both have and transmit baptism, why is it denied that it may exist among strange children, whom he yet exhorts, that, by keeping the heavenly commandments conveyed to them through the only-begotten Son, they should deserve to be His brethren and the sons of God?

Chapter 32. —61. Victoricus of Thabraca said: "If heretics may baptize, and give remission of sins, why do we destroy their credit, and call them heretics?"

62. What if another were to say: If the unrighteous may baptize, and give remission of sins, why do we destroy their credit, and call them unrighteous? The answer which we should give to such an one concerning the unrighteous may also be given to the other concerning heretics,—that is, in the first place, that the baptism with which they baptize is not theirs; and secondly, that it does not follow that whosoever has the baptism of Christ is also certain of the remission of his sins if he has this only in the outward sign, and is not converted with a true conversion of the heart, so that he

who gives remission should himself have remission of his sins.

Chapter 33. —63. Another Felix of Uthina said: "No one can doubt, most holy brethren in the priesthood, that human presumption has not so much power as the adorable and venerable majesty of our Lord Jesus Christ. Remembering then the danger, we ought not only to observe this ourselves, but to confirm it by our general consent, that all heretics who come to the bosom of our mother the Church be baptized, that the heretical mind, which has been polluted by long-continued corruption, may be reformed when cleansed by the sanctification of the laver."

64. Perhaps the man who has placed the strength of his case for the baptizing of heretics in the cleansing away of the long-continued corruption, would spare those who, having fallen headlong into some heresy, had remained in it a brief space, and presently being corrected, had passed from thence to the Catholic Church. Furthermore, he has himself failed to observe that it might be said that all unrighteous persons who come to that rock, in which is understood the Church, should be baptized, so that the unrighteous mind, which was building outside the rock upon the sand by hearing the words of Christ and not doing them, might be reformed when cleansed by the sanctification of the laver; and yet this is not done if they have been baptized already, even if it be proved that such was their character when they were baptized, that is, that they "renounced the world in words and not in deeds."

Chapter 34. —65. Quietus of Burug said: "We who live by faith ought with believing observance to obey what has been before foretold for our instruction. For it is written in Solomon, 'He that is washed by one dead, what availed his washing?' Which assuredly he says of those who are washed by heretics, and of those who wash. For if they who are baptized among them receive eternal life through the remission of their sins, why do they come to the Church? But if no salvation is received from a dead person, and they therefore, acknowledging their former error, return with penance to the truth, they ought to be sanctified with the one life-giving baptism which is in the Catholic Church."

66. What it is to be baptized by the dead, we have already, without prejudice to the more careful consideration of the same scripture, sufficiently declared before. But I would ask why it is that they wish heretics alone to be considered dead, when Paul the apostle has said generally of sin, "The wages of sin is death;" and again, "To be carnally minded is death." And when he says that a widow that lived in pleasure is dead, how are they not dead "who renounce the world in words and not in deeds"? What, therefore, is the profit of washing in him who is baptized by them, except, indeed, that if he himself also is of the same character, he has the laver indeed, but it does not profit him to salvation? But if he by whom he is baptized is such, but the man who is baptized is turned to the Lord with no false heart, he is not baptized by that dead person, but by that living One of whom it is said, "The same is He which baptizes." But to what he says of heretics, that if they who are baptized among them receive eternal life through the remission of their sins, why do they come to the Church? we answer:

They come for this reason, that although they have received the baptism of Christ up to the point of the celebration of the sacrament, yet they cannot attain to life eternal save through the charity of unity; just as neither would those envious and malicious ones attain to life eternal, who would not have their sins forgiven them, even if they entertained hatred only against those from whom they suffered wrong; since the Truth said, "If ye forgive not men their trespasses, neither will your Father forgive your trespasses," how much less when they were hating those towards whom they were rewarding evil for good? And yet these men, though "renouncing the world in words and not in deeds," would not be baptized again, if they should afterwards be corrected, but they would be made holy by the one living baptism. And this is indeed in the Catholic Church, but not in it alone, as neither is it in the saints alone who are built upon the rock, and of whom that one dove is composed.

Chapter 35. —67. Castus of Sicca said: He who presumes to follow custom in despite of truth is either envious and evilly disposed towards the brethren to whom the truth is revealed, or else he is ungrateful towards God, by whose inspiration His Church is instructed."

68. If this man proved that those who differed from him, and held the view that has since been held by the whole world under the sanction of a Christian Council, were following custom so as to despise truth, we should have reason for fearing these words; but seeing that this custom is found both to have had its origin in truth and to have been confirmed by truth, we have nothing to fear in this judgment. And yet, if they were envious or evilly disposed towards the brethren, or

ungrateful towards God, see with what kind of men they were willing to hold communion; see what kind of men, holding different opinions from their own, they treated as Cyprian enjoined them at the first, not removing them from the right of communion; see by what kind of men they were not polluted in the preservation of unity; see how greatly the bond of peace was to be loved; see what views they hold who bring charges against us, founded on the Council of bishops, their predecessors, whose example they do not imitate, and by whose example, when the rights of the case are considered, they are condemned. If it was the custom, as this judgment bears witness, that heretics coming to the Church should be received with the baptism which they already had, either this was done rightly, or the evil do not pollute the good in unity. If it was rightly done, why do they accuse the world because they are so received? But if the evil does not pollute the good in unity, how do they defend themselves against the charge of sacrilegious separation?

Chapter 36. —69. Eucratius of Theni said: "Our God and Lord Jesus Christ, teaching the apostles with His own mouth, fully laid down our faith, and the grace of baptism, and the rule of the law of the Church, saying, 'Go ye, and teach all nations, baptizing them in the name of the Father, and of the Son, and of the Holy Ghost.' Therefore, the false and unrighteous baptism of heretics is to be repudiated by us, and contradicted with all solemnity of witness, seeing that from their mouth issues not life, but poison, not heavenly grace, but blaspheming of the Trinity. And so it is plain that heretics coming to the Church ought to be baptized with perfect and Catholic baptism, that, being purified from the blasphemy of their presumption, they may be reformed by the grace of the Holy Spirit."

70. Clearly, if the baptism is not consecrated in the name of the Father, and of the Son, and of the Holy Ghost, it should be considered to be of the heretics, and repudiated as unrighteous by us with all solemnity of witness; but if we discern this name in it, we do better to distinguish the words of the gospel from heretical error, and approve what is sound in them, correcting what is faulty.

Chapter 37. —71. Libosus of Vaga said: "The Lord says in the gospel, 'I am the truth;' He did not say, I am custom. Therefore, when the truth is made manifest, let custom yield to truth; so that, if even in time past any one did not baptize heretics in the Church, he may now begin to baptize them."

72. Here he has in no way tried to show how that is the truth to which he says that custom ought to yield. But it is of more importance that he helps us against those who have separated themselves from unity, by confessing that the custom existed, than that he thinks it ought to yield to a truth which he does not show. For the custom is of such a nature, that if it admitted sacrilegious men to the altar of Christ without the cleansing of baptism, and polluted none of the good men who remained in unity, then all who have cut themselves off from the same unity, in which they could not be polluted by the contagion of any evil persons whatsoever, have separated themselves without reason, and have committed the manifest sacrilege of schism. But if all perished in pollution through that custom, from what cavern do they issue without the original truth, and with all the cunning of

calumny? If, however, the custom was a right one by which heretics were thus received, let them abandon their madness, let them confess their error; let them come to the Catholic Church, not that they may be bathed again with the sacrament of baptism, but that they may be cured from the wound of severance.

Chapter 38. —73. Lucius of Thebaste said: "I declare my judgment that heretics, and blasphemers, and unrighteous men, who with various words pluck away the sacred and adorable words of the Scriptures, should be held accursed, and therefore exorcised and baptized."

74. I too think that they should be held accursed, but not that therefore they should be exorcised and baptized; for it is their own falsehood which I hold accursed, but Christ's sacrament which I venerate.

Chapter 39. —75. Eugenius of Ammedera said: "I too pronounce this same judgment, that heretics should be baptized."

76. To him we answer: But this is not the judgment which the Church pronounces, to which also God has now revealed in a plenary Council the point in which ye were then still otherwise minded, but because saving charity was in you, ye remained in unity.

Chapter 40. —77. Also, another Felix of Ammacura said: "I too, following the authority of the holy Scriptures, give my judgment that heretics should be baptized, and with them those also who maintain that they have been baptized among schismatics. For if, according to the warning of Christ, our fountain is sealed to ourselves, let all the enemies of our Church understand that it cannot belong to others; nor can He who is the Shepherd of our flock give the water unto salvation to two different peoples. And therefore, it is clear that neither heretics nor schismatics can receive anything heavenly, who dare to accept from men that are sinners and aliens from the Church. When the giver has no ground to stand upon, surely neither can the receiver derive any profit."

78. To him we answer, that the holy Scriptures nowhere have enjoined that heretics baptized among heretics should be baptized afresh, but that they have shown in many places that all are aliens from the Church who are not on the rock, nor belong to the members of the dove, and yet that they baptize and are baptized and have the sacrament of salvation without salvation. But how our fountain is like the fountain of Paradise, in that, like it, it flows forth even beyond the bounds of Paradise, has been sufficiently set forth above; and that "He who is the Shepherd of our flock cannot give the water unto salvation to two different peoples," that is, to one that is His own, and to another that is alien, I fully agree in admitting. But does it follow that because the water is not unto salvation it is not the identical water? For the water of the deluge was for salvation unto those who were placed within the ark, but it brought death to those without, and yet it was the same water. And many aliens, that is to say, envious persons, whom Cyprian declares and proves from Scripture to be of the party of the devil, seem as it were to be within, and yet, if they were not without the ark, they would not perish by water. For such men are slain by baptism, as the sweet savor of Christ was unto death to those of whom the apostle speaks. Why then do not either heretics or schismatics receive anything heavenly, just as thorns or tares, like those who were

without the ark received indeed the rain from the floods of heaven, but to destruction, not to salvation? And so I do not take the pains to refute what he said in conclusion: "When the giver has no ground to stand upon, surely neither can the receiver derive any profit," since we also say that it does not profit the receivers while they receive it in heresy, consenting with the heretics; and therefore they come to Catholic peace and unity, not that they may receive baptism, but that what they had received may begin to profit them.

Chapter 41. —79. Also, another Januarius of Muzuli said: "I wonder that, while all acknowledge that there is one baptism, all do not understand the unity of the same baptism. For the Church and heresy are two distinct things. If heretics have baptism we have it not; but if we have it, heretics cannot have it. But there is no doubt that the Church alone possesses the baptism of Christ, since it alone possesses both the favor and the truth of Christ."

80. Another might equally say, and say with equal want of truth: I wonder that, while all confess there is one baptism, all do not understand the unity of baptism. For righteousness and unrighteousness are two distinct things. If the unrighteous have baptism, the righteous have it not; but if the righteous have it, the unrighteous cannot have it. But there is no doubt that the righteous alone possess the baptism of Christ, since they alone possess both the favor and the truth of Christ. This is certainly false, as they confess themselves. For those envious ones also who are of the party of the devil, though placed within the Church, as Cyprian tells us, and who were well known to the Apostle Paul, had baptism, but did not belong to the members of that dove which is

safely sheltered on the rock.

Chapter 42. —81. Adelphius of Thasbalte said: "It is surely without cause that they find fault with the truth in false and invidious terms, saying that we rebaptize, since the Church does not rebaptize heretics, but baptizes them."

82. Truly enough it does not rebaptize them, because it only baptizes those who were not baptized before; and this earlier custom has only been confirmed in a later Council by a more careful perfecting of the truth.

Chapter 43. —83. Demetrius of the Lesser Leptis said: "We uphold one baptism, because we claim for the Catholic Church alone what is her own. But those who say that heretics baptize truly and lawfully are themselves the men who make, not two, but many baptisms; for since heresies are many in number, the baptisms, too, will be reckoned according to their number."

84. To him we answer: If this were so, then would as many baptisms be reckoned as there are works of the flesh, of which the apostle says, "that they which do such things shall not inherit the kingdom of God;" among which are reckoned also heresies; and so many of those very works are tolerated within the Church as though in the chaff, and yet there is one baptism for them all, which is not vitiated by any work of unrighteousness.

Chapter 44. —85. Vincentius of Thibari said: "We know that heretics are worse than heathens. If they, being converted, wish to come to God, they have assuredly a rule of truth, which the Lord by His divine precept committed to the apostles, saying, 'Go ye, lay on hands in my name, cast out devils;' and in another place, 'Go ye, and teach all nations, baptizing them in the name of the Father, and of the Son, and of the Holy Ghost.' Therefore, first by the laying on of hands in exorcism, secondly by regeneration in baptism, they may come to the promises of Christ; but my judgment is that in no other way should this be done."

86. By what rule he asserts that heretics are worse than heathens I do not know, seeing that the Lord says, "If he neglect to hear the Church, let him be unto thee as a heathen man and a publican." Is a heretic worse even than such? I do not gainsay it. I do not, however, allow that because the man himself is worse than a heathen, that is, than a Gentile and pagan, therefore whatever the sacrament contains that is Christ's is mingled with his vices and character, and perishes through the corruption of such admixture. For if even those who depart from the Church, and become not the followers but the founders of heresies, have been baptized before their secession, they continue to have baptism, although, according to the above rule, they are worse than heathens; for if on correction they return, they do not receive it, as they certainly would do if they had lost it. It is therefore possible that a man may be worse than a heathen, and yet that the sacrament of Christ may not only be in him, but be not a whit inferior to what it is in a holy and righteous man. For although to the extent of his powers he has not preserved the sacrament, but done it violence in heart and will, yet so far as the sacrament's own nature is concerned, it has remained unhurt in its integrity even in the man who despised and rejected it.

Were not the people of Sodom heathens, that is to say, Gentiles? The Jews therefore were worse, to whom the Lord says, "It shall be more tolerable for the land of Sodom in the day of judgment than for thee;" and to whom the prophet says, "Thou hast justified Sodom," that is to say, in comparison with thee Sodom is righteous. Shall we, however, maintain that on this account the holy sacraments which existed among the Jews partook of the nature of the Jews themselves, —those sacraments which the Lord Himself also accepted, and sent the lepers whom He had cleansed to fulfill them, of which when Zacharias was administering them, the angel stood by him, and declared that his prayer had been heard while he was sacrificing in the temple? These same sacraments were both in the good men of that time, and in those bad men who were worse than are the heathens, seeing that they were ranked before the Sodomites for wickedness, and yet those sacraments were perfect and holy in both.

87. For even if the Gentiles themselves could have anything holy and right in their doctrines, our saints did not condemn it, however much the Gentiles themselves were to be detested for their superstitions and idolatry and pride, and the rest of their corruptions, and to be punished with judgment from heaven unless they submitted to correction. For when Paul the apostle also was saying something concerning God before the Athenians, he adduced as a proof of what he said, that certain of them had said something to the same effect, which certainly would not be condemned but recognized in them if they should come to Christ. And the holy Cyprian uses similar evidence against the same heathens; for, speaking of the magi, he says, "The chief of them, however, Hostanes, asserts both that the form of the true

God cannot be seen, and also that true angels stand beside His seat. In which Plato also agrees in like manner, and, maintaining the existence of one God, he calls the others angels or demons. Hermes Trismegistus also speaks of one God, and confesses that He is incomprehensible, and past our powers of estimation." If, therefore, they were to come to the perception of salvation in Christ, it surely would not be said to them, This that ye have is bad, or false; but clearly it would deservedly be said, Though this in you is perfect and true, yet it would profit nothing unless ye came to the grace of Christ. If, therefore, anything that is holy can be found and rightly approved in the very heathens, although the salvation which is of Christ is not yet to be granted to them, we ought not, even though heretics are worse than they, to be moved to the desire of correcting what is bad in them belonging to themselves, without being willing to acknowledge what is good in them of Christ. But we will set forth from a fresh preface to consider the remaining judgments of this Council.

Book VII.

In which the remaining judgments of the Council of Carthage are examined.

Chapter 1. —1. Let us not be considered troublesome to our readers, if we discuss the same question often and from different points of view. For although the Holy Catholic Church throughout all nations be fortified by the authority of primitive custom and of a plenary Council against those arguments which throw some darkness over the question about baptism, whether it can be the same among heretics and schismatics that it is in the Catholic Church, yet, since a different opinion has at one time been entertained in the unity of the Church itself, by men who are in no wise to be despised, and especially by Cyprian, whose authority men endeavor to use against us who are far removed from his charity, we are therefore compelled to make use of the opportunity of examining and considering all that we find on this subject in his Council and letters, in order, as it were, to handle at some considerable length this same question, and to show how it has more truly been the decision of the whole body of the Catholic Church, that heretics or schismatics, who have received baptism already in the body from which they came, should be admitted with it into the communion of the Catholic Church, being corrected in their error and rooted and grounded in the faith, that, so far as concerns the sacrament of baptism, there should not be an addition of something that was wanting, but a turning to profit of what was in them. And the holy Cyprian indeed, now that the corruptible body no longer presses down the soul, nor the earthly tabernacle presses down the mind that muses upon many things, sees with greater clearness that truth to which his charity made him deserving to attain. May he therefore help us by his prayers, while we labor in the mortality of the flesh as in a darksome cloud, that if the Lord so grant it, we may imitate so far as we can the good that was in him. But if he thought otherwise than right on any point, and persuaded certain of his brethren and colleagues to entertain his views in a matter which he now sees clearly through the revelation of Him whom he loved, let us, who are far inferior to his merits, yet following, as our weakness will allow, the authority of the

Catholic Church of which he was himself a conspicuous and most noble member, strive our utmost against heretics and schismatics, seeing that they, being cut off from the unity which he maintained, and barren of the love with which he was fruitful, and fallen away from the humility in which he stood, are disavowed and condemned the more by him, in proportion as he knows that they wish to search out his writings for purposes of treachery, and are unwilling to imitate what he did for the maintenance of peace,—like those who, calling themselves Nazarene Christians, and circumcising the foreskin of their flesh after the fashion of the Jews, being heretics by birth in that error from which Peter, when straying from the truth, was called by Paul persist in the same to the present day.

As therefore they have remained in their perversity cut off from the body of the Church, while Peter has been crowned in the primacy of the apostles through the glory of martyrdom, so these men, while Cyprian, through the abundance of his love, has been received into the portion of the saints through the brightness of his passion, are obliged to recognize themselves as exiles from unity, and, in defense of their calumnies, set up a citizen of unity as an opponent against the very home of unity. Let us, therefore, go on to examine the other judgments of that Council after the same fashion.

Chapter 2. —2. Marcus of Mactaris said: "It is not to be wondered at if heretics, being enemies and opponents of the truth, claim to themselves what has been entrusted and vouchsafed to other men. What is marvelous is that some of us, traitors to the truth, uphold heretics and oppose Christians; therefore we decree that heretics should be baptized."

3. To him we answer: It is indeed much more to be wondered at, and deserving of expressions of great praise, that Cyprian and his colleagues had such love for unity that they continued in unity with those whom they considered to be traitors to the truth, without any apprehension of being polluted by them. For when Marcus said, "It is marvelous that some of us, traitors to the truth, uphold heretics and oppose Christians," it seemed natural that he should add, Therefore we decree that communion should not be held with them. This he did not say; but what he does say is, "Therefore we decree that heretics should be baptized," adhering to what the peaceful Cyprian had enjoined in the first instance, saying, "Judging no man, nor removing any from the right of communion if he entertain a different opinion." While, therefore, the Donatists calumniate us and call us traditors, I should be glad to know, supposing that any Jew or pagan were found, who, after reading the records of that Council should call both us and them, according to their own rules, traitors to the truth, how we should be able to make our joint defense so as to refute and wash away so grave a charge. They give the name of traditors to men whom they were never able in times past to convict of the offense, and whom they cannot now show to be involved in it, being themselves rather shown to be liable to the same charge. But what has this to do with us? What shall we say of them who, by their own showing, are unquestionably traitors? For if we, however falsely, are called traditors, because, as they allege, we took part in the same communion with traditors, we have all taken part with the traditors in question, seeing that in the time of the blessed Cyprian the party of Donatus had not yet separated itself from unity. For the delivery of the

sacred books, from which they began to be called traditors, occurred somewhat more than forty years after his martyrdom. If, therefore, we are traditors, because we sprang from traditors, as they believe or pretend, we both of us derive our origin from those other traitors. For there is no room for saying that they did not communicate with these traitors, since they call them men of their own party. In the words of the Council which they are most forward to quote, "Some of us," it declares, "traitors to the truth, uphold heretics." To this is added the testimony of Cyprian, showing clearly that he remained in communion with them, when he says, "Judging no man, nor removing any from the right of communion if he entertains a different opinion." For those who entertained a different opinion were the very persons whom Marcus calls traitors to the truth because they upheld heretics, as he maintains, by receiving them into the Church without baptism. That it was, moreover, the custom that they should be so received, is testified both by Cyprian himself in many passages, and by some bishops in this Council. Whence it is evident that, if heretics have not baptism, the Church of Christ of those days was full of traitors, who upheld them by receiving them in this way. I would urge, therefore, that we plead our cause in common against the charge of treason which they cannot disavow, and therein our special case will be argued against the charge of delivering the books, which they could not prove against us. But let us argue the point as though they had convicted us; and what we shall answer jointly to those who urge against both of us the general treason of our forefathers, that we will answer to these men who urge against us that our forefathers gave up the sacred books. For as we were dead because our forefathers delivered up the books, which caused them to divide themselves from us, so both we and they themselves are dead through the treason of our forefathers, from whom both we and they are sprung. But since they say they live, they hold that that treason does not in any way affect them, therefore neither are we affected by the delivery of the books. And it should be observed that, according to them, the treason is indisputable: while, according to us, there is no truth either in the former charge of treason, because we say that heretics also may have the baptism of Christ; nor in the latter charge of delivering the books, because in that they were themselves beaten. They have therefore no reason for separating themselves by the wicked sin of schism, because, if our forefathers were not guilty of delivering up the books, as we say, there is no charge which can affect us at all; but if they were guilty of the sin, as these men say, then it is just as far from affecting us as the sin of those other traitors is from affecting either us or them. And hence, since there is no charge that can implicate us from the unrighteousness of our forefathers, the charge arising against them from their own schism is manifestly proved.

Chapter 3. —4. Satius of Sicilibba said: "If heretics receive forgiveness of their sins in their own baptism, it is without reason that they come to the Church. For since it is for sins that men are punished in the day of judgment, heretics have nothing to fear in the judgment of Christ if they have obtained remission of their sins."

5. This too might also have been our own judgment; but let its author beware in what spirit it was said. For it is expressed in terms of such import, that I

should feel no compunction in consenting and subscribing to it in the same spirit in which I too believe that heretics may indeed have the baptism of Christ, but cannot have the remission of their sins. But he does not say, If heretics baptize or are baptized, but "If heretics," he says, "receive forgiveness of their sins in their own baptism, it is without reason that they come to the Church." For if we were to set in the place of heretics those whom Cyprian knew within the Church as "renouncing the world in words alone and not in deeds," we also might express this same judgment, in just so many words, with the most perfect truth. If those who only seem to be converted receive forgiveness of their sins in their own baptism, it is without reason that they are afterwards led on to a true conversion. For since it is for sins that men are punished in the day of judgment, "those who renounce the world in words and not in deeds" have nothing to fear in the judgment of Christ if they have obtained remission of their sins. But this reasoning is only made perfect by some such context as is formed by the addition of the words. But they ought to fear the judgment of Christ, and to lose no time in being converted in the truth of their hearts; and, when they have done this, it is certainly not necessary that they should be baptized a second time. It was possible, therefore, for them to receive baptism, and either not to receive remission of their sins, or to be burdened again at once with the load of sins which were forgiven them; and so the same is the case also with the heretics.

Chapter 4. —6. Victor of Gor said: "Seeing that sins are forgiven only in the baptism of the Church, he who admits heretics to communion without baptism is guilty of two errors contrary to reason; for, on the one hand, he does not cleanse the heretics, and, on the other, he defiles the Christians."

7. To this we answer that the baptism of the Church exists even among heretics, though they themselves are not within the Church; just as the water of Paradise was found in the land of Egypt, though that land was not itself in Paradise. We do not therefore admit heretics to communion without baptism; and since they come with their waywardness corrected, we receive not their sins, but the sacraments of Christ. And, in respect of the remission of their sins, we say again here exactly what we said above. And certainly, in regard of what he says at the end of his judgment, declaring that he "is guilty of two errors contrary to reason, seeing that on the one hand he does not cleanse the heretics, and on the other he defiles the Christians," Cyprian himself is the first and the most earnest in repudiating this with the colleagues who agreed with him. For neither did he think that he was defiled, when, because the bond of peace, he decreed that it was right to hold communion with such men, when he used the words, "Judging no one, nor removing any from the right of communion if he entertain a different opinion." Or, if heretics defile the Church by being admitted to communion without being baptized, then the whole Church has been defiled in virtue of that custom which has been so often recorded here. And just as those men call us traditors because of our forefathers, in whom they could prove nothing of the sort when they laid the charge against them, so, if every man partakes of the character of those with whom he may have held communion, all were then made heretics. And if everyone who asserts this is mad, it must be false that Victor says, when he declares

that "he who admits heretics to communion without baptism, not only fails to cleanse the heretics, but pollutes the Christians as well." Or if this be true, they were then not admitted without baptism, but those men had the baptism of Christ, although it was given and received among heretics, who were so admitted in accordance with that custom which these very men acknowledged to exist; and on the same grounds they are even now rightly admitted in the same manner.

Chapter 5. —8. Aurelius of Utica said: "Since the apostle says that we ought not to be partakers with the sins of other men, what else does he do but make himself partaker with the sins of other men, who holds communion with heretics without the baptism of the Church? And therefore, I pronounce my judgment that heretics should be baptized, that they may receive remission of their sins, and so communion be allowed to them."

9. The answer is: Therefore Cyprian and all those bishops were partakers in the sins of other men, inasmuch as they remained in communion with such men, when they removed no one from the right of communion who entertained a different opinion. Where, then, is the Church? Then, to say nothing for the moment of heretics, —since the words of this judgment are applicable also to other sinners, such as Cyprian saw with lamentation to be in the Church with him, whom, while he confuted them, he yet tolerated, —where is the Church, which, according to these words must be held to have perished from that very moment by the contagion of their sins? But if, as is the most firmly established truth, the Church both has remained and does remain, the partaking of the sins of

others, which is forbidden by the apostle, must be considered only to consist in consenting to them. But let heretics be baptized again, that they may receive remission of their sins, if the wayward and the envious are baptized again, who, seeing that "they renounced the world in words and not in deeds," were indeed able to receive baptism, but did not obtain remission of their sins, as the Lord says, "If ye forgive not men their trespasses, neither will your Father forgive your trespasses."

Chapter 6. —10. Iambus of Germaniciana said: "Those who approve the baptism of heretics disapprove ours, so as to deny that such as are, I will not say washed, but defiled outside the Church, ought to be baptized within the Church."

11. To him we answer, that none of our party approves the baptism of heretics, but all the baptism of Christ, even though it be found in heretics who are as it were chaff outside the Church, as it may be found in other unrighteous men who are as chaff within the Church. For if those who are baptized without the Church are not washed, but defiled, assuredly those who are baptized outside the rock on which the Church is built are not washed, but defiled. But all are without the said rock who hear the words of Christ and do them not. Or if it be the case that they are washed indeed in baptism, but yet continue in the defilement of their unrighteousness, from which they were unwilling to be changed for the better, the same is true also of the heretics.

Chapter 7. —12. Lucianus of Rucuma said: "It is written, 'And God saw the light that it was good, and God divided the light from the darkness.' If light and darkness can agree, then can there be something in common between us and heretics. Therefore, I give my judgment that heretics should be baptized."

13. To him the answer is: If light and darkness can agree, then can there be something common between the righteous and unrighteous. Let him therefore declare his judgment that those unrighteous should be baptized afresh whom Cyprian confuted within the Church itself; or let him who can say if those are not unrighteous "who renounce the world in words and not in deeds."

Chapter 8. —14. Pelagianus of Luperciana said: "It is written, 'Either the Lord is God, or Baal is God.' So now either the Church is the Church, or heresy is the Church. Further, if heresy be not the Church, how can the baptism of the Church exist among heretics?"

15. To him we may answer as follows: Either Paradise is Paradise, or Egypt is Paradise. Further, if Egypt be not Paradise, how can the water of Paradise be in Egypt? But it will be said to us that it extends even thither by flowing forth from Paradise. In like manner, therefore, baptism extends to heretics. Also we say: Either the rock is the Church, or the sand is the Church. Further, since the sand is not the Church, how can baptism exist with those who build upon the sand by hearing the words of Christ and doing them not? And yet it does exist with them; and in like manner also it exists among the heretics.

Chapter 9. —16. Jader of Midila said: "We know that there is but one baptism in the Catholic Church, and therefore we ought not to admit a heretic unless he has been baptized in our body, lest he should think that he has been baptized outside the Catholic Church."

17. To him our answer is, that if this were said of those unrighteous men who are outside the rock, it certainly would be falsely said. And so it is therefore also in the case of heretics.

Chapter 10. —18. Likewise, another Felix of Marazana said: "There is one faith, one baptism, but of the Catholic Church, to which alone is given authority to baptize."

19. What if another were to say as follows: One faith, one baptism, but of the righteous only, to whom alone authority is given to baptize? As these words might be refuted, so also may the judgment of Felix be refuted. Do even the unrighteous who are not changed in heart in baptism, while "they renounce the world in words and not in deeds" yet belong to the members of the Church? Let them consider whether such a Church is the actual rock, the very dove, the bride herself without spot or wrinkle.

Chapter 11. —20. Paul of Bobba said: "I for my part am not moved if some fail to uphold the faith and truth of the Church, seeing that the apostle says 'For what if some did not believe? shall their unbelief make the faith of God without effect? God forbid: yea let God be true, but every man a liar.' But if God be true, how can the truth of baptism be in the company of heretics, where God is not?"

21. To him we answer: What is God among the covetous? And yet baptism exists among them; and so also it exists among heretics. For they among whom God is, are the temple of God. "But what agreement hath the

temple of God with idols?" Further, Paul considers, and Cyprian agrees with him, that covetousness is idolatry; and Cyprian himself again associates with his colleagues, who were robbers, but yet baptized, with great reward of toleration.

Chapter 12. —22. Pomponius of Dionysiana said: "It is manifest that heretics cannot baptize and give remission of sins, seeing that no power is given to them that they should be able either to loose or bind anything on earth."

23. The answer is: This power is not given to murderers either, that is, to those who hate their brothers. For it was not said to such as these, "whosesoever sins ye remit, they are remitted unto them; and whosesoever sins ye retain, they are retained." And yet they baptize, and both Paul tolerates them in the same communion of baptism, and Cyprian acknowledges them.

Chapter 13. —24. Venantius of Tinisa said: "If a husband, going on a journey into foreign countries, had entrusted the guardianship of his wife to a friend, he would surely keep her that was entrusted to his care with the utmost diligence, that her chastity and holiness might not be defiled by anyone. Christ our Lord and God, when going to the Father, committed His bride to our care: do we keep her uncorrupt and undefiled, or do we betray her purity and chastity to adulterers and corrupters? For he who makes the baptism of Christ common with heretics betrays the bride of Christ to adulterers."

25. We answer: What of those who, when they are baptized, turn themselves to the Lord with their lips and not with their heart? do not they possess an adulterous

mind? Are not they themselves lovers of the world, which they renounce in words and not in deeds; and they corrupt good manners through evil communications, saying, "Let us eat and drink; for to-morrow we die?" Did not the discourse of the apostle take heed even against such as these, when he says, "But I fear, lest by any means, as the serpent beguiled Eve through his subtilty, so your minds [also] should be corrupted from the simplicity that is in Christ?" When, therefore, Cyprian held the baptism of Christ to be in common with such men, did he therefore betray the bride of Christ into the hands of adulterers, or did he not rather recognize the necklace of the Bridegroom even on an adulteress?

Chapter 14. —26. Aymnius of Ausuaga said: "We have received one baptism, which same also we administer; but he who says that authority is given to heretics also to baptize, the same makes two baptisms."

27. To him we answer: Why does not he also make two baptisms who maintains that the unrighteous also can baptize? For although the righteous and unrighteous are in themselves opposed to one another, yet the baptism which the righteous give, such as was Paul, or such as was also Cyprian, is not contrary to the baptism which those unrighteous men were wont to give who hated Paul, whom Cyprian understands to have been not heretics, but bad Catholics; and although the moderation which was found in Cyprian, and the covetousness which was found in his colleagues, are in themselves opposed to one another, yet the baptism which Cyprian used to give was not contrary to the baptism which his colleagues who opposed him used to give, but one and the same with it, because in both cases it is He that baptizes of whom it is

said, "The same is He which baptizes."

Chapter 15. —28. Saturninus of Victoriana said: "If heretics may baptize, they are excused and defended in doing unlawful things; nor do I see why either Christ called them His adversaries, or the apostle called them antichrists."

29. To him we answer: We say that heretics have no authority to baptize in the same sense in which we say that defrauders have no authority to baptize. For not only to the heretic, but to the sinner, God says, "What hast thou to do to declare my statutes, or that thou shouldest take my covenant in thy mouth?" To the same person He assuredly says, "When thou saw a thief, then thou consented with him." How much worse, therefore, are those who did not consent with thieves, but themselves were wont to plunder farms with treacherous deceits? Yet Cyprian did not consent with them, though he did tolerate them in the corn-field of the Catholic Church, lest the wheat should be rooted out together with it. And yet at the same time the baptism which they themselves conferred was the very selfsame baptism, because it was not of them, but of Christ. As therefore they, although the baptism of Christ be recognized in them, were yet not excused and defended in doing unlawful things, and Christ rightly called those His adversaries who were destined, by persevering in such things, to hear the doom, "Depart from me, ye that work iniquity," whence also they are called antichrists, because they are contrary to Christ while they live in opposition to His words, so likewise is it the case with heretics.

Chapter 16. —30. Another Saturninus of Tucca said: "The Gentiles, although they worship idols, yet acknowledge and confess the supreme God, the Father and Creator. Against Him Marcion blasphemes, and some men do not blush to approve the baptism of Marcion. How do such priests either maintain or vindicate the priesthood of God, who do not baptize the enemies of God, and hold communion with them while they are thus unbaptized?"

31. The answer is this: Truly when such terms as this are used, all moderation is passed; nor do they take into consideration that even they themselves hold communion with such men, "judging no one, nor removing any from the right of communion if he entertains a contrary opinion." But Saturninus has used an argument in this very judgment of his, which might furnish materials for his admonition (if he would pay attention to it), that in each man what is wrong should be corrected, and what is right should be approved, since he says, "The Gentiles, although they worship idols, yet acknowledge and confess the supreme God, the Father and Creator." If, then, any Gentile of such a kind should come to God, would he wish to correct and change this point in him, that he acknowledged and confessed God the Father and Creator? I trow not. But he would amend in him his idolatry, which was an evil in him; and he would give to him the sacraments of Christ, which he did not possess; and anything that was wayward which he found in him he would correct; and anything which had been wanting he would supply. So also in the Marcionist heretic he would acknowledge the perfectness of baptism, he would correct his waywardness, he would teach him Catholic truth.

Chapter 17. —32. Marcellus of Zama said: "Since sins are remitted only in the baptism of the Church, he who does not baptize a heretic holds communion with a sinner."

33. What, does he who holds communion with one who does this not hold communion with a sinner? But what else did all of them do, "in judging no one, or removing from the right of communion anyone who entertained a different opinion"? Where, then, is the Church? Are those things not an obstacle to those who are patient, and tolerate the tares lest the wheat should be rooted out together with them? I would have them therefore say, who have committed the sacrilege of schism by separating themselves from the whole world, how it comes that they have in their mouths the judgment of Cyprian, while they do not have in their hearts the patience of Cyprian. But to this Marcellus we have an answer in what has been said above concerning baptism and the remission of sins, explaining how there can be baptism in a man although there be in him no remission of his sins.

Chapter 18. —34. Irenæus of Ululi said: "If the Church does not baptize a heretic, because it is said that he has been baptized already, then heresy is the greater."

35. The answer is: On the same principle it might be said, If therefore the Church does not baptize the covetous man, because it is said that he has been baptized already, then covetousness is the greater. But this is false, therefore the other is also false.

Chapter 19. —36. Donatus of Cibaliana said: "I acknowledge one Church, and one baptism that appertains thereto. If there is anyone who says that the grace of baptism exists among heretics, he must first show and prove that the Church exists with them."

37. To him we answer: If you say that the grace of baptism is identical with baptism, then it exists among heretics; but if baptism is the sacrament or outward sign of grace, while the grace itself is the abolition of sins, then the grace of baptism does not exist with heretics. But so there is one baptism and one Church, just as there is one faith. As therefore the good and bad, not having one hope, can yet have one baptism, so those who have not one common Church can have one common baptism.

Chapter 20. —38. Zozimus of Tharassa said: "When a revelation has been made of the truth, error must give way to truth; inasmuch as Peter also, who before was wont to circumcise, gave way to Paul when he declared the truth."

39. The answer is: This may also be considered as the expression of our judgment too, and this is just what has been done in respect of this question of baptism. For after that the truth had been more clearly revealed, error gave way to truth, when that most wholesome custom was further confirmed by the authority of a plenary Council. It is well, however, that they so constantly bear in mind that it was possible even for Peter, the chief of the apostles, to have been at one time minded otherwise than the truth required; which we believe, without any disrespect to Cyprian, to have been the case with him, and that with all our love for Cyprian, for it is not right that he should be loved with greater love

than Peter.

Chapter 21. —40. Julianus of Telepte said: "It is written, 'A man can receive nothing, except it be given him from heaven;' if heresy is from heaven, it can give baptism."

41. Let him hear another also saying: If covetousness is from heaven, it can give baptism. And yet the covetous do confer it; so therefore also may the heretics.

Chapter 22. —42. Faustus of Timida Regia said: "Let not these persons flatter themselves who favor heretics. He who interferes with the baptism of the Church on behalf of heretics makes them Christians, and us heretics."

43. To him we answer: If anyone was to say that a man who, when he received baptism had not received remission of his sins, because he entertained hatred towards his brother in his heart, was nevertheless not to be baptized again when he dismissed that hatred from his heart, does such a man interfere with the baptism of the Church on behalf of murderers, or does he make them righteous and us murderers? Let him therefore understand the same also in the case of heretics.

Chapter 23. —44. Geminius of Furni said: "Certain of our colleagues may prefer heretics to themselves, they cannot prefer them to us: and therefore what we have once decreed we hold, that we should baptize those who come to us from heretics."

45. This man also acknowledges most openly that certain of his colleagues entertained opinions contrary to

his own: whence again and again the love of unity is confirmed, because they were separated from one another by no schism, till God should reveal to one or other of them anything wherein they were otherwise minded. But to him our answer is, that his colleagues did not prefer heretics to themselves, but that, as the baptism of Christ is acknowledged in the covetous, in the fraudulent, in robbers, in murderers, so also they acknowledged it in heretics.

Chapter 24. —46. Rogatianus of Nova said: "Christ established the Church, the devil heresy: how can the synagogue of Satan have the baptism of Christ?"

47. To him our answer is: Is it true that because Christ established the well-affectioned, and the devil the envious, therefore the party of the devil, which is proved to be among the envious, cannot have the baptism of Christ?

Chapter 25. —48. Therapius of Bulla said: "If a man gives up and betrays the baptism of Christ to heretics, what else can he be said to be but a Judas to the Bride of Christ?"

49. How great a condemnation have we here of all schismatics, who have separated themselves by wicked sacrilege from the inheritance of Christ dispersed throughout the whole world, if Cyprian held communion with such as was the traitor Judas, and yet was not defiled by them; or if he was defiled, then were all made such as Judas; or if they were not, then the evil deeds of those who went before do not belong to those who came after even though they were the offspring of the same communion. Why, therefore, do they cast in our teeth the

traditores, against whom they did not prove their charge, and do not cast in their own teeth Judas, with whom Cyprian and his colleagues held communion? Behold the Council in which these men are wont to boast! We indeed say, that he who approves the baptism of Christ even in heretics, does not betray to heretics the baptism of Christ; just in the same way as he does not betray to murderers the baptism of Christ who approves the baptism of Christ even in murderers: but since they profess to prescribe to us from the decrees of this Council what opinions we ought to hold, let them first assent to it themselves. See how therein were compared to the traitor Judas, all who said that heretics, although baptized in heresy, should not be baptized again. Yet with such Cyprian was willing to hold communion, when he said, "Judging no man, nor depriving any of the right of communion if he entertain a contrary opinion." But that there had been men of such a sort in former times within the Church, is made clear by the sentence in which he says: "But some one will say, What, then, shall be done with these men who in times past were admitted into the Church without baptism?" That such had been the custom of the Church, is testified again and again by the very men who compose this Council. If, therefore, anyone who does this "can be said to be nothing else but a Judas to the Bride of Christ," according to the terms in which the judgment of Therapius is couched; but Judas, according to the teaching of the gospel, was a traitor; then all those men held communion with traitors who at that time uttered those very judgments, and before they uttered them they all had become traitors through that custom which at that time was retained by the Church. All, therefore—that is to say, both we and they themselves who were the offspring of that unity—are traitors. But we defend ourselves in two ways: first, because without prejudice to the right of unity, as Cyprian himself declared in his opening speech, we do not assent to the decrees of this Council in which this judgment was pronounced; and secondly, because we hold that the wicked in no way hurt the good in Catholic unity, until at the last the chaff be separated from the wheat. But our opponents, since they both shelter themselves as it were under the decrees of this Council, and maintain that the good perish as by a kind of infection from communion with the wicked, have no resource to save them from allowing both that the earlier Christians, whose offspring they are, were traitors, since they are convicted by their own Council; and that the deeds of those who went before them do reflect on them, since they throw in our teeth the deeds of our ancestors.

Chapter 26. —50. Also, another Lucius of Membresa said: "It is written, 'God hears not sinners.' How can he who is a sinner be heard in baptism?"

51. We answer: How is the covetous man heard, or the robber, and usurer, and murderer? Are they not sinners? And yet Cyprian, while he finds fault with them in the Catholic Church, yet tolerates them.

Chapter 27. —52. Also, another Felix of Buslaceni said: "In admitting heretics to the Church without baptism, let no one place custom before reason and truth; for reason and truth always exclude custom."

53. To him our answer is: You do not show the truth; you confess the existence of the custom. We should therefore do right in maintaining the custom which has

since been confirmed by a plenary Council, even if the truth were still concealed, which we believe to have been already made manifest.

Chapter 28. —54. Another Saturninus of Abitini said: "If Antichrist can give to anyone the grace of Christ, then can heretics also baptize, who are called Antichrists."

55. What if another were to say, If a murderer can give the grace of Christ, then can they also baptize that hate their brethren who are called murderers? For certainly he would seem in a way to speak the truth, and yet they can baptize; in like manner, therefore, can the heretics as well.

Chapter 29. —56. Quintus of Aggya said: "He who has a thing can give it; but what can the heretics give, who are well known to have nothing?"

57. To him our answer is: If, then, any man can give a thing who has it, it is clear that heretics can give baptism: for when they separate from the Church, they have still the sacrament of washing which they had received while in the Church; for when they return they do not again receive it, because they had not lost it when they withdrew from the Church.

Chapter 30. —58. Another Julianus of Marcelliana said: "If a man can serve two masters, God and mammon, then baptism also can serve two, the Christian and the heretic."

59. Truly, if it can serve the self-restrained and the covetous man, the sober and the drunken, the well-affectioned and the murderer, why should it not also serve

the Christian and the heretic? —whom, indeed, it does not really serve; but it ministers to them, and is administered by them, for salvation to those who use it right, and for judgment to such as use it wrong.

Chapter 31. —60. Tenax of Horrea Celiæ said: "There is one baptism, but of the Church; and where the Church is not, there baptism also cannot be."

61. To him we answer: How then comes it that it may be where the rock is not, but only sand; seeing that the Church is on the rock, and not on sand?

Chapter 32. —62. Another Victor of Assuras said: "It is written, that 'there is one God and one Christ, one Church and one baptism.' How then can anyone baptize in a place where there is not either God, or Christ, or the Church?"

63. How can anyone baptize either in that sand, where the Church is not, seeing that it is on the rock; nor God and Christ, seeing that there is not there the temple of God and Christ?

Chapter 33. —64. Donatulus of Capse said: "I also have always entertained this opinion, that heretics, who have gained nothing outside the Church, should be baptized when they are converted to the Church."

65. To this the answer is: They have, indeed, gained nothing outside the Church, but that is nothing towards salvation, not nothing towards the sacrament. For salvation is peculiar to the good; but the sacraments are common to the good and bad alike.

Chapter 34. —66. Verulus of Rusiccade said: "A man that is a heretic cannot give that which he has not; much more is this the case with a schismatic, who has lost what he had."

67. We have already shown that they still have it, because they do not lose it when they separate themselves. For they do not receive it again when they return: wherefore, if it was thought that they could not give it because they were supposed not to have it, let it now be understood that they can give it, because it is understood that they also have it.

Chapter 35. —68. Pudentianus of Cuiculi said: "My recent ordination to the episcopate induced me, brethren, to wait and hear what my elders would decide. For it is plain that heresies have and can have nothing; and so, if any come from them, it is determined righteously that they should be baptized."

69. As, therefore, we have already answered those who went before, for whose judgment this man was waiting, so be it understood that we have answered himself.

Chapter 36. —70. Peter of Hippo Diarrhytus said: "Since there is one baptism in the Catholic Church, it is clear that a man cannot be baptized outside the Church; and therefore I give my judgment, that those who have been bathed in heresy or in schism ought to be baptized on coming to the Church."

71. There is one baptism in the Catholic Church, in such a sense that, when any have gone out from it, it does not become two in those who go out, but remains one and the same. What, therefore, is recognized in those

who return, should also be recognized in those who received it from men who have separated themselves, since they did not lose it when they went apart into heresy.

Chapter 37. —72. Likewise, another Lucius of Ausafa said: "According to the motion of my mind and of the Holy Spirit, since there is one God, the Father of our Lord Jesus Christ, and one Christ, and one hope, one Spirit, one Church, there ought also to be only one baptism. And therefore I say, both that if anything has been set on foot or done among the heretics, that it ought to be rescinded; and also, that they who come out from among the heretics should be baptized in the Church."

73. Let it therefore be pronounced of no effect that they baptize, who hear the words of God and do them not, when they shall begin to pass from unrighteousness to righteousness, that is, from the sand to the rock. And if this is not done, because what there was in them of Christ was not violated by their unrighteousness, then let this also be understood in the case of heretics: for neither is there the same hope in the unrighteous, so long as they are on the sand, as there is in those who are upon the rock; and yet there is in both the same baptism, although as it is said that there is one hope, so also is it said that there is one baptism.

Chapter 38. —74. Felix of Gurgites said: "I give my judgment, that, according to the precepts of the holy Scriptures, those who have been unlawfully baptized outside the Church by heretics, if they wish to flee to the Church, should obtain the grace of baptism where it is lawfully given."

75. Our answer is: Let them indeed begin to have in a lawful manner to salvation what they before had unlawfully to destruction; because each man is justified under the same baptism, when he has turned himself to God with a true heart, as that under which he was condemned, when on receiving it he "renounced the world in words alone, and not in deeds."

Chapter 39. —76. Pusillus of Lamasba said: "I believe that baptism is not unto salvation except within the Catholic Church. Whatsoever is without the Catholic Church is mere pretense."

77. This indeed is true, that "baptism is not unto salvation except within the Catholic Church." For in itself it can indeed exist outside the Catholic Church as well; but there it is not unto salvation, because there it does not work salvation; just as that sweet savor of Christ is certainly not unto salvation in them that perish, though from a fault not in itself, but in them. But "whatsoever is without the Catholic Church is mere pretense," yet only in so far as it is not Catholic. But there may be something Catholic outside the Catholic Church, just as the name of Christ could exist outside the congregation of Christ, in which name he who did not follow with the disciples was casting out devils. For there may be pretense also within the Catholic Church, as is unquestionable in the case of those "who renounce the world in words and not in deeds," and yet the pretense is not Catholic. As, therefore, there is in the Catholic Church something which is not Catholic, so there may be something which is Catholic outside the Catholic Church.

Chapter 40. —78. Salvianus of Gazaufala said: "It is generally known that heretics have nothing; and therefore they come to us, that they may receive what previously they did not have."

79. Our answer is: On this theory, the very men who founded heresies are not heretics themselves, because they separated themselves from the Church, and certainly they previously had what they received there. But if it is absurd to say that those are not heretics through whom the rest became heretics, it is therefore possible that a heretic should have what turns to his destruction through his evil use of it.

Chapter 41. —80. Honoratus of Tucca said: "Since Christ is the truth, we ought to follow the truth rather than custom; that we may sanctify by the baptism of the Church the heretics who come to us, simply because they could receive nothing outside."

81. This man, too, is a witness to the custom, in which he gives us the greatest assistance, whatever else he may appear to say against us. But this is not the reason why heretics come over to us, because they have received nothing outside, but that what they did receive may begin to be of use to them: for this it could not be outside in any wise.

Chapter 42. —82. Victor of Octavus said: "As ye yourselves also know, I have not been long appointed a bishop, and therefore I waited for the counsel of my seniors. This therefore I express as my opinion, that whosoever comes from heresy should undoubtedly be baptized."

83. What, therefore, has been answered to those

for whom he waited, may be taken as the answer also to himself.

Chapter 43. —84. Clarus of Mascula said: "The sentence of our Lord Jesus Christ is manifest, when He sent forth His apostles, and gave the power which had been given Him of His Father to them alone, whose successors we are, governing the Church of the Lord with the same power, and baptizing those who believe the faith. And therefore heretics, who, being without, have neither power nor the Church of Christ, cannot baptize anyone with His baptism."

85. Are, then, ill-affectioned murderers successors of the apostles? Why, then, do they baptize? Is it because they are not outside? But they are outside the rock, to which the Lord gave the keys, and on which He said that He would build His Church.

Chapter 44. —86. Secundianus of Thambei said: "We ought not to deceive heretics by our too great forwardness, that not having been baptized in the Church of our Lord Jesus Christ, and having therefore not received remission of their sins, they may not impute to us, when the day of judgment comes, that we have been the cause of their not being baptized, and not having obtained the indulgence of the grace of God. On which account, since there is one Church and one baptism, when they are converted to us, let them receive together with the Church the baptism also of the Church."

87. Nay, when they are transferred to the rock, and joined to the society of the Dove, let them receive the remission of their sins, which they could not have outside the rock and outside the Dove, whether they were openly

without, like the heretics, or apparently within, like the abandoned Catholics; of whom, however, it is clear that they both have and confer baptism without remission of sins, when even from themselves it is received by men, who, being not changed for the better, honor God with their lips, while their heart is far from Him. Yet it is true that there is one baptism, just as there is one Dove, though those who are not in the one communion of the Dove may yet have baptism in common.

Chapter 45. —88. Also, another Aurelius of Chullabi said: "The Apostle John has laid down in his epistle the following precept: 'If there come any unto you, and bring not this doctrine, receive him not into your house, neither bid him God speed: for he that bides him God speed is partaker of his evil deeds.' How can such men be admitted without consideration into the house of God, who are forbidden to be admitted into our private house? Or how can we hold communion with them without the baptism of Christ, when, if we only so much as bid them God speed, we are partakers of their evil deeds?"

89. In respect of this testimony of John there is no need of further disputation, since it has no reference at all to the question of baptism, which we are at present discussing. For he says, "If any come unto you, and bring not the doctrine of Christ." But heretics leaving the doctrine of their error are converted to the doctrine of Christ, that they may be incorporated with the Church, and may begin to belong to the members of that Dove whose sacrament they previously had; and therefore, what previously they lacked belonging to it is given to them, that is to say, peace and charity out of a pure heart, and of

a good conscience, and of faith unfeigned. But what they previously had belonging to the Dove is acknowledged, and received without any depreciation; just as in the adulteress God recognizes His gifts, even when she is following her lovers; because when after her fornication is corrected she is turned again to chastity, those gifts are not laid to her charge, but she herself is corrected. But just as Cyprian might have defended himself if this testimony of John had been cast in his teeth whilst he was holding communion with men like these, so let those against whom it is spoken make their own defense. For to the question before us, as I said before, it has no reference at all. For John says that we are not to bid God speed to men of strange doctrine; but Paul the apostle says, with even greater vehemence, "If any man that is called a brother be covetous, or a drunkard," or anything of the sort, with such a one no not to eat; and yet Cyprian used to admit to fellowship, not with his private table, but with the altar of God, his colleagues who were usurers, and treacherous, and fraudulent, and robbers. But in what manner this may be defended has been sufficiently set forth in other books already.

Chapter 46. —90. Litteus of Gemelli said: "'If the blind lead the blind, both shall fall into the ditch.' Since, therefore, it is clear that heretics can give no light to anyone, as being blind themselves, therefore their baptism is invalid."

91. Neither do we say that it is valid for salvation so long as they are heretics, just as it is of no value to those murderers of whom we spoke, so long as they hate their brethren: for they also themselves are in darkness, and if anyone follows them they fall together into the

ditch; and yet it does not follow that they either have not baptism or are unable to confer it.

Chapter 47. —92. Natalis of Oëa said: "It is not only I myself who am present, but also Pompeius of Sabrati, and Dioga of Leptis Magna, who commissioned me to represent their views, being absent indeed in body, but present in spirit, who deliver this same judgment as our colleagues, that heretics cannot have communion with us, unless they have been baptized with the baptism of the Church."

93. He means, I suppose, that communion which belongs to the society of the Dove; for in the partaking of the sacraments they doubtless held communion with them, judging no man, nor removing any from the right of communion if he held a different opinion. But with whatever reference he spoke, there is no great need for these words being refuted. For certainly a heretic would not be admitted to communion, unless he had been baptized with the baptism of the Church. But it is clear that the baptism of the Church exists even among heretics if it be consecrated with the words of the gospel; just as the gospel itself belongs to the Church, and has nothing to do with their waywardness, but certainly retains its own holiness.

Chapter 48. —94. Junius of Neapolis said: "I do not depart from the judgment which we once pronounced, that we should baptize heretics on their coming to the Church."

95. Since this man has adduced no argument nor proof from the Scriptures, he need not detain us long.

Chapter 49. —96. Cyprian of Carthage said: "My opinion has been set forth with the greatest fullness in the letter which has been written to our colleague Jubaianus, that heretics being called enemies of Christ and antichrists according to the testimony of the gospel and the apostles, should, when they come to the Church, be baptized with the one baptism of the Church, that from enemies they may be made friends, and that from antichrists they may be made Christians."

97. What need is there of further disputation here, seeing that we have already handled with the utmost care that very epistle to Jubaianus of which he has made mention? And as to what he has said here, let us not forget that it might be said of all unrighteous men who, as he himself bears witness, are in the Catholic Church, and whose power of possessing and of conferring baptism is not questioned by any of us. For they come to the Church, who pass to Christ from the party of the devil, and build upon the rock, and are incorporated with the Dove, and are placed in security in the garden enclosed and fountain sealed; where none of those are found who live contrary to the precepts of Christ, wherever they may seem to be. For in the epistle which he wrote to Magnus, while discussing this very question, he himself warned us at sufficient length, and in no ambiguous terms, of what kind of society we should understand that the Church consists. For he says, in speaking of a certain man, "Let him become an alien and profane, an enemy to the peace and unity of the Lord, not dwelling in the house of God, that is to say, in the Church of Christ, in which none dwell save those who are of one heart and of one mind." Let those, therefore, who would lay injunctions on us on the authority of Cyprian, pay attention for a time to what we

here say. For if only those who are of one heart and of one mind dwell in the Church of Christ, beyond all question those were not dwelling in the Church of Christ, however much they might appear to be within, who of envy and contention were announcing Christ without charity; by whom he understands, not the heretics and schismatics who are mentioned by the Apostle Paul, but false brethren holding conversation with him within, who certainly ought not to have baptized, because they were not dwelling in the Church, in which he himself says that none dwell save those who are of one heart and of one mind: unless, indeed, anyone be so far removed from the truth as to say that those were of one heart and of one mind who were envious and malevolent, and contentious without charity; and yet they used to baptize: nor did the detestable waywardness which they displayed in any degree violate or diminish from the sacrament of Christ, which was handled and dispensed by them.

Chapter 50. —98. It is indeed worthwhile to consider the whole of the passage in the aforesaid letter to Magnus, which he has put together as follows: "Not dwelling," he says, "in the house of God—that is to say, in the Church of Christ—in which none dwell save those that are of one heart and of one mind, as the Holy Spirit says in the Psalms, speaking of 'God that makes men to be of one mind in a house.' Finally, the very sacrifices of the Lord declare that Christians are united among themselves by a firm and inseparable love for one another. For when the Lord calls bread, which is compacted together by the union of many grains, His body, He is signifying one people, whom He bore, compacted into one body; and when He calls wine, which is pressed out from a multitude of branches and clusters and brought together into one, His blood, He also signifies one flock joined together by the mingling of a multitude united into one." These words of the blessed Cyprian show that he both understood and loved the glory of the house of God, which house he asserted to consist of those who are of one heart and of one mind, proving it by the testimony of the prophets and the meaning of the sacraments, and in which house certainly were not found those envious persons, those malevolent without charity, who nevertheless used to baptize. From whence it is clear that the sacrament of Christ can both be in and be administered by those who are not in the Church of Christ, in which Cyprian himself bears witness that there are none dwelling save those who are of one heart and of one mind. Nor can it indeed be said that they can baptize so long as they are undetected, seeing that the Apostle Paul did not fail to detect those of whose ministry he bears unquestionable testimony in his epistle, saying that he rejoices that they also were proclaiming Christ. For he says of them, "Whether in pretense or in truth, Christ is preached; and I therein do rejoice, yea, and will rejoice."

Chapter 51. —99. Taking all these things, therefore, into consideration, I think that I am not rash in saying that there are some in the house of God after such a fashion as not to be themselves the very house of God, which is said to be built upon a rock, which is called the one dove, which is styled the beauteous bride without spot or wrinkle, and a garden enclosed, a fountain sealed, a well of living water, an orchard of pomegranates with pleasant fruits; which house also received the keys, and the power of binding and loosing. If anyone shall neglect this house when it arrests and corrects him, the Lord says, "Let him be unto thee as a heathen man and a publican." Of this house it is said, "Lord, I have loved the habitation of Thy house, and the place where Thine honor dwelleth;" and, "He makes men to be of one mind in a house;" and, "I was glad when they said unto me, Let us go into the house of the Lord;" and, "Blessed are they that dwell in Thy house, O Lord; they will be still praising Thee;" with countless other passages to the same effect. This house is also called wheat, bringing forth fruit with patience, some thirty-fold, some sixtyfold, and some a hundredfold. This house is also in vessels of gold and of silver, and in precious stones and imperishable woods. To this house it is said, "Forbearing one another in love, endeavoring to keep the unity of the Spirit in the bond of peace;" and, "For the temple of God is holy, which temple ye are." For this house is composed of those that are good and faithful, and of the holy servants of God dispersed throughout the world, and bound together by the unity of the Spirit, whether they know each other personally or not. But we hold that others are said to be in the house after such a sort, that they belong not to the substance of the house, nor to the society of fruitful and peaceful justice, but only as the chaff is said to be among the corn; for that they are in the house we cannot deny, when the apostle says, "But in a great house there are not only vessels of gold and of silver, but also of wood and of earth; and some to honor, and some to dishonor." Of this countless multitude are found to be not only the crowd which within the Church afflicts the hearts of the saints, who are so few in comparison with so vast a host, but also the heresies and schisms which exist in those who have burst the meshes of the net, and may now be said to be rather out of the house than in the house, of whom it is said, "They went out from us, but they were not of us." For they are more thoroughly separated, now that they are also divided from us in the body, than are those who live within the Church in a carnal and worldly fashion, and are separated from us in the spirit.

Chapter 52. —100. Of all these several classes, then, no one doubts respecting those first, who are in the house of God in such a sense as themselves to be the house of God, whether they be already spiritual, or as yet only babes nurtured with milk, but still making progress with earnestness of heart, towards that which is spiritual, that such men both have baptism so as to be of profit to themselves, and transmit it to those who follow their example so as to benefit them; but that in its transmission to those who are false, whom the Holy Spirit shuns, though they themselves, so far as lies with them, confer it so as to be of profit, yet the others receive it in vain, since they do not imitate those from whom they receive it. But they who are in the great house after the fashion of vessels to dishonor, both have baptism without profit to themselves, and transmit it without profit to those who follow their example: those, however, receive it with profit, who are united in heart and character, not to their ministers, but to the holy house of God. But those who are more thoroughly separated, so as to be rather out of the house than in the house, have baptism without any profit to themselves; and, moreover, there is no profit to those who receive it from them, unless they be compelled by urgent necessity to receive it, and their heart in receiving it does not depart from the bond of unity: yet nevertheless they possess it, though the possession be of no avail; and it is received from them, even when it is of no profit to those who so receive it, though, in order that it may become of use, they must depart from their heresy or schism, and cleave to that house of God. And this ought to be done, not only by heretics and schismatics, but also by those who are in the house through communion in the sacraments, yet so as to be outside the house through the perversity of their character. For so the sacrament begins to be of profit even to themselves, which previously was of no avail.

Chapter 53. —101. The question is also commonly raised, whether baptism is to be held valid which is received from one who had not himself received it, if, from some promptings of curiosity, he had chanced to learn how it ought to be conferred; and whether it makes no difference in what spirit the recipient receives it, whether in mockery or in sincerity: if in mockery, whether the difference arises when the mockery is of deceit, as in the Church, or in what is thought to be the Church; or when it is in jest, as in a play: and which is the more accursed, to receive it deceitfully in the Church, or in heresy or schism without deceit, that is to say, with full sincerity of heart: or whether it be worse to receive it deceitfully in heresy or in good faith in a play, if any one were to be moved by a sudden feeling of religion in the midst of his acting. And yet, if we compare such a one even with him who receives it deceitfully in the Catholic Church itself, I should be surprised if any one was to doubt which of the two should be preferred; for I do not see of what avail the intention of him who gives in truth can be to him who receives deceitfully. But let us consider, in the case of someone also giving it in deceit when both the given and the recipient are acting deceitfully in the unity of the Catholic Church itself, whether this should rather be acknowledged as baptism, or that which is given in a play, if anyone should be found who received it faithfully from a sudden impulse of religion: or whether it be not true that, so far as the men themselves are concerned, there is a very great difference between the believing recipient in a play, and the mocking recipient in the Church; but that in regard to the genuineness of the sacrament there is no difference. For if it makes no difference in respect to the genuineness of the sacrament within the Catholic Church itself, whether certain persons celebrate it in truth or in deceit, so long as both still celebrate the same thing, I cannot see why it should make a difference outside, seeing that he who receives it is not cloaked by his deceit, but he is changed by his religious impulse. Or have those truthful persons among whom it is celebrated more power for the confirmation of the sacrament, than those deceitful men by whom and in whom it is celebrated can exert for its invalidation? And yet, if the deceit be subsequently brought to light, no one seeks a repetition of the sacrament; but the fraud is either punished by excommunication or set right by penitence.

102. But the safe course for us is, not to advance 'th any rashness of judgment in setting forth a view ·h has neither been started in any regionary Council Catholic Church nor established in a plenary one; ·sert, with all the confidence of a voice that cannot ·d, what has been confirmed by the consent of ι Church, under the direction of our Lord God ·us Christ. Nevertheless, if any one were to ·osing I were duly seated in a Council in

which a question were raised on points like these—to declare what my own opinion was, without reference to the previously expressed views of others, whose judgment I would rather follow, if I were under the influence of the same feelings as led me to assert what I have said before, I should have no hesitation in saying that all men possess baptism who have received it in any place, from any sort of men, provided that it were consecrated in the words of the gospel, and received without deceit on their part with some degree of faith; although it would be of no profit to them for the salvation of their souls if they were without charity, by which they might be grafted into the Catholic Church. For "though I have faith," says the apostle, "so that I could remove mountains, but have not charity, I am nothing." Just as already, from the established decrees of our predecessors, I have no hesitation in saying that all those have baptism who, though they receive it deceitfully, yet receive it in the Church, or where the Church is thought to be by those in whose society it is received, of whom it was said, "They went out from us." But when there was no society of those who so believed, and when the man who received it did not himself hold such belief, but the whole thing was done as a farce, or a comedy, or a jest,—if I were asked whether the baptism which was thus conferred should be approved, I should declare my opinion that we ought to pray for the declaration of God's judgment through the medium of some revelation seeking it with united prayer and earnest groanings of suppliant devotion, humbly deferring all the time to the decision of those who were to give their judgment after me, in case they should set forth anything as already known and determined. And, therefore, hov much the more must I be considered to have given m opinion now without prejudice to the utterance of more diligent research or authority higher than my own!

Chapter 54. —103. But now I think that it is fully time for me to bring to their due termination these books also on the subject of baptism, in which our Lord God has shown to us, through the words of the peaceful Bishop Cyprian and his brethren who agreed with him, how great is the love which should be felt for catholic unity; so that even where they were otherwise minded until God should reveal even this to them, they should rather bear with those who thought differently from themselves, than sever themselves from them by a wicked schism; whereby the mouths of the Donatists are wholly closed, even if we say nothing of the followers of Maximian. For if the wicked pollute the good in unity, then even Cyprian himself already found no Church to which he could be joined. But if the wicked do not infect the good in unity, then the sacrilegious Donatist has no ground to set before himself for separation. But if baptism is both possessed and transferred by the multitude of others who work the works of the flesh, of which it is said, that "they which do such things shall not inherit the kingdom of God," then it is possessed and transferred also by heretics, who are numbered among those works; because they could have transferred it had they remained, and did not lose it by their secession. But men of this kind confer it on their own as fruitlessly and uselessly as the others who while them, since they shall not inherit the kingdom of God as, when those others are brought into the right not that baptism begins to be present, having before, but that it begins to profit them, already in them; so is it the case with heretics as well. Whence Cyprian and those who thought with him could not impose limits on the Catholic Church, which they would not mutilate. But in that they were otherwise minded we feel no fear, seeing that we too share in their veneration for Peter; yet in that they did not depart from unity we rejoice, seeing that we, like them, are founded on the rock.

product-compliance